SEVEN SEAS ENTERTAINMENT PRESENTS

Black & White
TOUGH LOVE AT THE OFFICE

story and art by **SAL JIANG**　　VOLUME ONE

TRANSLATION
Alexa Frank

ADAPTATION
Asha Bardon

LETTERING
Danya Shevchenko

COVER DESIGN
H. Qi

PROOFREADER
Krista Grandy

SENIOR COPY EDITOR
Dawn Davis

EDITOR
Anne Elk

PRODUCTION DESIGNER
Christina McKenzie

PRODUCTION MANAGER
Lissa Pattillo

PREPRESS TECHNICIAN
Melanie Ujimori

PRINT MANAGER
Rhiannon Rasmussen-Silverstein

EDITOR-IN-CHIEF
Julie Davis

ASSOCIATE PUBLISHER
Adam Arnold

PUBLISHER
Jason DeAngelis

Shiro to Kuro-Black & White- volume 1
© Sal Jiang 2021
This edition originally published in Japan in 2021
by Jitsugyo no Nihon Sha, Ltd., Tokyo.
English translation rights arranged with Jitsugyo no Nihon Sha, Ltd.
through TOHAN CORPORATION, Tokyo.

No portion of this book may be reproduced or transmitted in any form without written permission from the copyright holders. This is a work of fiction. Names, characters, places, and incidents are the products of the author's imagination or are used fictitiously. Any resemblance to actual events, locales, or persons, living or dead, is entirely coincidental. Any information or opinions expressed by the creators of this book belong to those individual creators and do not necessarily reflect the views of Seven Seas Entertainment or its employees.

Seven Seas press and purchase enquiries can be sent to Marketing Manager Lianne Sentar at press@gomanga.com. Information regarding the distribution and purchase of digital editions is available from Digital Manager CK Russell at digital@gomanga.com.

Seven Seas and the Seven Seas logo are trademarks of
Seven Seas Entertainment. All rights reserved.

ISBN: 978-1-63858-528-2
Printed in USA
First Printing: October 2022
10 9 8 7 6 5 4 3 2 1

READING DIRECTIONS

This book reads from *right to left*, Japanese style. If this is your first time reading manga, you start reading from the top right panel on each page and take it from there. If you get lost, just follow the numbered diagram here. It may seem backwards at first, but you'll get the hang of it! Have fun!!

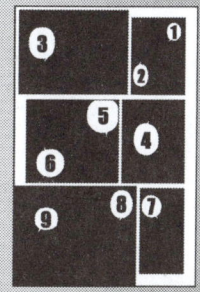

Follow us online: www.SevenSeasEntertainment.com

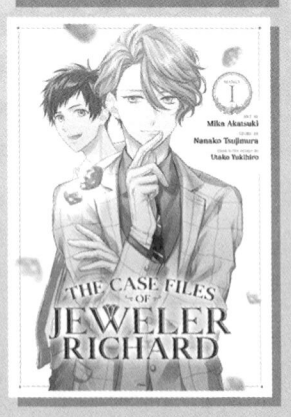

Available now from SEVEN SEAS ENTERTAINMENT

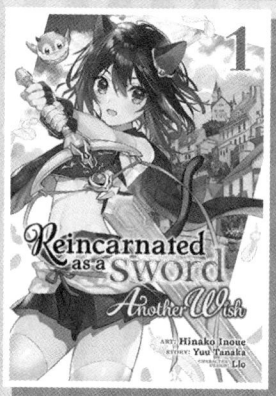

Explore all these and more at
SevenSeasEntertainment.com

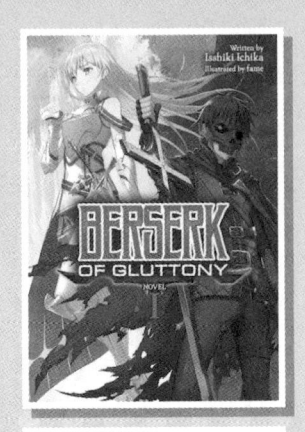

Available now from
SEVEN SEAS' AIRSHIP

Take flight with more **NOVELS** at
AirShipNovels.com

Experience all that SEVEN SEAS has to offer!

SEVENSEASENTERTAINMENT.COM
Visit and follow us on Twitter at twitter.com/gomanga/

Black & White
TOUGH LOVE AT THE OFFICE

BLACK AND WHITE CHARACTER DESIGNS

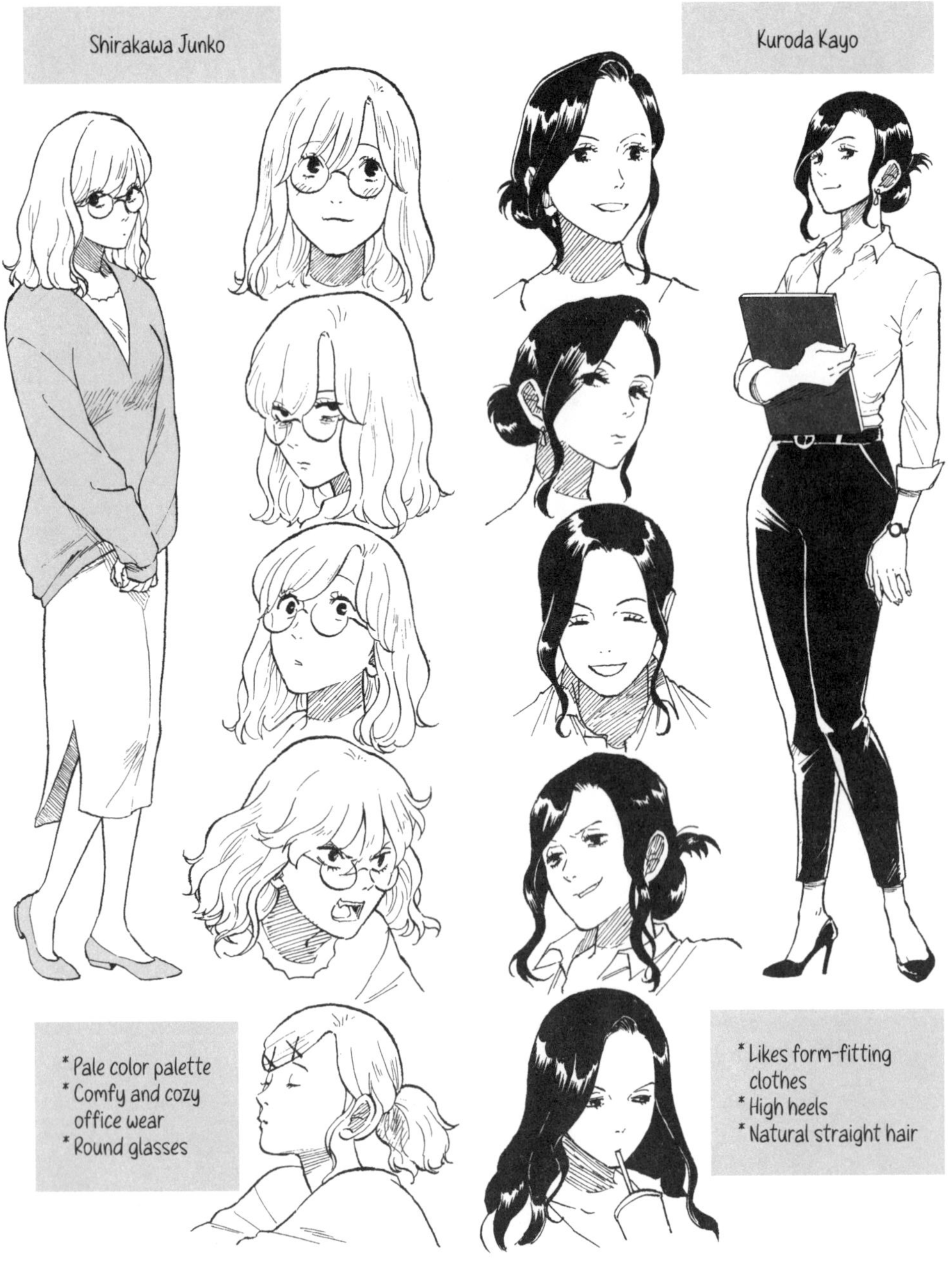
Shirakawa Junko
Kuroda Kayo
* Pale color palette
* Comfy and cozy office wear
* Round glasses
* Likes form-fitting clothes
* High heels
* Natural straight hair

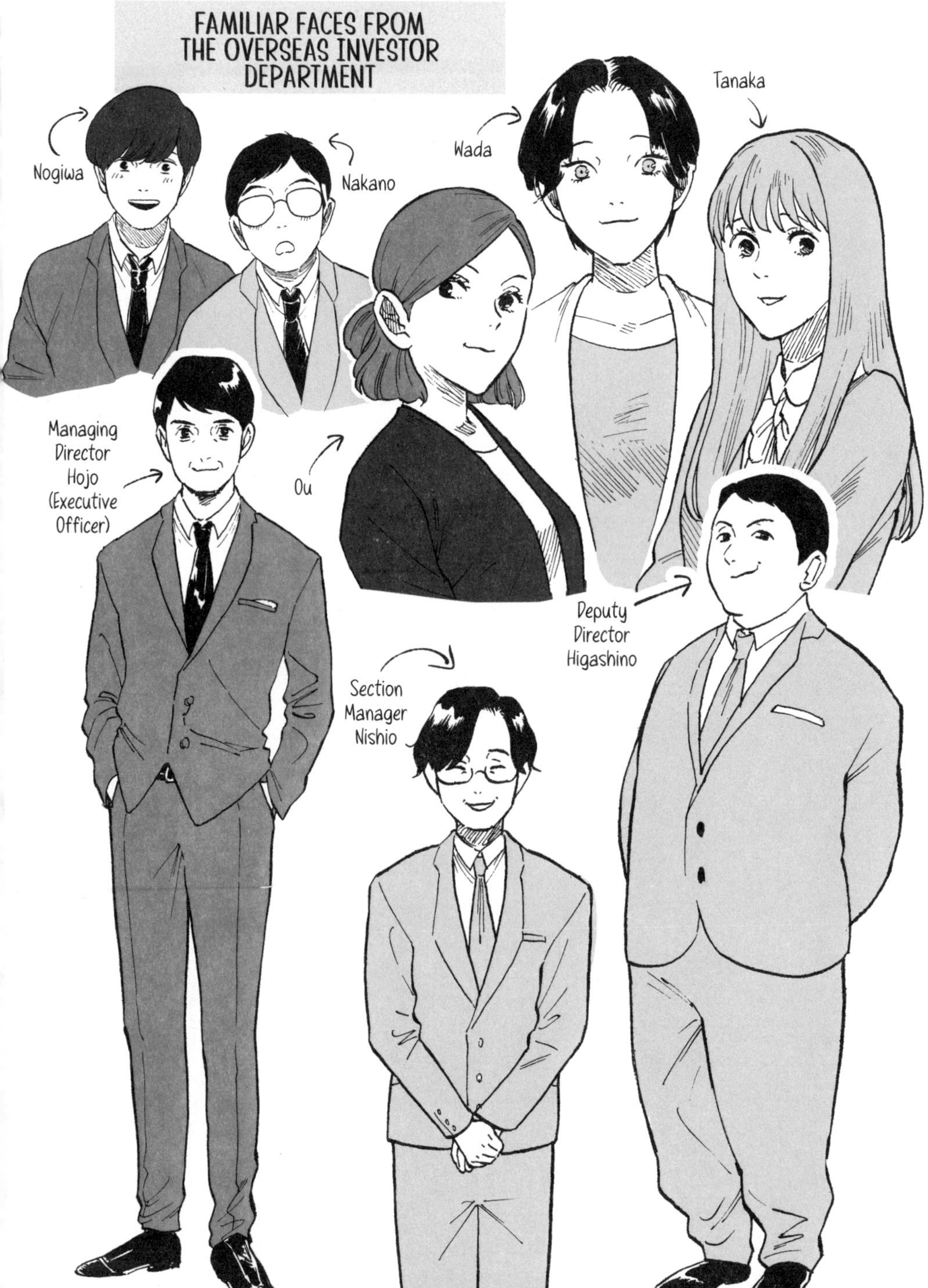
FAMILIAR FACES FROM THE OVERSEAS INVESTOR DEPARTMENT
Nogiwa
Nakano
Wada
Tanaka
Ou
Managing Director Hojo (Executive Officer)
Deputy Director Higashino
Section Manager Nishio

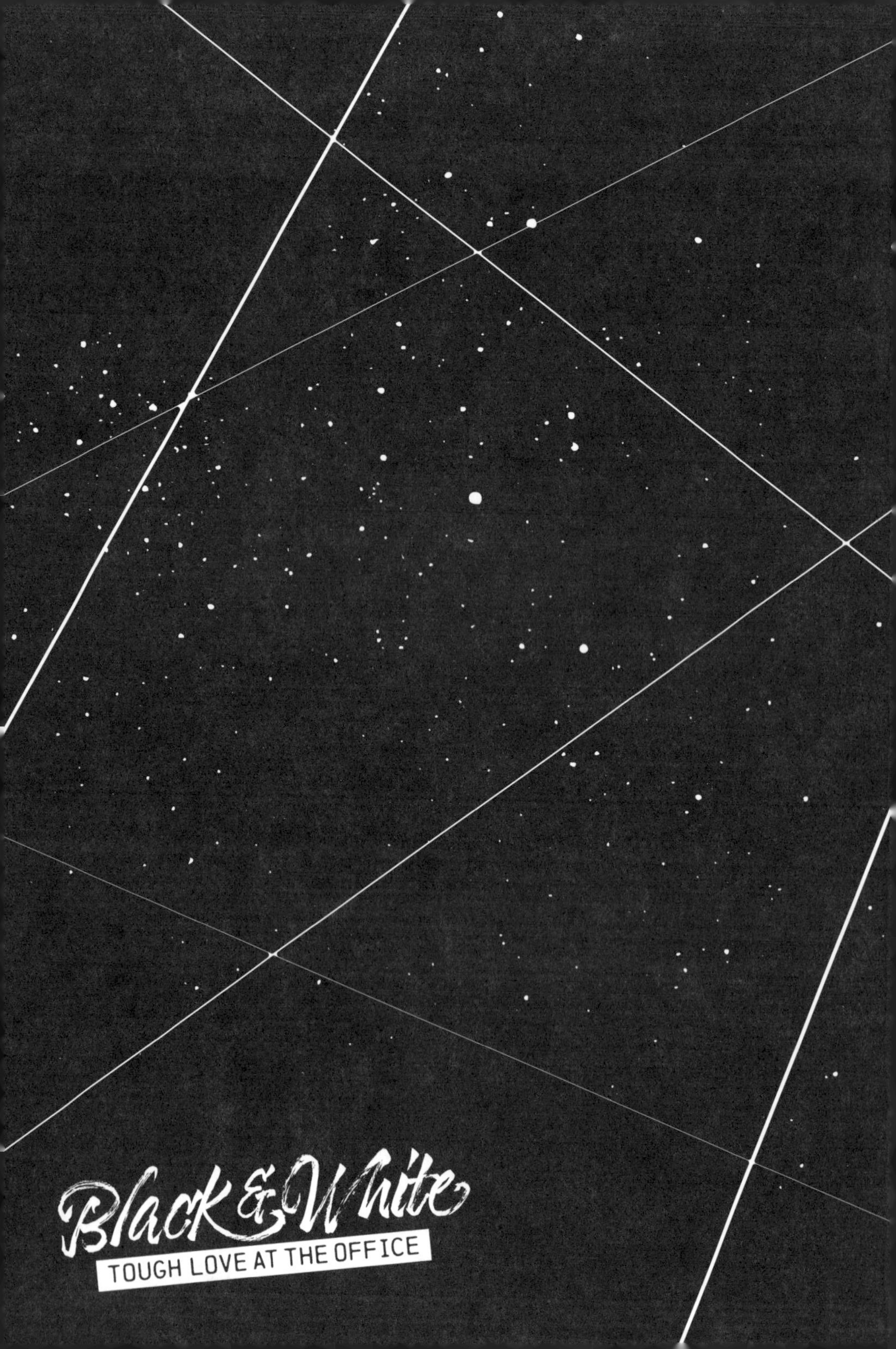
Black & White
TOUGH LOVE AT THE OFFICE

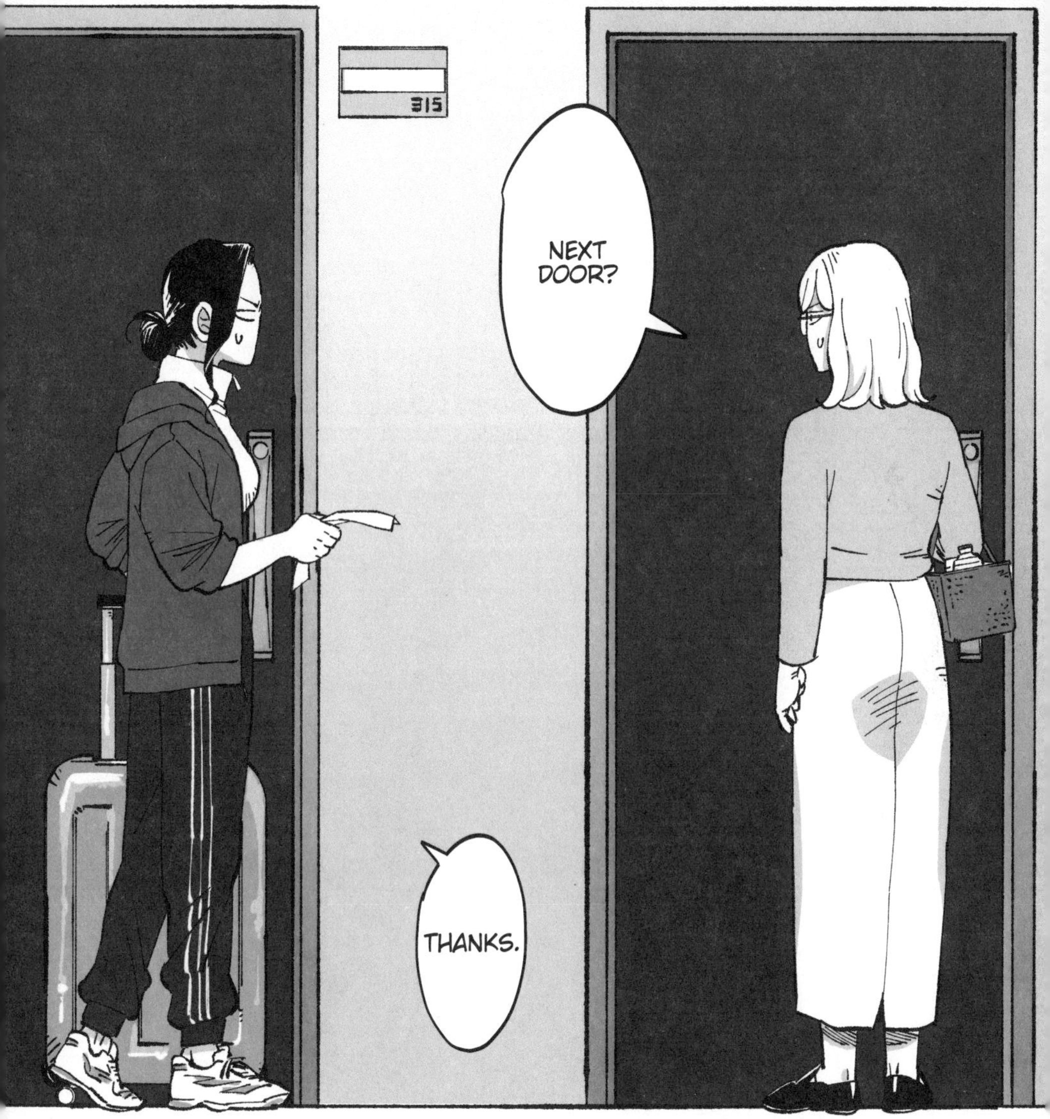
315
NEXT DOOR?
THANKS.

Chapter 6 – Fin

RUSTLE
RUSTLE
315...
315...
IS THAT THE PERSON WHO LIVES NEXT DOOR?
OH...
315 IS...
HERE?
HM?

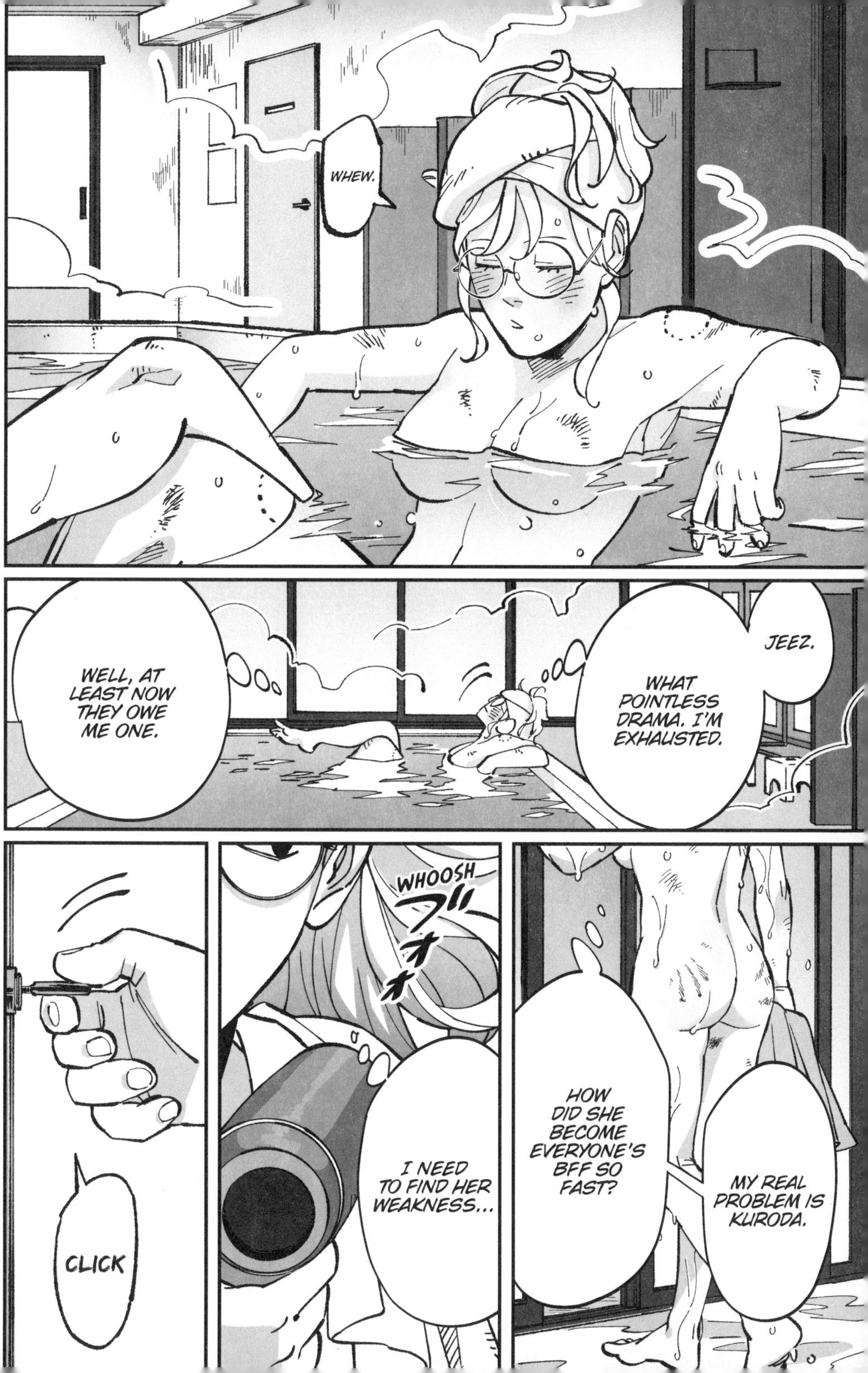
WHEW.
JEEZ.
WHAT POINTLESS DRAMA. I'M EXHAUSTED.
WELL, AT LEAST NOW THEY OWE ME ONE.
MY REAL PROBLEM IS KURODA.
HOW DID SHE BECOME EVERYONE'S BFF SO FAST?
WHOOSH
I NEED TO FIND HER WEAKNESS...
CLICK

THUD THUD

THE TRAINING COURSE?

GREAT, NOW I'LL HAVE TO MAKE MORE REVISIONS.

SPIN

WOULD YOU TAKE A LOOK?

WE MADE SOME NEW MATERIAL FOR THE TRAINING COURSE.

UM, WELL...

OH, WADA-CHAN AND TANAKA-CHAN! WHAT'S UP?

SMILE

GLANCE

FIDGET

......

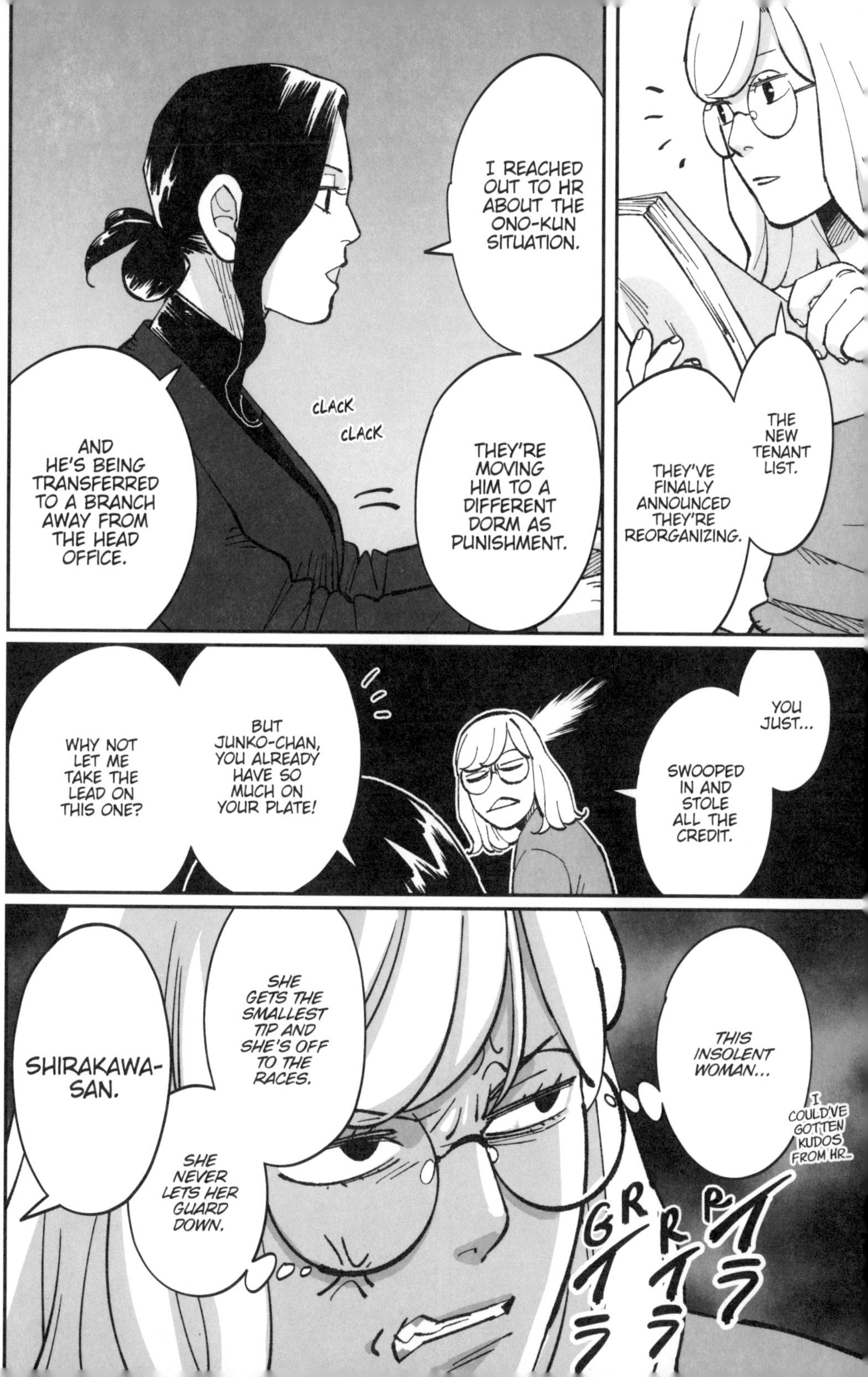
THE NEW TENANT LIST.
THEY'VE FINALLY ANNOUNCED THEY'RE REORGANIZING.
I REACHED OUT TO HR ABOUT THE ONO-KUN SITUATION.
THEY'RE MOVING HIM TO A DIFFERENT DORM AS PUNISHMENT.
CLACK
CLACK
AND HE'S BEING TRANSFERRED TO A BRANCH AWAY FROM THE HEAD OFFICE.
YOU JUST...
SWOOPED IN AND STOLE ALL THE CREDIT.
BUT JUNKO-CHAN, YOU ALREADY HAVE SO MUCH ON YOUR PLATE!
WHY NOT LET ME TAKE THE LEAD ON THIS ONE?
THIS INSOLENT WOMAN...
I COULD'VE GOTTEN KUDOS FROM HR...
SHE GETS THE SMALLEST TIP AND SHE'S OFF TO THE RACES.
SHE NEVER LETS HER GUARD DOWN.
SHIRAKAWA-SAN.
GRRR
イライラ
イライラ
イライラ

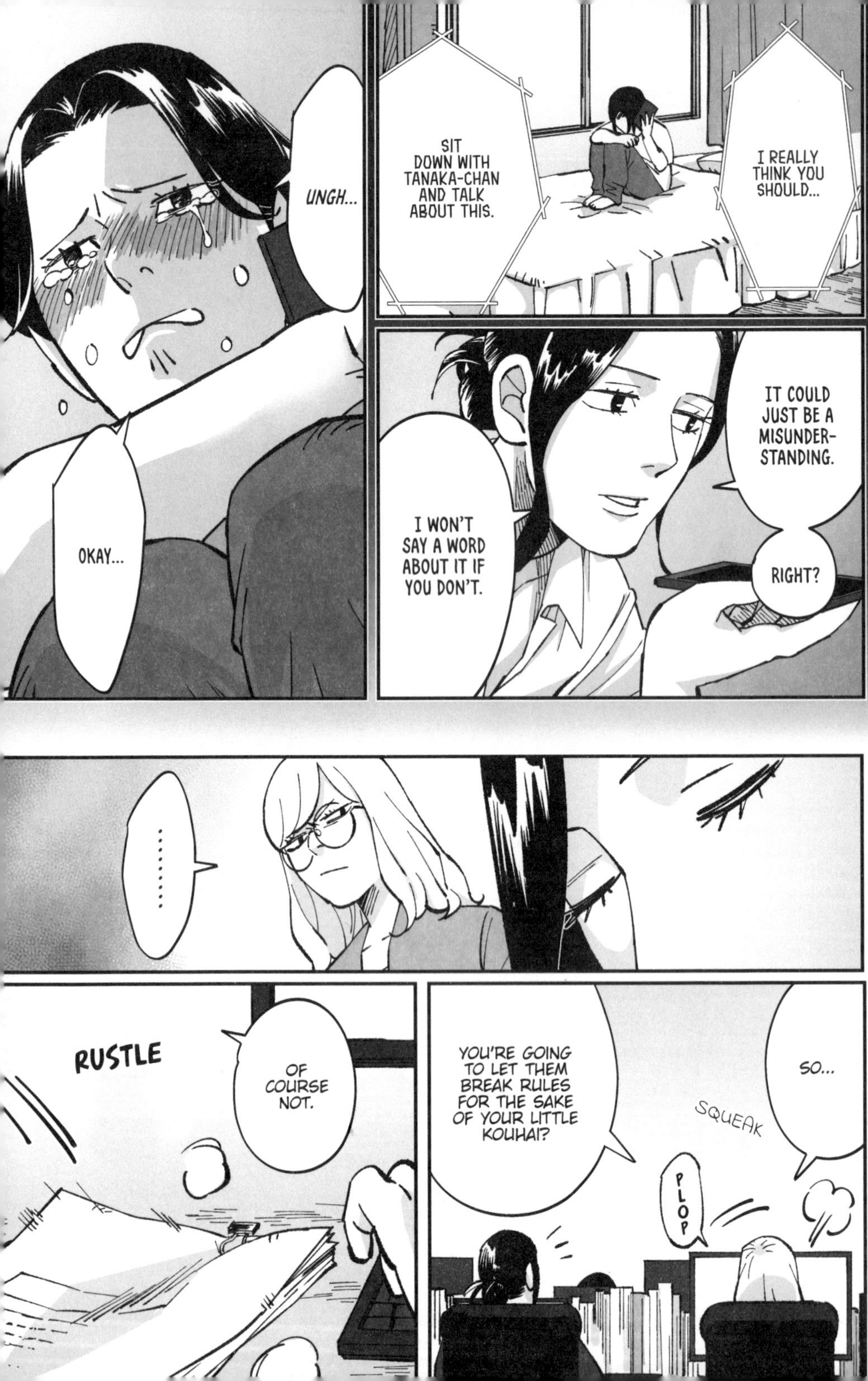
I REALLY THINK YOU SHOULD...
SIT DOWN WITH TANAKA-CHAN AND TALK ABOUT THIS.
IT COULD JUST BE A MISUNDER-STANDING.
RIGHT?
I WON'T SAY A WORD ABOUT IT IF YOU DON'T.
UNGH...
OKAY...
......
SO...
SQUEAK
PLOP
YOU'RE GOING TO LET THEM BREAK RULES FOR THE SAKE OF YOUR LITTLE KOUHAI?
OF COURSE NOT.
RUSTLE

PATCHED THINGS UP?

SEEMS LIKE THEY'VE PATCHED THINGS UP AND THEN SOME.

WHAT'S UP WITH THEM?

ISN'T IT WONDERFUL?

YOU TOLD HER THEY'RE SIBLINGS?

I JUST GAVE HER A LITTLE ENCOURAGEMENT.

THE BOND THAT THOSE TWO HAVE...

IS TOO STRONG TO BE BROKEN BY SOME GUY.

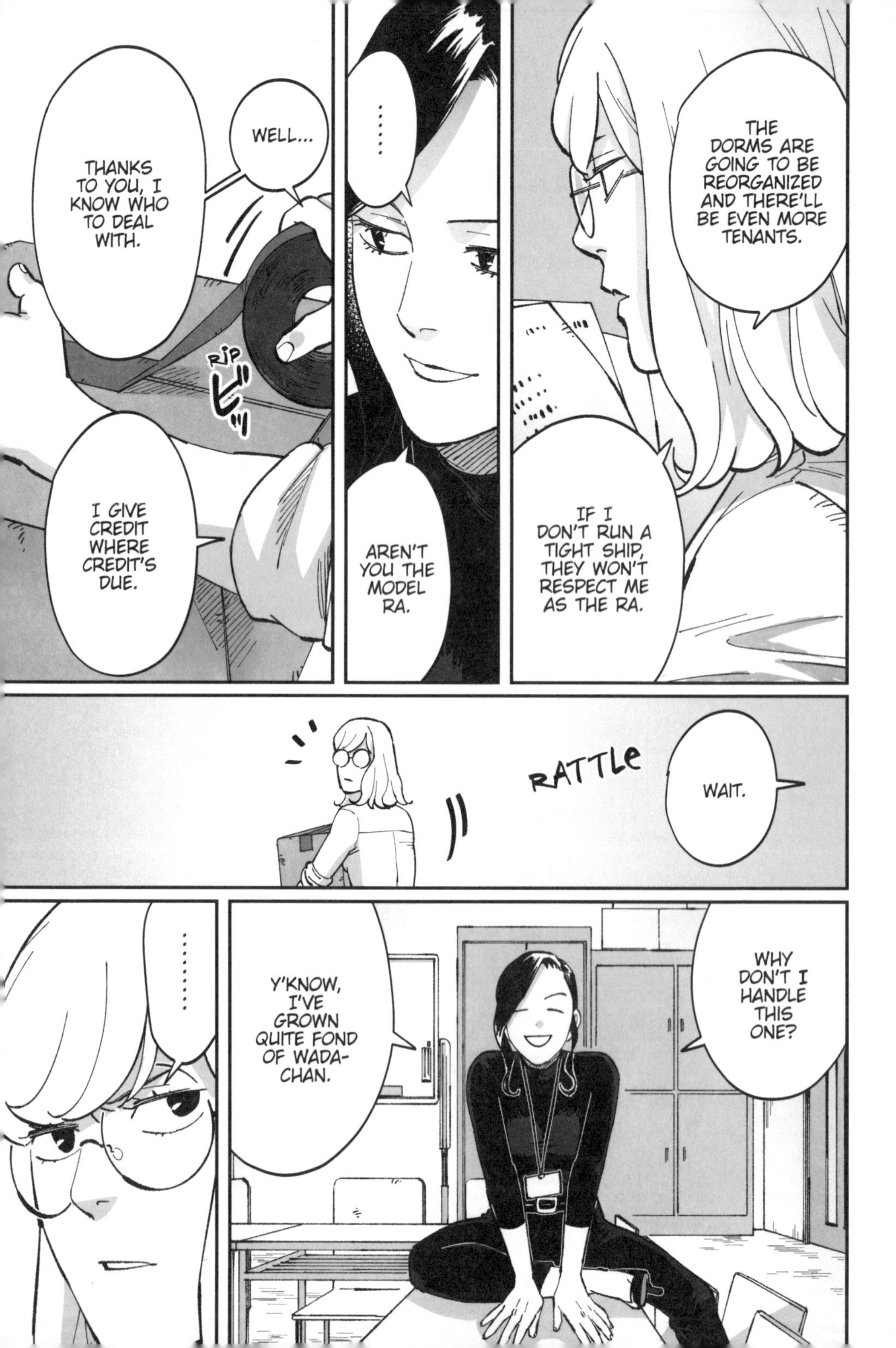
THE DORMS ARE GOING TO BE REORGANIZED AND THERE'LL BE EVEN MORE TENANTS.
IF I DON'T RUN A TIGHT SHIP, THEY WON'T RESPECT ME AS THE RA.
......
AREN'T YOU THE MODEL RA.
WELL...
THANKS TO YOU, I KNOW WHO TO DEAL WITH.
RIP
ビッ
I GIVE CREDIT WHERE CREDIT'S DUE.
WAIT.
RATTLE
WHY DON'T I HANDLE THIS ONE?
Y'KNOW, I'VE GROWN QUITE FOND OF WADA-CHAN.
......

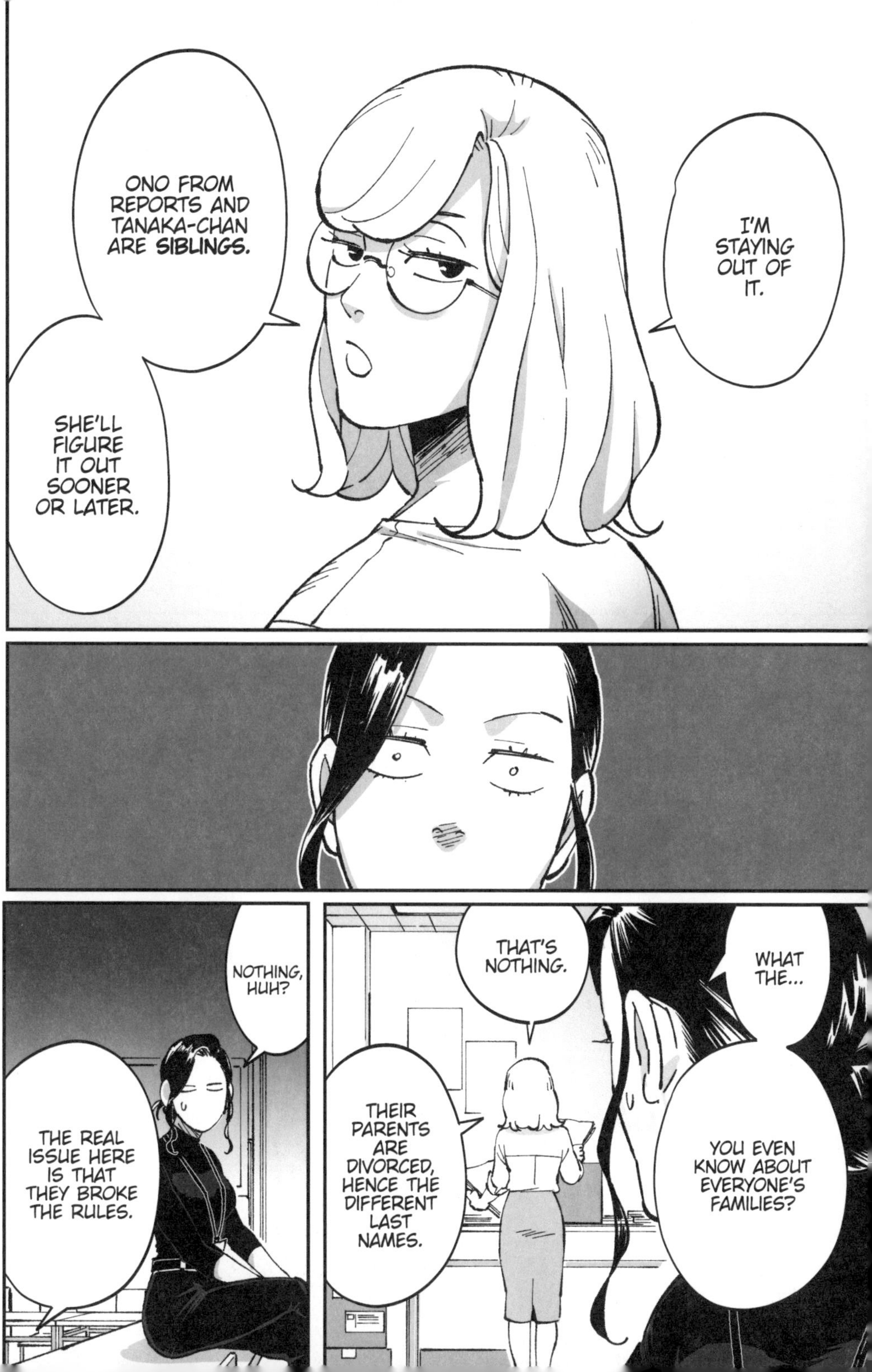
I'M STAYING OUT OF IT.
ONO FROM REPORTS AND TANAKA-CHAN ARE **SIBLINGS.**
SHE'LL FIGURE IT OUT SOONER OR LATER.
WHAT THE...
THAT'S NOTHING.
YOU EVEN KNOW ABOUT EVERYONE'S FAMILIES?
THEIR PARENTS ARE DIVORCED, HENCE THE DIFFERENT LAST NAMES.
NOTHING, HUH?
THE REAL ISSUE HERE IS THAT THEY BROKE THE RULES.

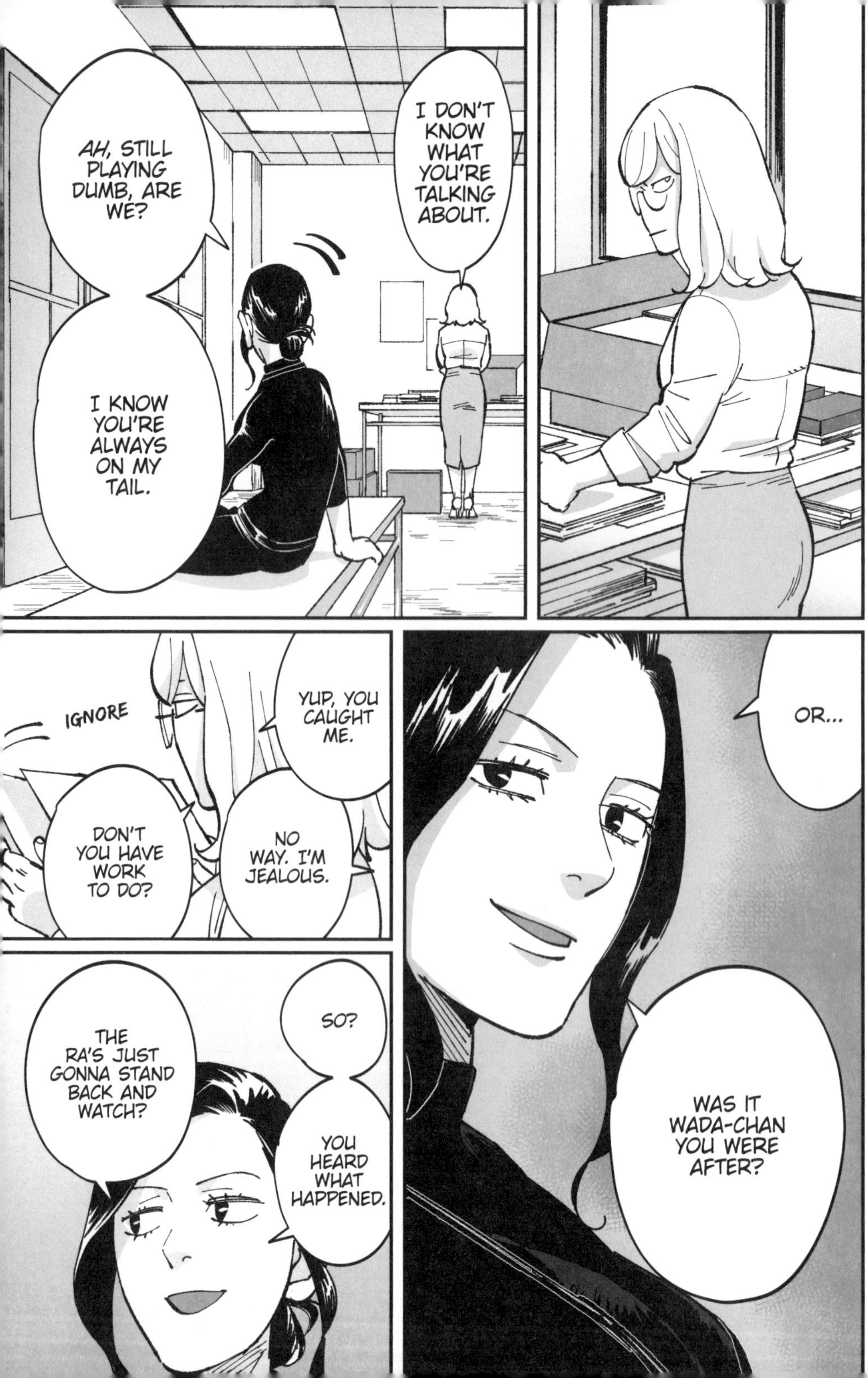
I DON'T KNOW WHAT YOU'RE TALKING ABOUT.
AH, STILL PLAYING DUMB, ARE WE?
I KNOW YOU'RE ALWAYS ON MY TAIL.
OR...
WAS IT WADA-CHAN YOU WERE AFTER?
YUP, YOU CAUGHT ME.
IGNORE
NO WAY. I'M JEALOUS.
DON'T YOU HAVE WORK TO DO?
SO?
YOU HEARD WHAT HAPPENED.
THE RA'S JUST GONNA STAND BACK AND WATCH?

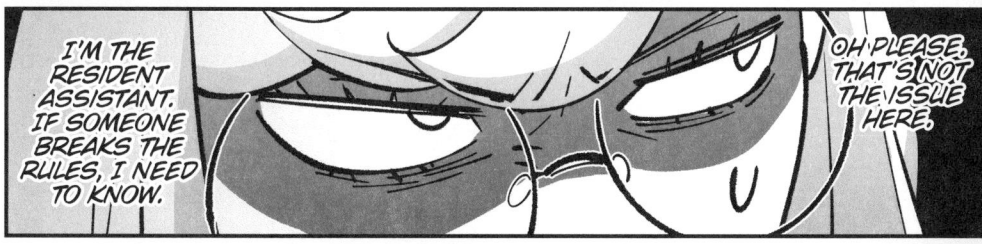

"WADA-CHAN..."

"I'M THE RESIDENT ASSISTANT. IF SOMEONE BREAKS THE RULES, I NEED TO KNOW."

"OH PLEASE, THAT'S NOT THE ISSUE HERE."

"DON'T YOU THINK SO?"

"MISS DEN MOTHER?"

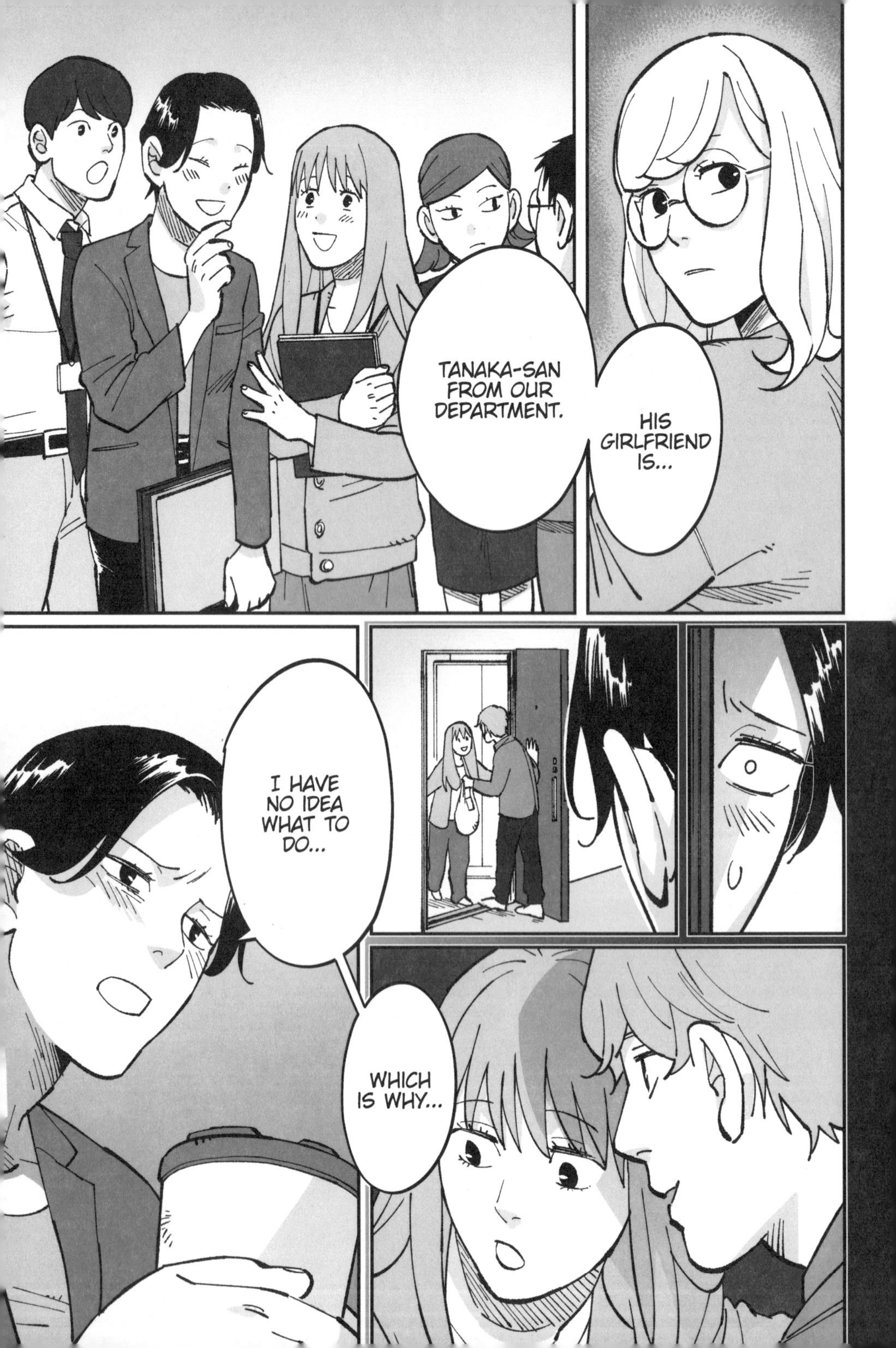
HIS GIRLFRIEND IS...
TANAKA-SAN FROM OUR DEPARTMENT.
I HAVE NO IDEA WHAT TO DO...
WHICH IS WHY...

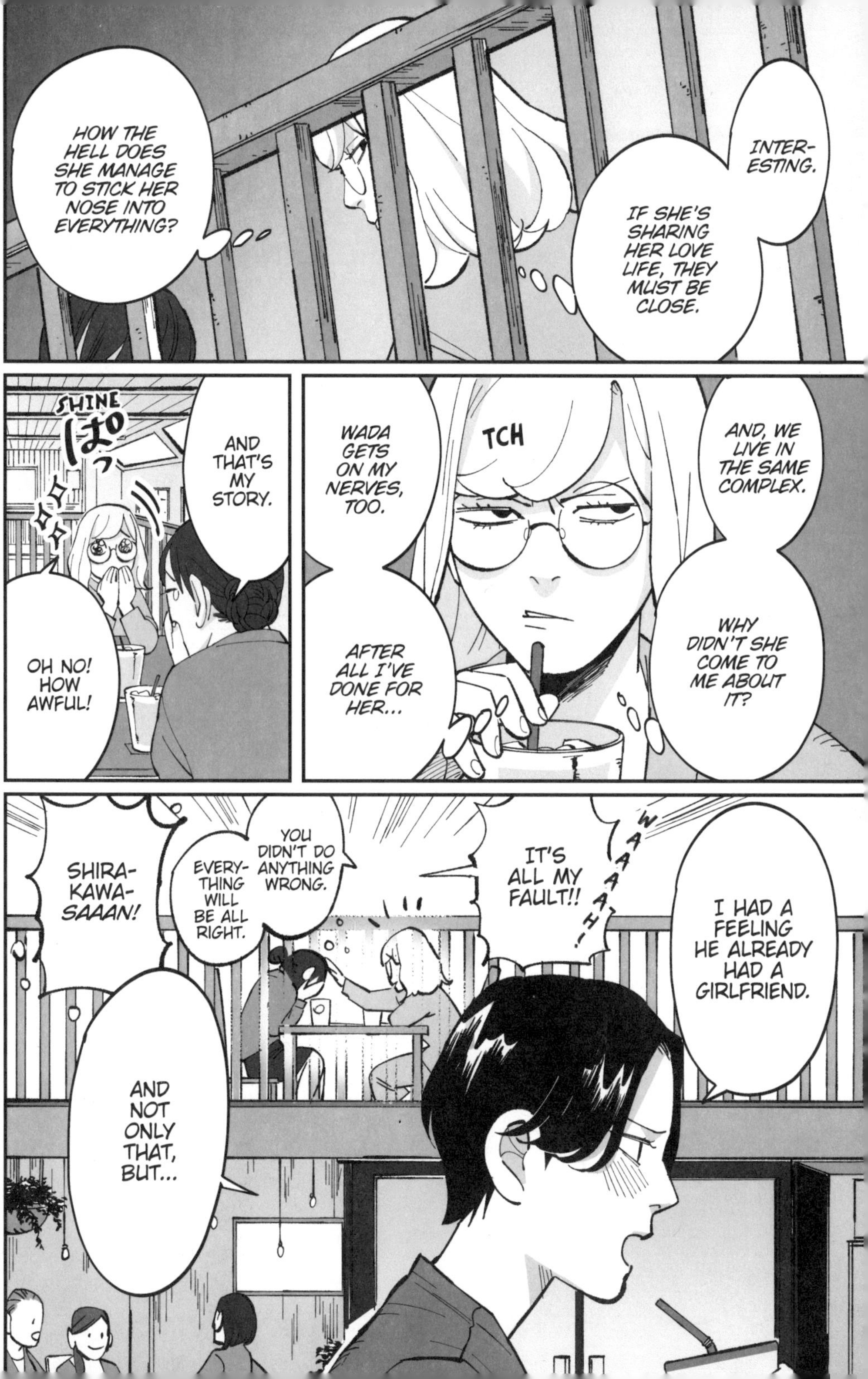
INTER-ESTING.
IF SHE'S SHARING HER LOVE LIFE, THEY MUST BE CLOSE.
HOW THE HELL DOES SHE MANAGE TO STICK HER NOSE INTO EVERYTHING?
AND, WE LIVE IN THE SAME COMPLEX.
TCH
WADA GETS ON MY NERVES, TOO.
WHY DIDN'T SHE COME TO ME ABOUT IT?
AFTER ALL I'VE DONE FOR HER...
AND THAT'S MY STORY.
SHINE
ぱっ
OH NO! HOW AWFUL!
I HAD A FEELING HE ALREADY HAD A GIRLFRIEND.
WAAAAH!
IT'S ALL MY FAULT!!
YOU DIDN'T DO ANYTHING WRONG.
EVERY-THING WILL BE ALL RIGHT.
SHIRA-KAWA-SAAAN!
AND NOT ONLY THAT, BUT...

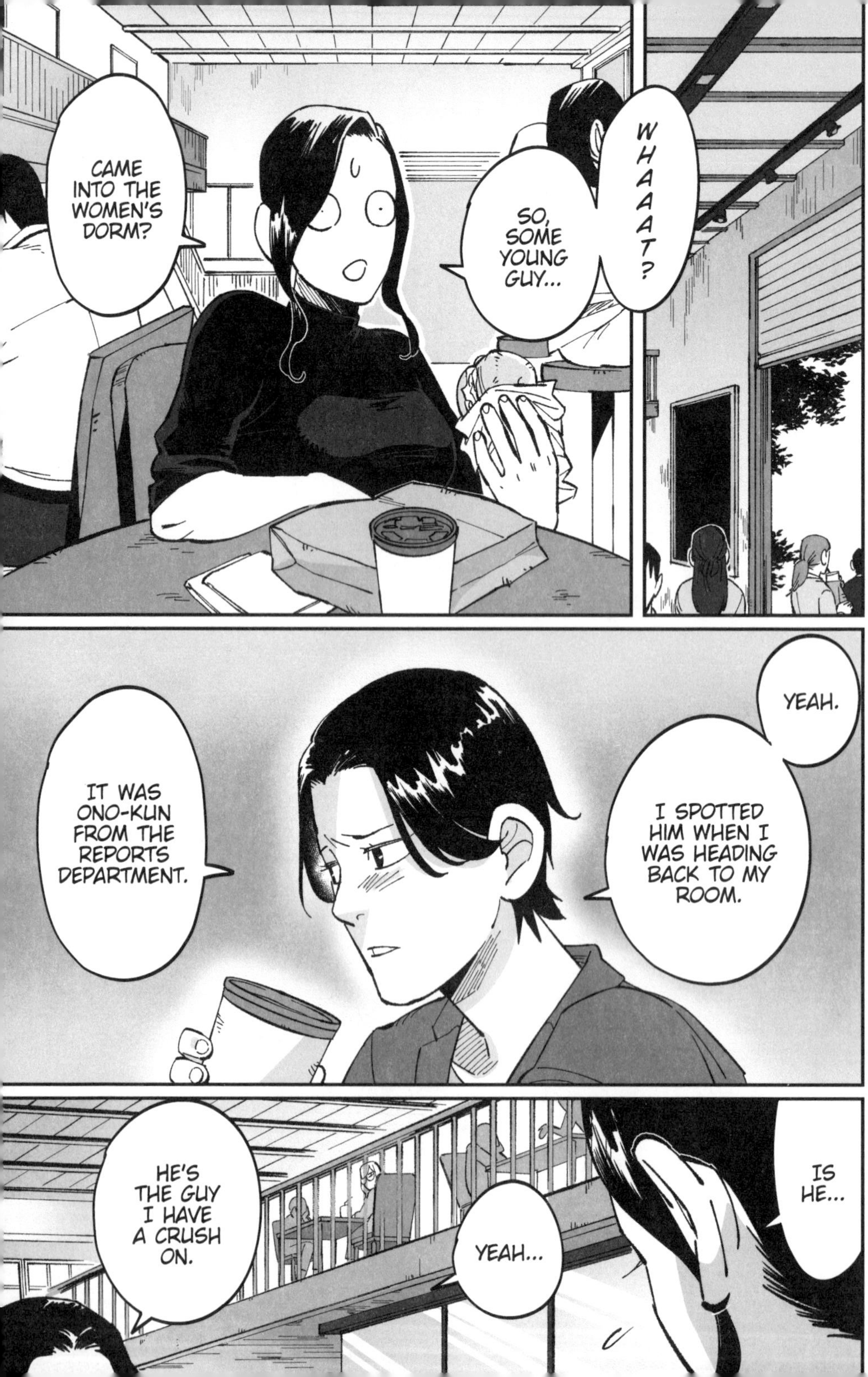
WHAAAAT?
SO, SOME YOUNG GUY...
CAME INTO THE WOMEN'S DORM?
YEAH.
I SPOTTED HIM WHEN I WAS HEADING BACK TO MY ROOM.
IT WAS ONO-KUN FROM THE REPORTS DEPARTMENT.
IS HE...
YEAH...
HE'S THE GUY I HAVE A CRUSH ON.

"THAT WOMAN IS GOING TO DRIVE ME TO DRINK."

"SHE'S GOT BITE MARKS ALL OVER HER BODY, AND YET..."

※ PERPETRATOR.

"SHE HAS SOME NERVE LYING TO HER KOUHAI LIKE THAT."

......

"THOSE TWO..."

"HAVE BEEN ATTACHED AT THE HIP LATELY."

......

THE TRAINING MATERIALS FOR THIS AFTERNOON.
SHIRAKAWA-SAN REVISED THE CURRICULUM FOR US.
TCH.
JUST MY LUCK.
WOW.
JUNKO-CHAN'S ALWAYS ONE STEP AHEAD.
IT'S INCREDIBLE THAT YOU GOT THIS ALL DONE SO FAST.
I'M SORRY, IT'S ALL MY FAULT FOR NOT CONSULTING YOU FIRST...
DON'T WORRY ABOUT IT!
BEAM
SUPPORTING THE TRAINING STAFF IS A PART OF MY JOB!
SHIRAKAWA-SAAAN...

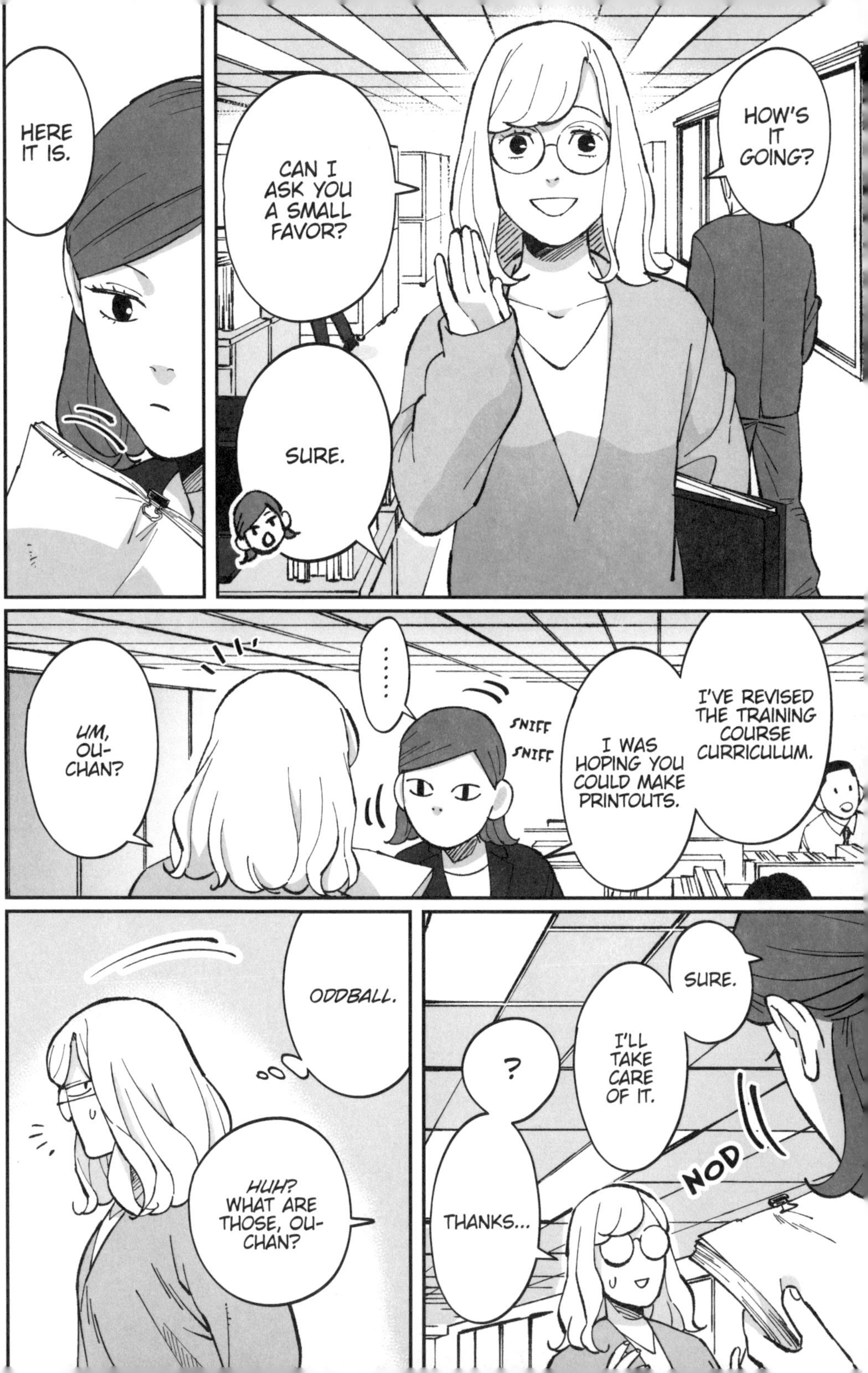
HOW'S IT GOING?
CAN I ASK YOU A SMALL FAVOR?
SURE.
HERE IT IS.
I'VE REVISED THE TRAINING COURSE CURRICULUM.
I WAS HOPING YOU COULD MAKE PRINTOUTS.
SNIFF
SNIFF
......
UM, OU-CHAN?
SURE.
I'LL TAKE CARE OF IT.
?
NOD
THANKS...
ODDBALL.
HUH? WHAT ARE THOSE, OU-CHAN?

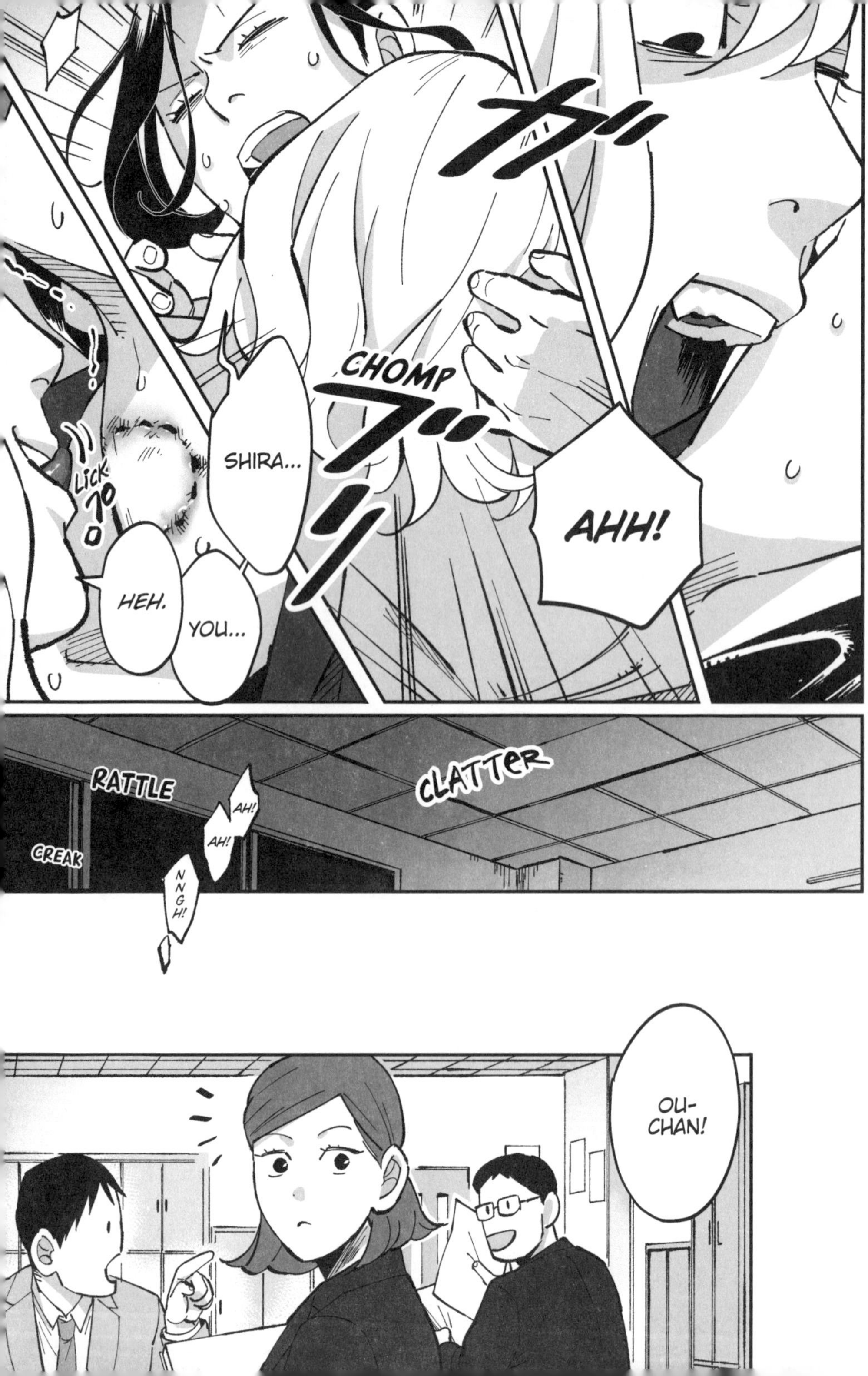
CHOMP
AHH!
SHIRA...
YOU...
HEH.
LICK
CLATTER
AH!
AH!
RATTLE
NNGH!
CREAK
OU-CHAN!

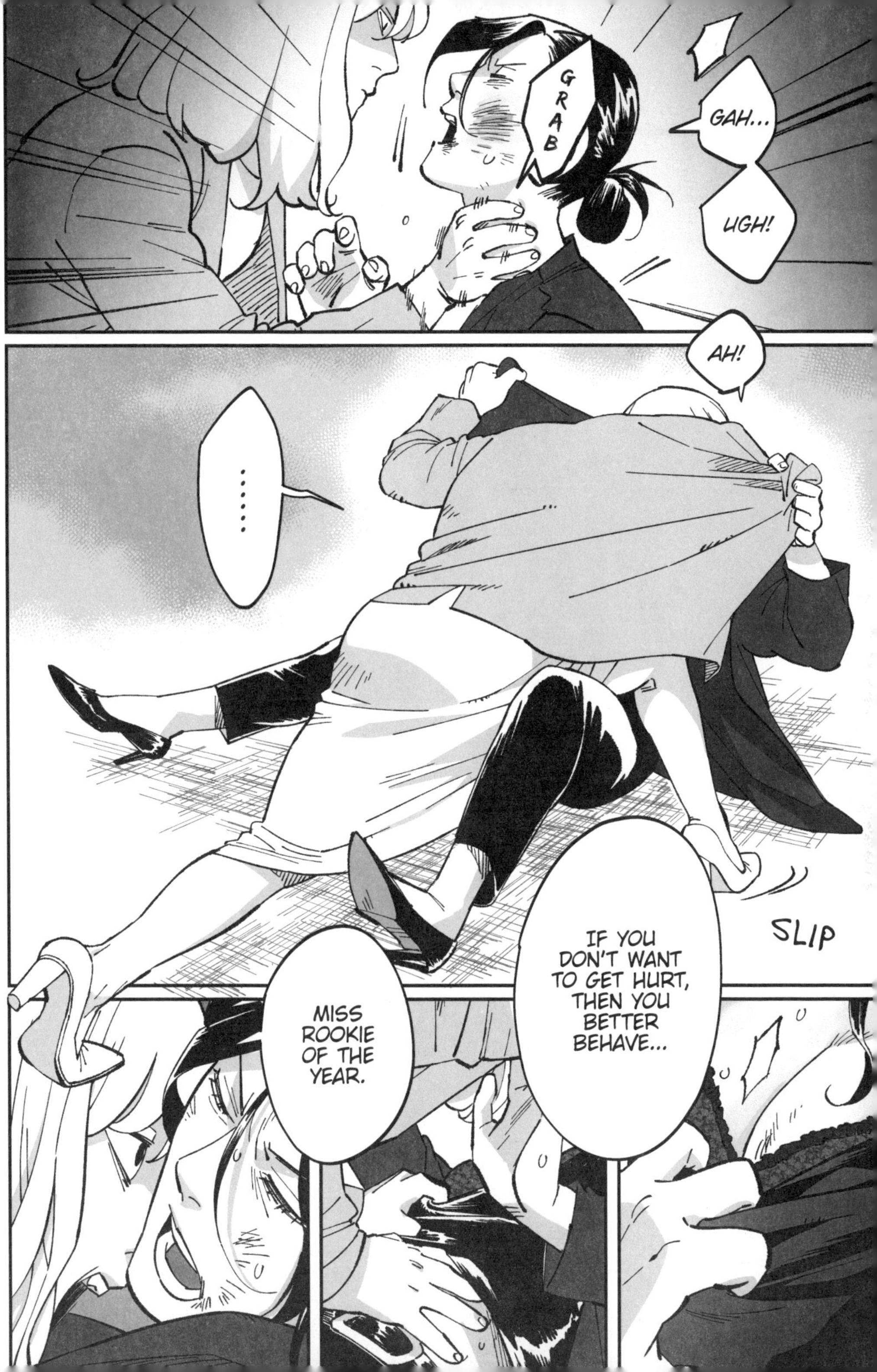
GAH...
UGH!
GRAB
AH!
......
SLIP
IF YOU DON'T WANT TO GET HURT, THEN YOU BETTER BEHAVE...
MISS ROOKIE OF THE YEAR.

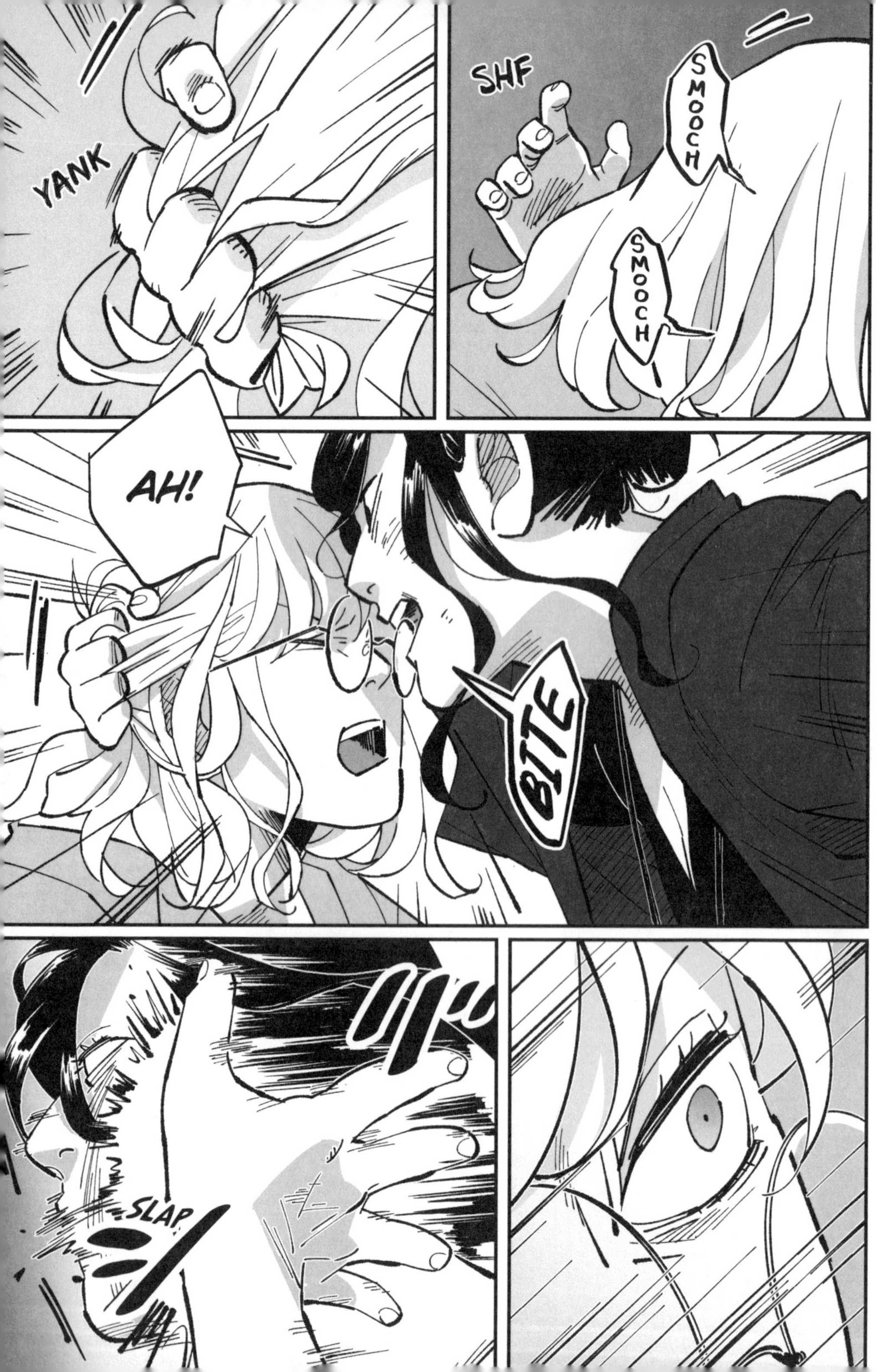
SHF
SMOOCH
SMOOCH
YANK
AH!
BITE
SLAP

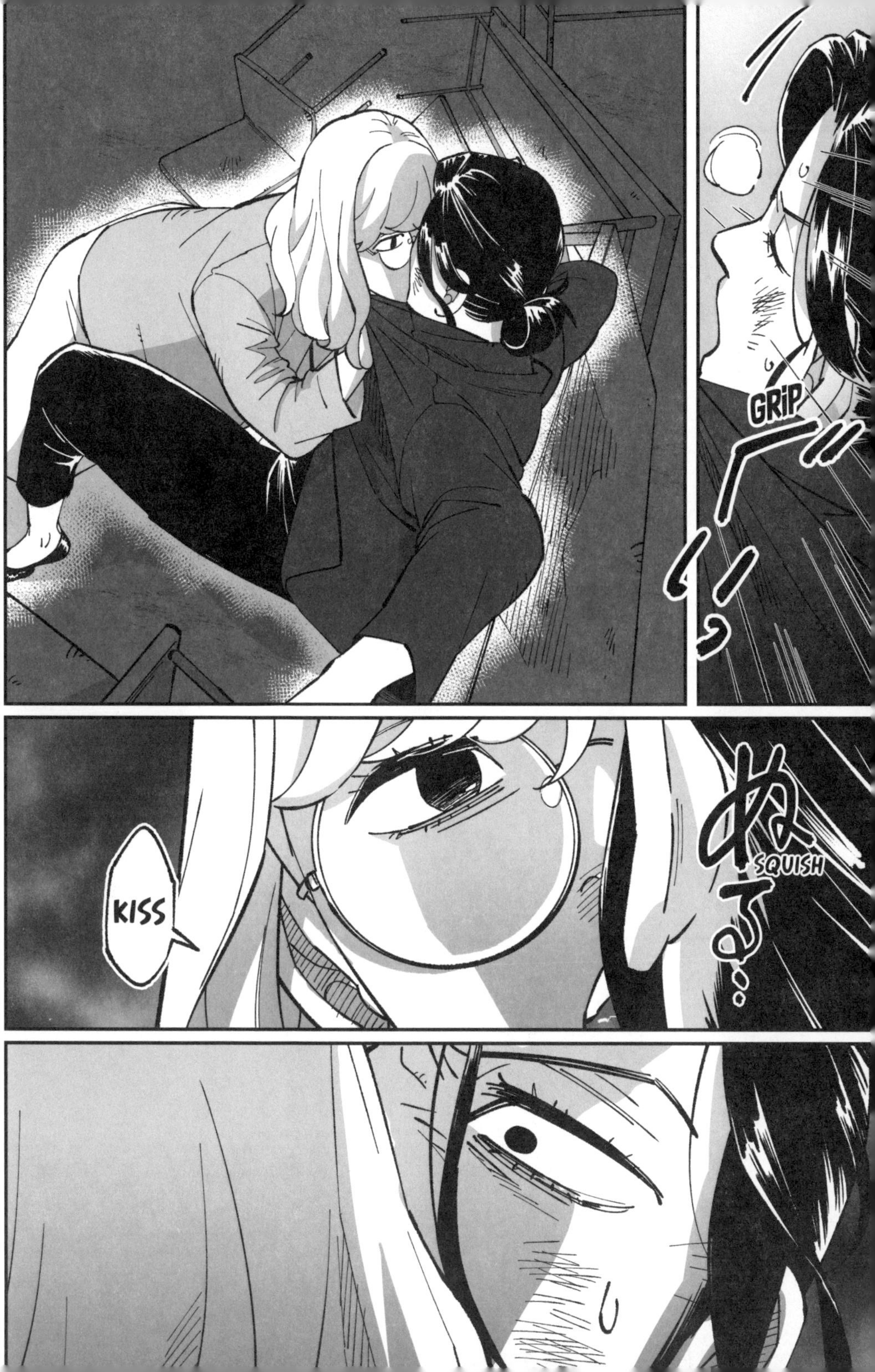
GRIP
KISS
ぬる…
SQUISH

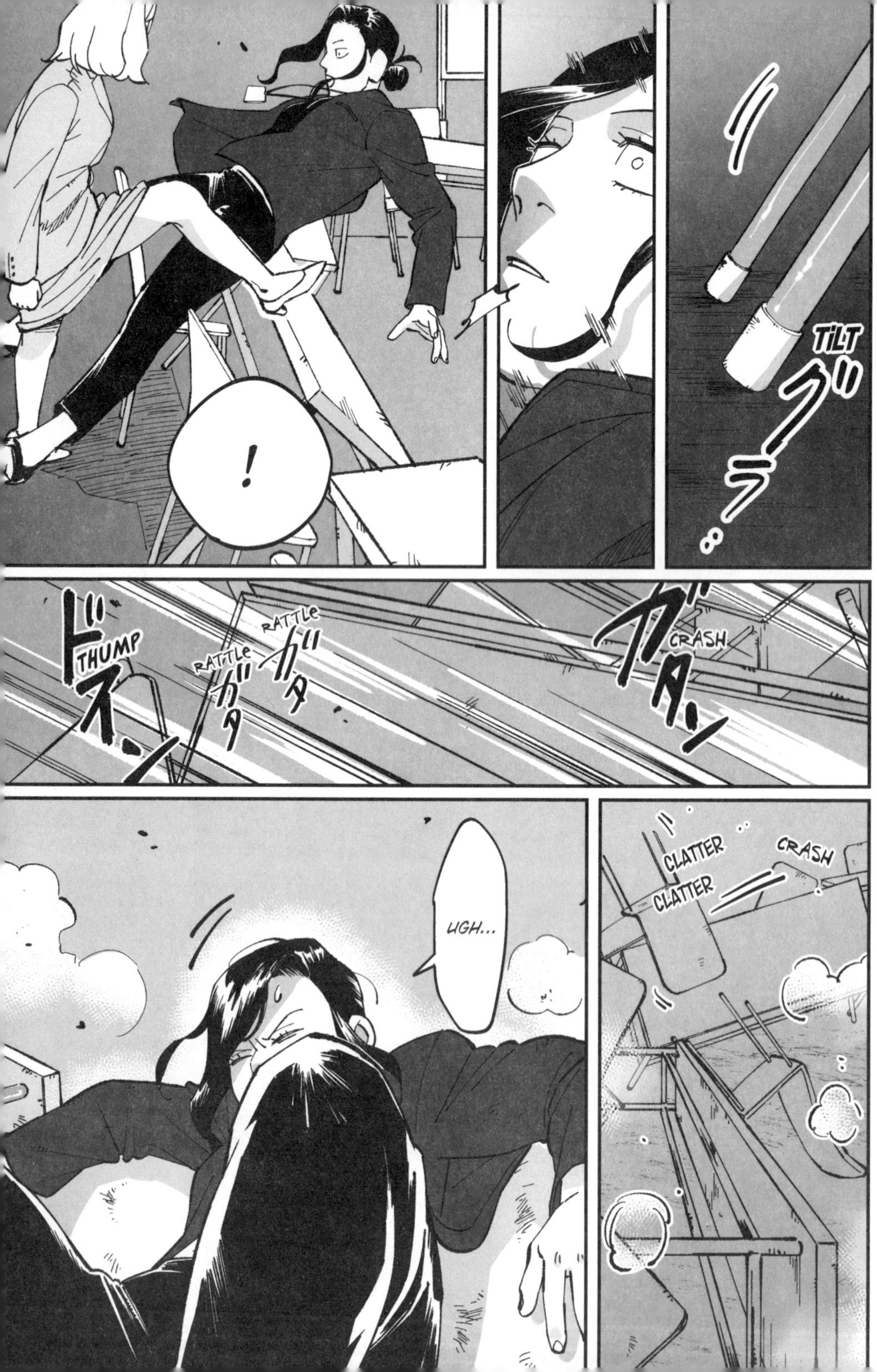
TILT
!
CRASH
RATTLE
RATTLE
THUMP
CRASH
CLATTER
CLATTER
UGH...

GOTTA HAND IT TO YOU.
YOU REALLY KNOW HOW TO PISS ME OFF.
CRACK
TAP
TAP
MAYBE I SHOULD'VE TOLD YOU THIS EARLIER, BUT...
TAP
TAP
YOU NEED TO STAY IN YOUR LANE.
THUD

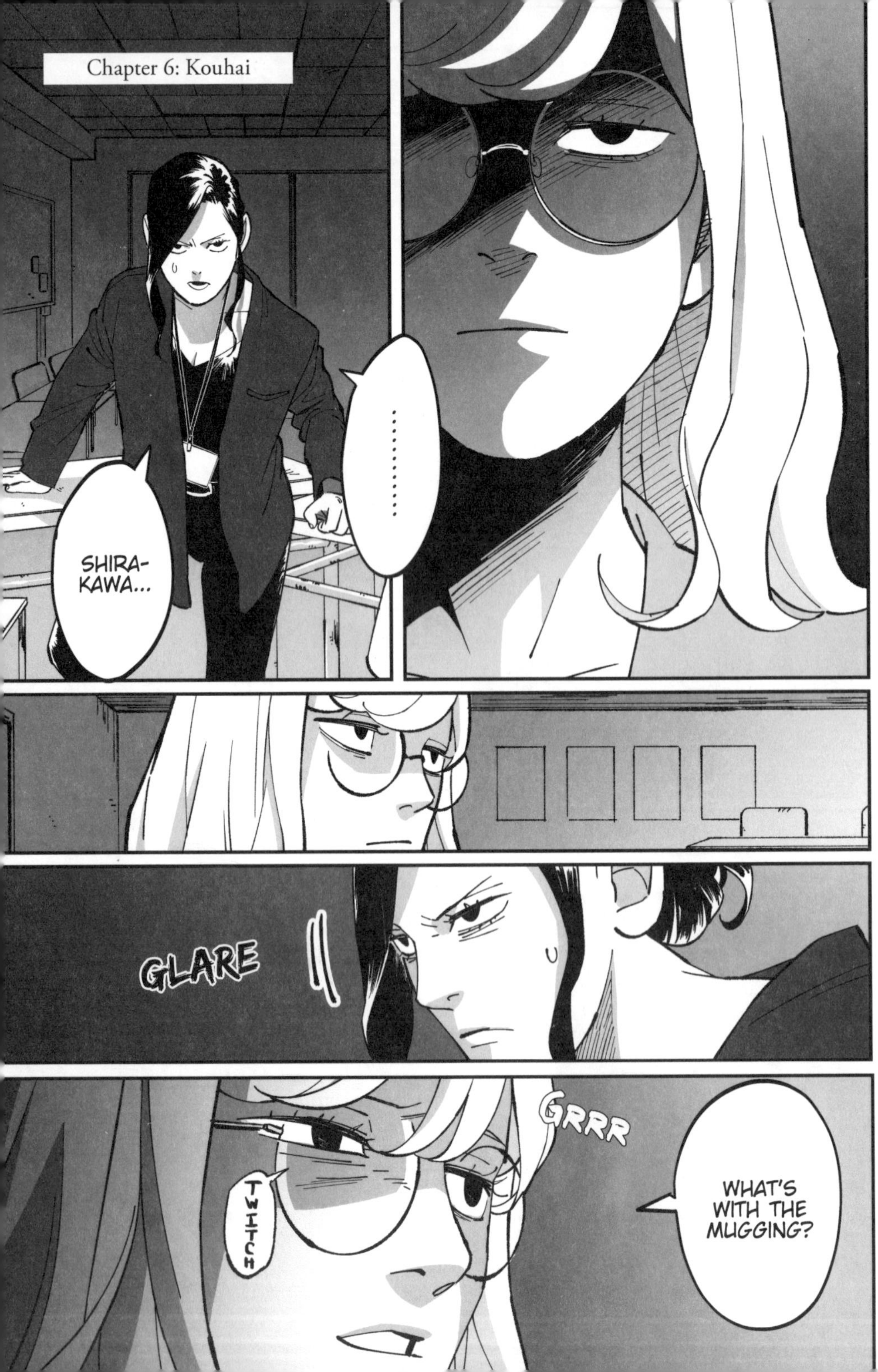

......
Chapter 6: Kouhai
SHIRA-KAWA...
GLARE
GRRR
WHAT'S WITH THE MUGGING?
TWITCH

Black & White
TOUGH LOVE AT THE OFFICE

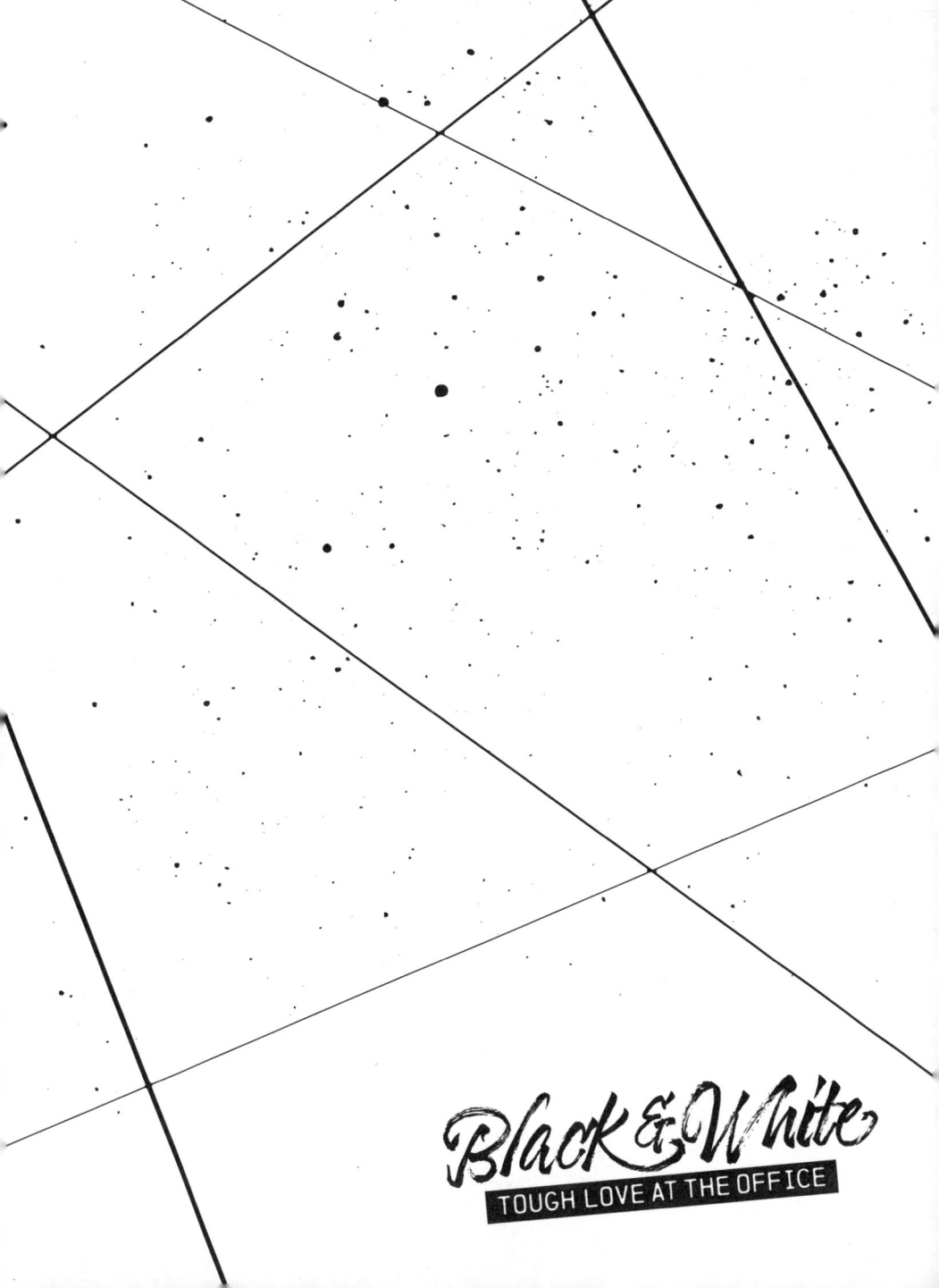

CLICK

!

SHIRA-KAWA...

Chapter 5 – Fin

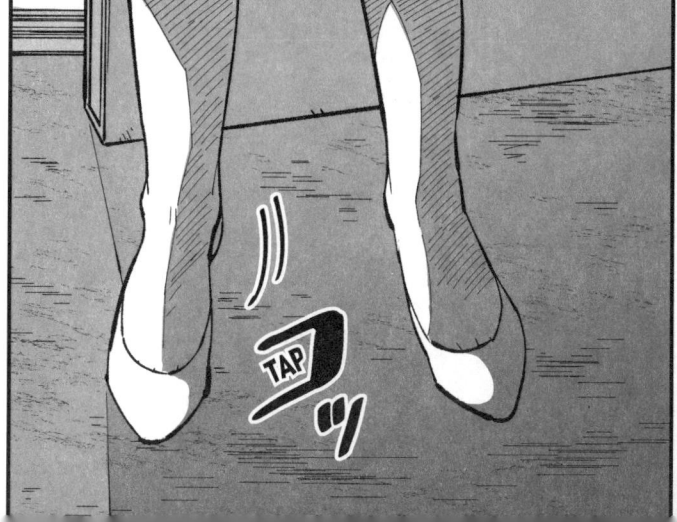

TUMBLE

?!
CREAK
CLATTER
OUCH...

NNGH!

TAP

HER BAGS WERE GONE LAST TIME I CHECKED.
SHIRAKAWA MUST'VE GONE HOME ALREADY.
TAP
IT'S PAST EIGHT P.M...
!

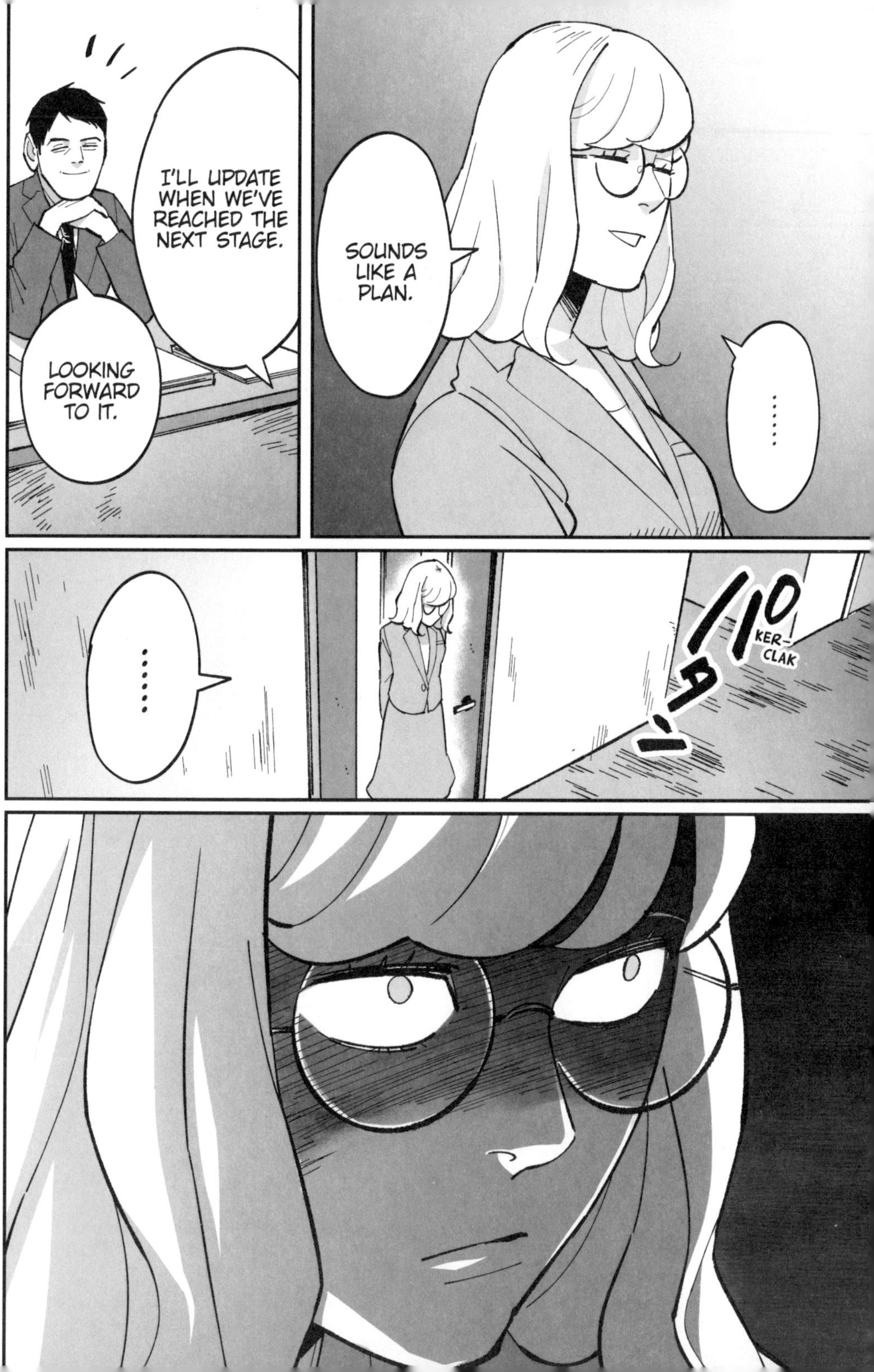
SOUNDS LIKE A PLAN.
......
I'LL UPDATE WHEN WE'VE REACHED THE NEXT STAGE.
LOOKING FORWARD TO IT.
KER-CLAK
......

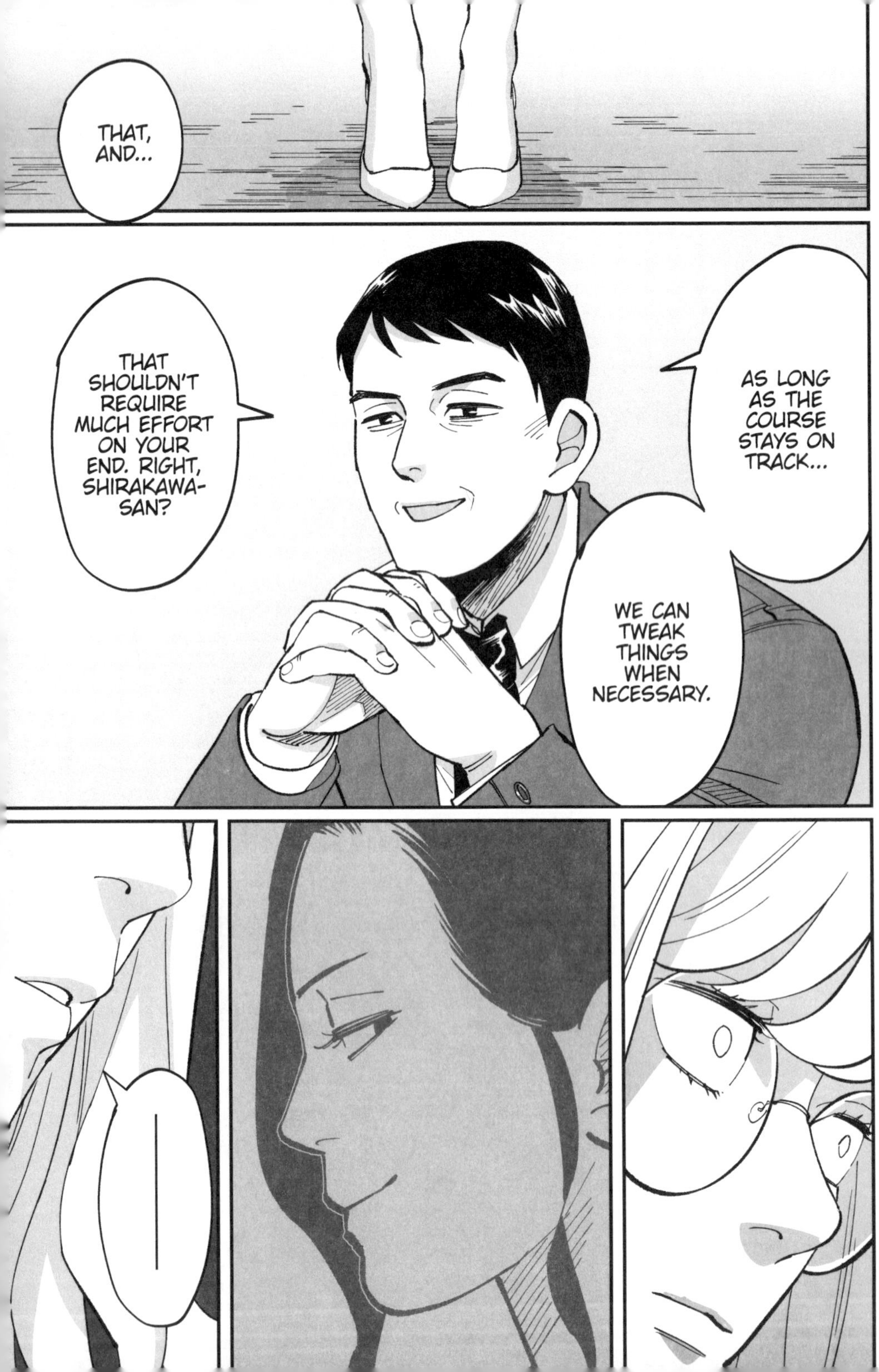
THAT, AND...
AS LONG AS THE COURSE STAYS ON TRACK...
WE CAN TWEAK THINGS WHEN NECESSARY.
THAT SHOULDN'T REQUIRE MUCH EFFORT ON YOUR END. RIGHT, SHIRAKAWA-SAN?

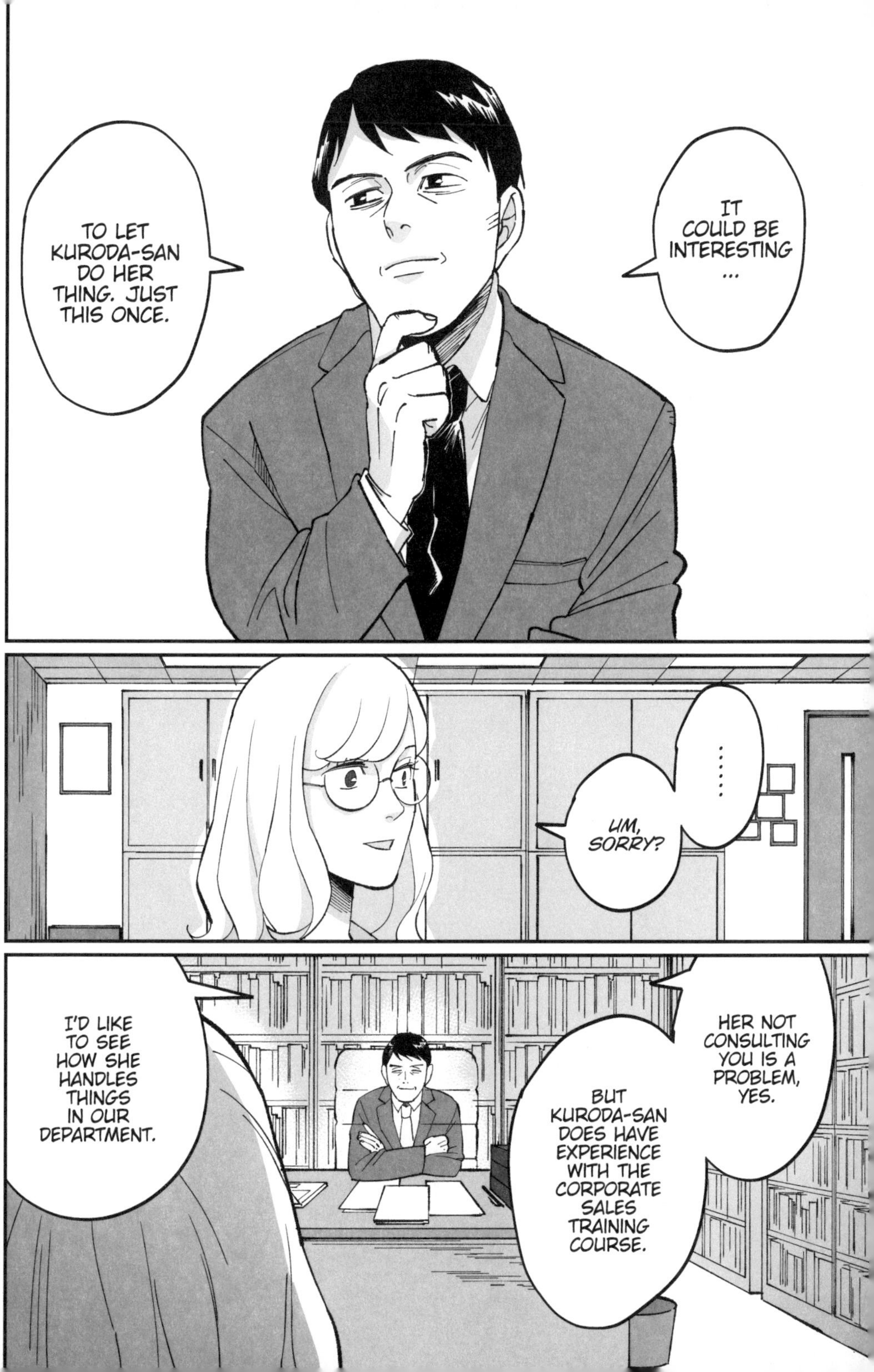
IT COULD BE INTERESTING ...
TO LET KURODA-SAN DO HER THING. JUST THIS ONCE.
......
UM, SORRY?
HER NOT CONSULTING YOU IS A PROBLEM, YES.
BUT KURODA-SAN DOES HAVE EXPERIENCE WITH THE CORPORATE SALES TRAINING COURSE.
I'D LIKE TO SEE HOW SHE HANDLES THINGS IN OUR DEPARTMENT.

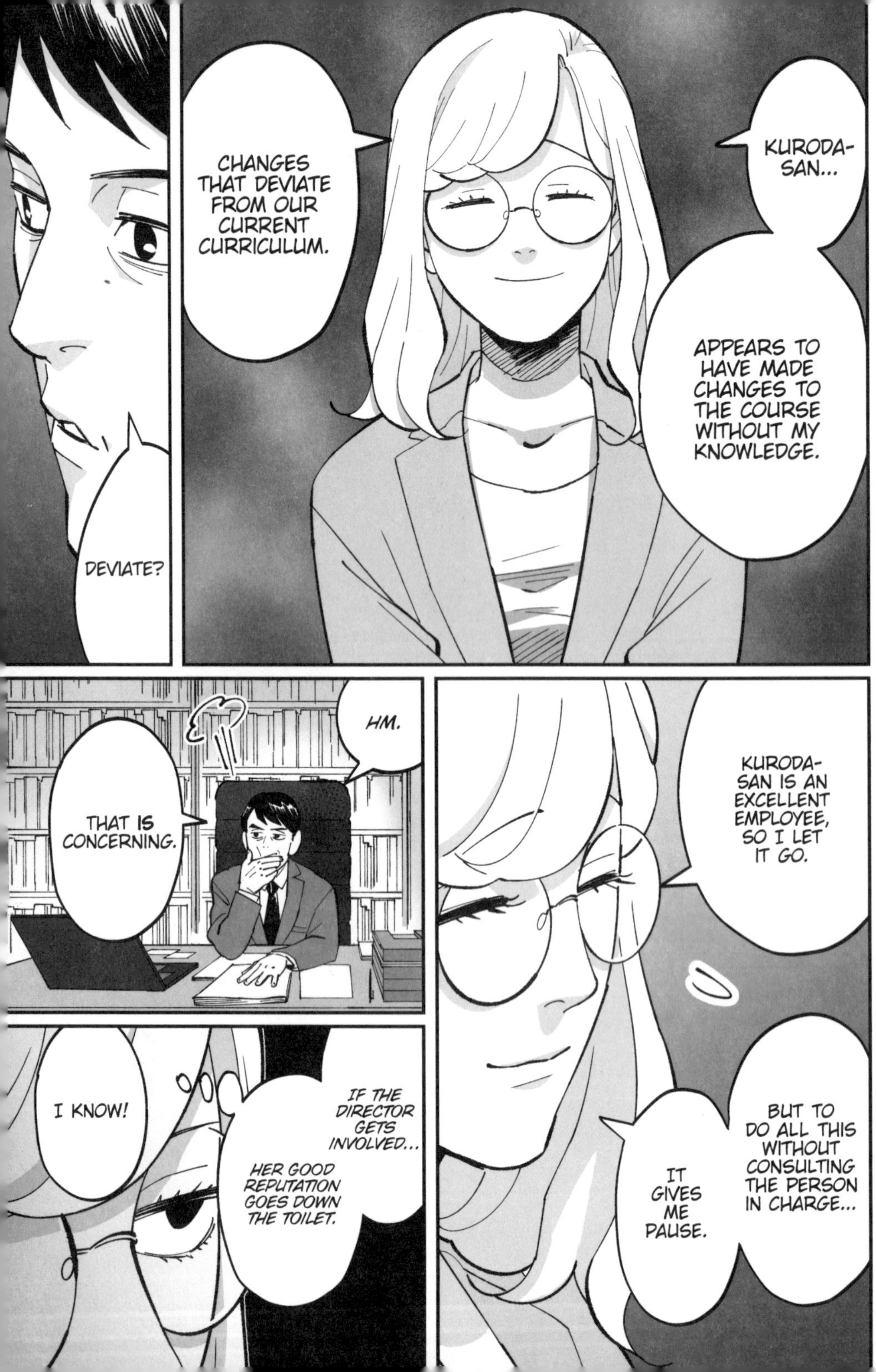
KURODA-SAN...
APPEARS TO HAVE MADE CHANGES TO THE COURSE WITHOUT MY KNOWLEDGE.
CHANGES THAT DEVIATE FROM OUR CURRENT CURRICULUM.
DEVIATE?
KURODA-SAN IS AN EXCELLENT EMPLOYEE, SO I LET IT GO.
BUT TO DO ALL THIS WITHOUT CONSULTING THE PERSON IN CHARGE...
IT GIVES ME PAUSE.
HM.
THAT IS CONCERNING.
IF THE DIRECTOR GETS INVOLVED...
HER GOOD REPUTATION GOES DOWN THE TOILET.
I KNOW!

AS I EXPECTED...
PUTTING YOU IN CHARGE WAS THE RIGHT DECISION.
FLIP パラ
FLIP パラ
FLIP パラ
LOOKS LIKE EVERY-THING'S GOING ACCORDING TO PLAN.
I BET THEY'LL BE READY FOR ACTUAL WORK BEFORE THE COURSE IS EVEN OVER.
NICE JOB.
OH, NO.
THE TRAINING STAFF DESERVES ALL THE CREDIT.
HOWEVER...
I DO HAVE A FEW CONCERNS.
CONCERNS?

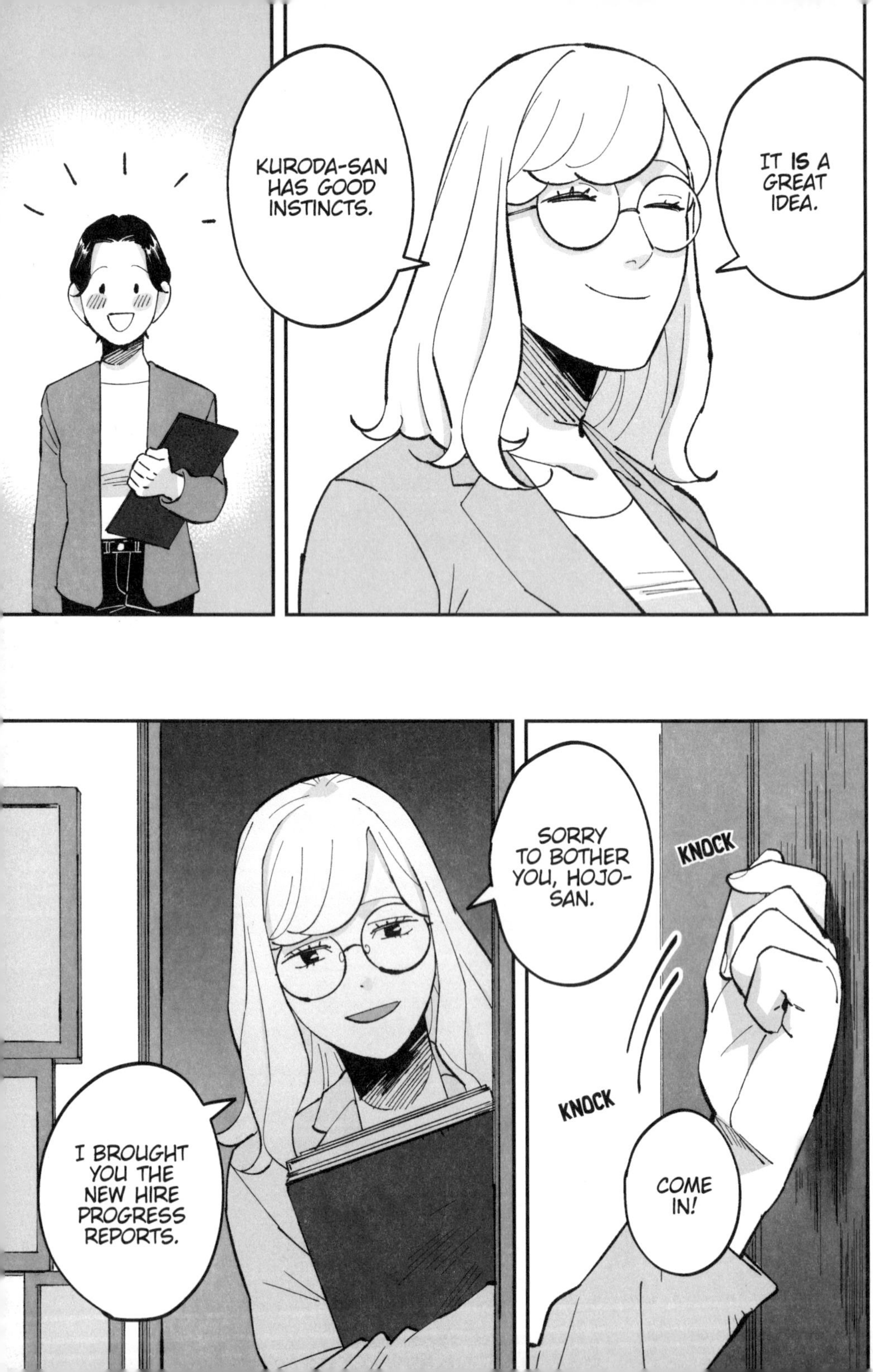
IT IS A GREAT IDEA.
KURODA-SAN HAS GOOD INSTINCTS.
KNOCK
KNOCK
COME IN!
SORRY TO BOTHER YOU, HOJO-SAN.
I BROUGHT YOU THE NEW HIRE PROGRESS REPORTS.

OH, THAT?

I KNOW WE'RE SUPPOSED TO COVER APPROVAL REQUESTS AT THE END, BUT..

I THOUGHT IT'D BE NICE TO MIX THINGS UP A LITTLE FOR THE NEWBIES.

WHEN I ASKED **KURODA-SAN** ABOUT IT...

SHE SAID IT WAS A GREAT IDEA..

SHE'S RIGHT.

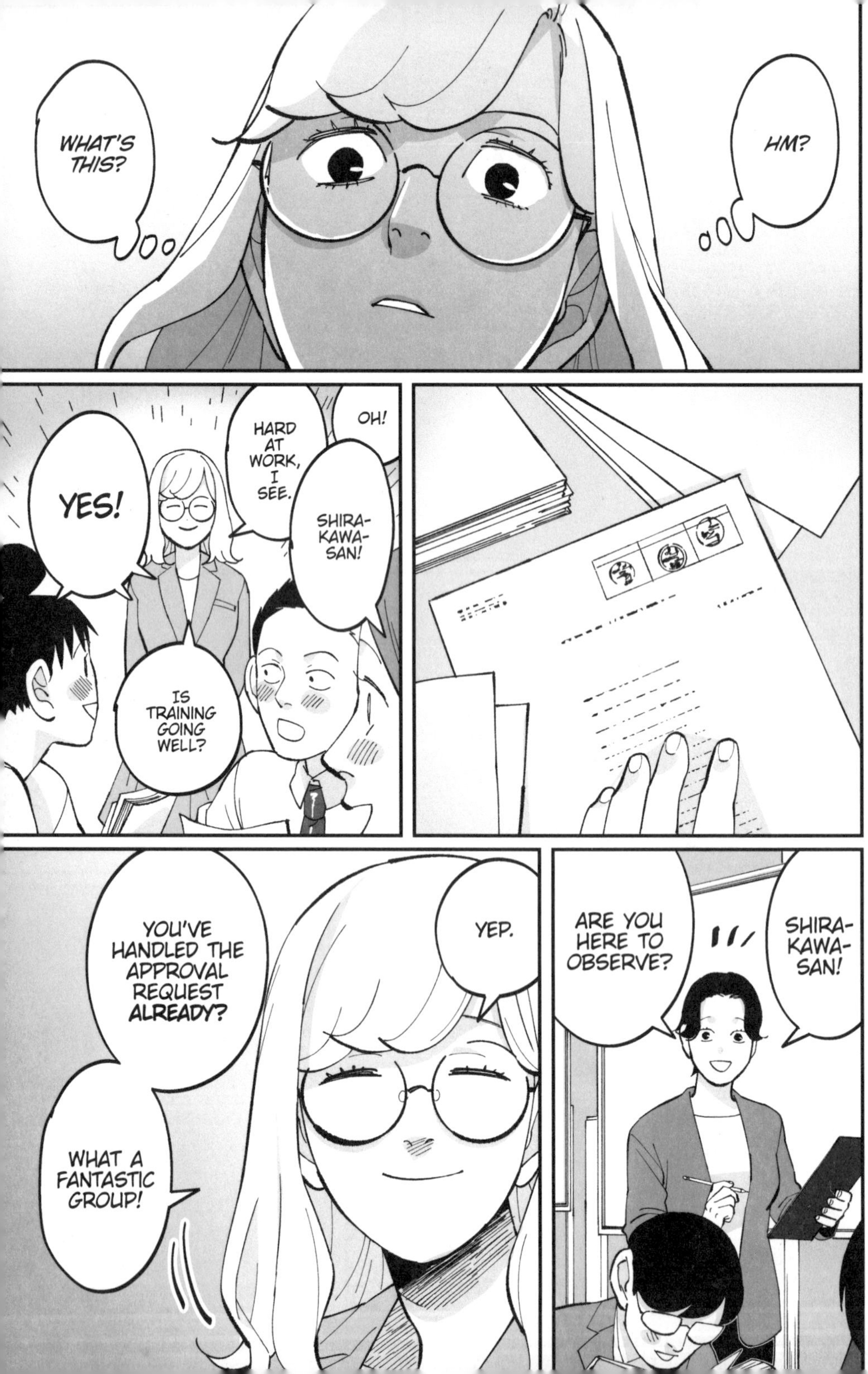
HM?
WHAT'S THIS?
OH!
SHIRA-KAWA-SAN!
HARD AT WORK, I SEE.
YES!
IS TRAINING GOING WELL?
SHIRA-KAWA-SAN!
ARE YOU HERE TO OBSERVE?
YEP.
YOU'VE HANDLED THE APPROVAL REQUEST **ALREADY?**
WHAT A FANTASTIC GROUP!

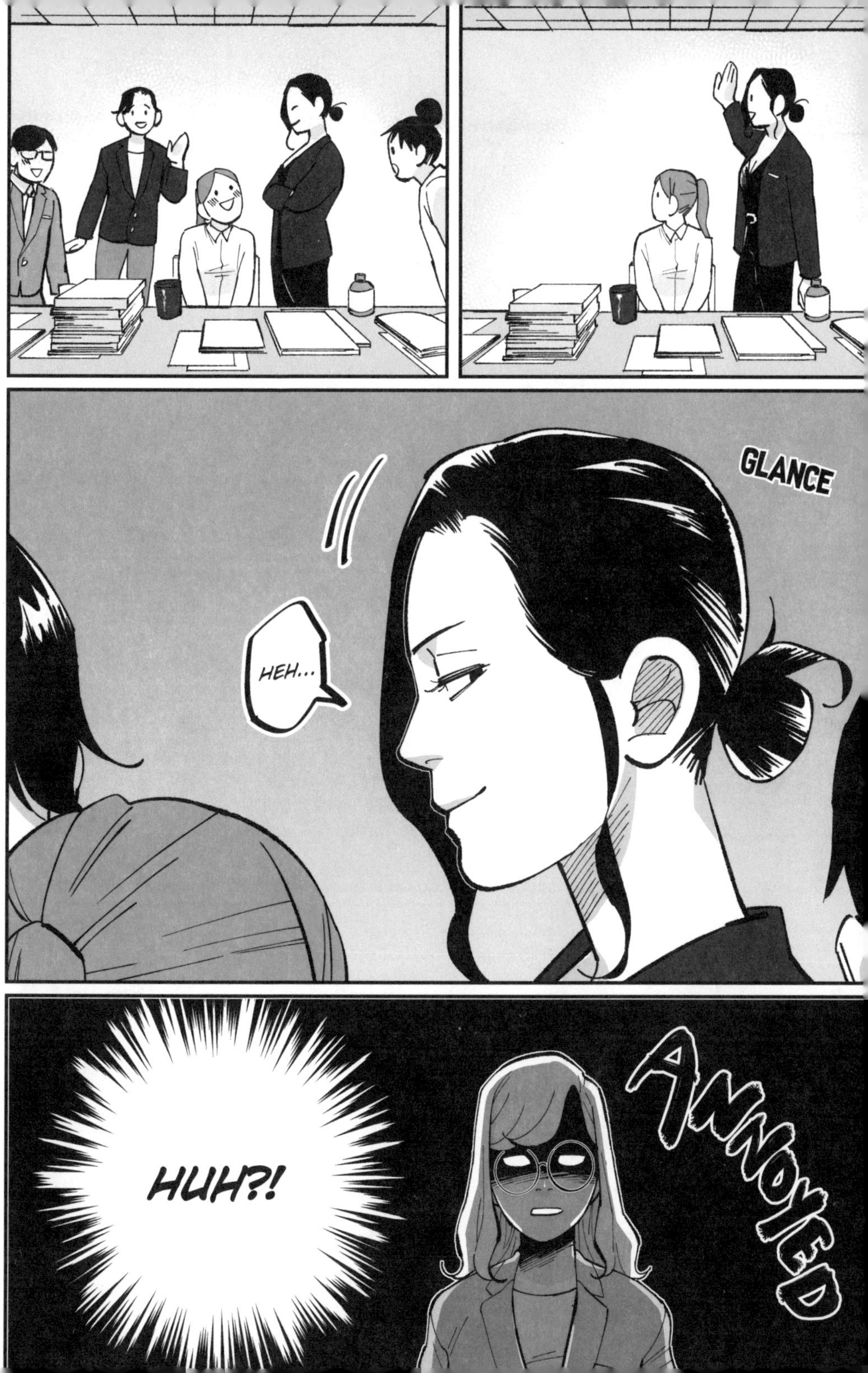
GLANCE
HEH...
HUH?!
ANNOYED

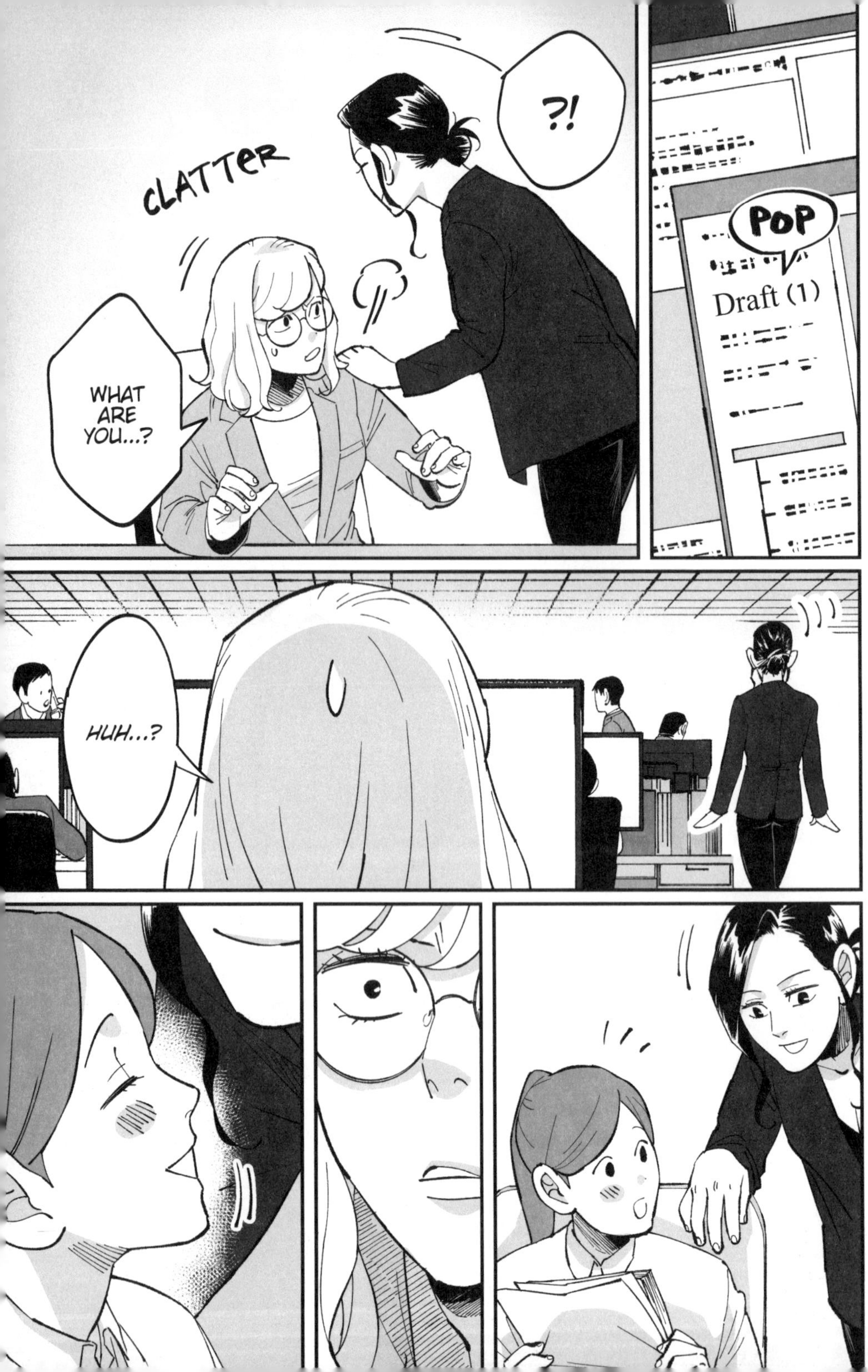

?!
CLATTER
POP
Draft (1)
WHAT ARE YOU...?
HUH...?

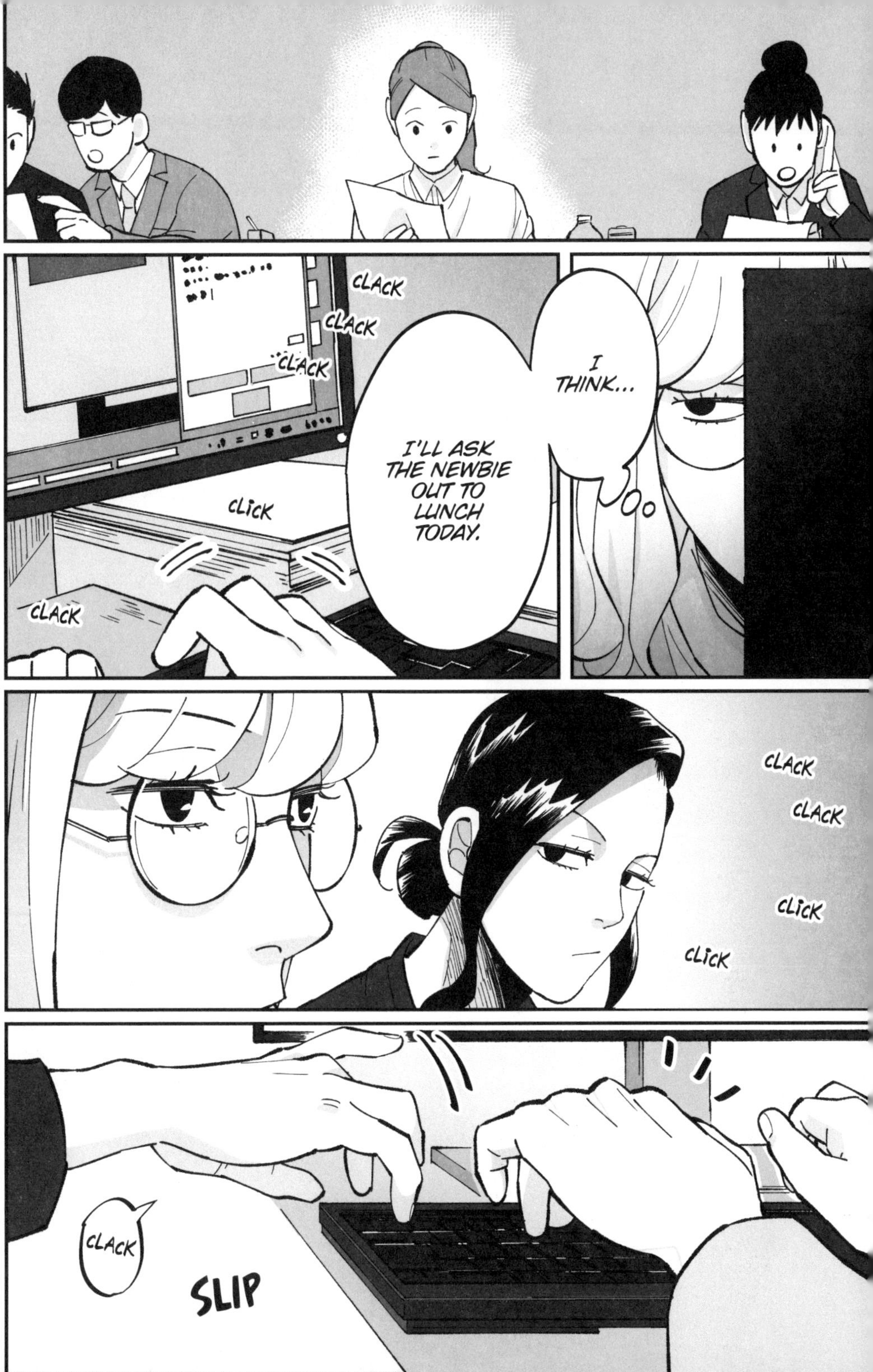
I THINK...
I'LL ASK THE NEWBIE OUT TO LUNCH TODAY.
CLACK
CLACK
CLACK
CLICK
CLACK
CLACK
CLACK
CLICK
CLICK
CLACK
SLIP

MAYBE... I'D JUST BE GETTING IN THEIR WAY.	IT DOESN'T SEEM LIKE ANYONE NEEDS THE EXTRA HELP...

HOW ABOUT YOU INVITE THEM TO LUNCH?

I'LL COME TOO.

WADA-CHAN.

SIGH...
OH!
NICE, ARE THOSE TRAINING MATERIALS?
JOLT
!
KURODA-SAN!
DID YOU MAKE 'EM YOURSELF?
......
......
I JUST THOUGHT THEY'D HELP CLARIFY THINGS.
HOW SWEET! YOU'RE A PEACH, WADA-CHAN!
YOU REALLY THINK SO...?
HM?

As previously discussed...
we didn't purchase them per official guidelines.
AND THAT'S WHY YOUR WORK JOURNALS NEED TO BE COMPLETED DURING OFFICE HOURS.
SO COOL!
GUYS...
ARE YOU LISTEN-ING?
HELLO?
....

New Hires
AND THAT'S THE BUSINESS WORKFLOW. YOU'LL LEARN ALL THE DETAILS NEXT WEEK.
I KNOW THERE'S A LOT TO LEARN, BUT...
DON'T WORRY. KURODA-SAN AND I ARE HERE TO HELP.
IF YOU RUN INTO ANY ISSUES, PLEASE DON'T HESITATE TO ASK.
I'M HERE FOR YOU IF YOU NEED ANYTHING.
SMILE
AAAAH...
SCRIBBLE
SCRIBBLE
......
WE WILL!

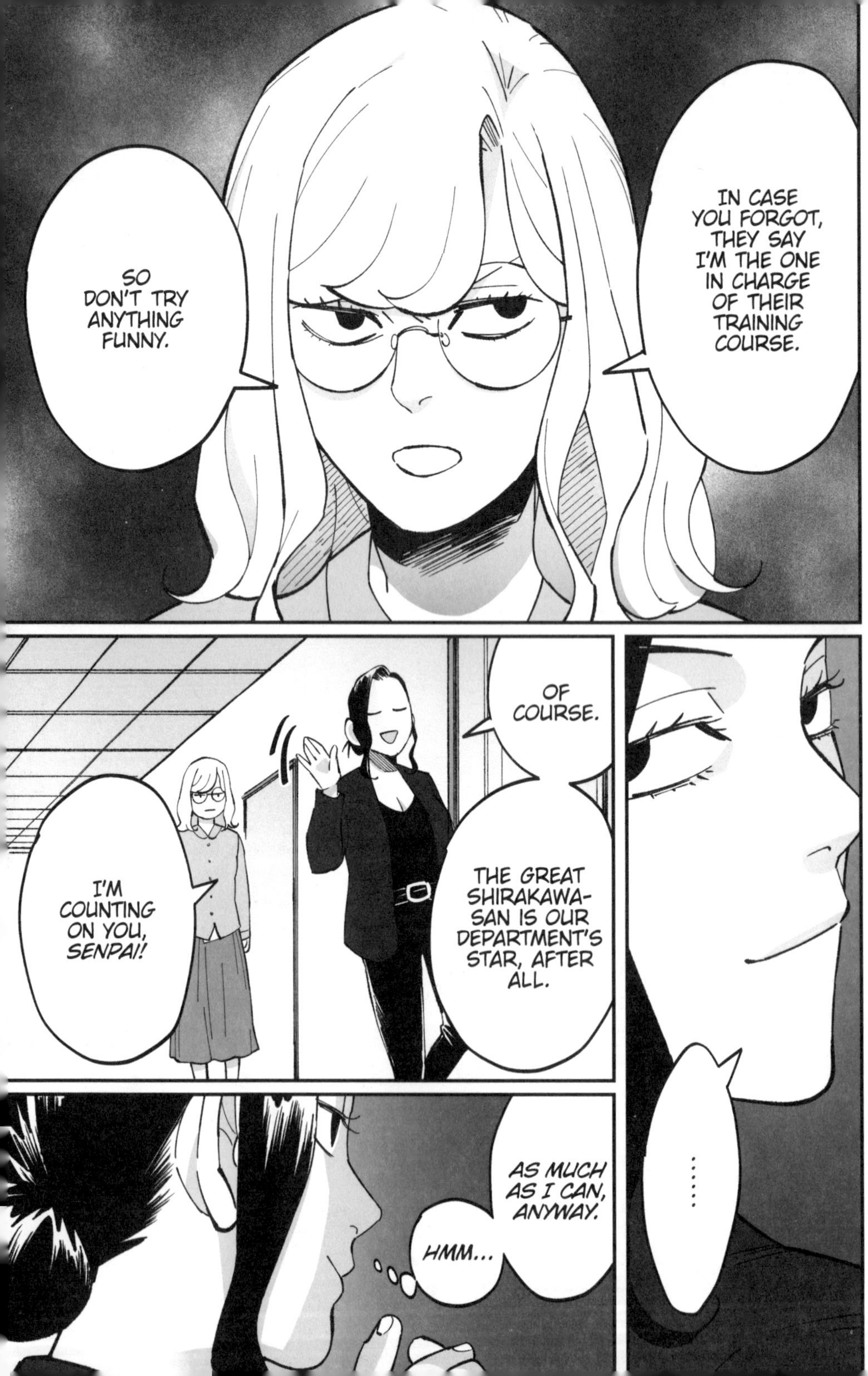
IN CASE YOU FORGOT, THEY SAY I'M THE ONE IN CHARGE OF THEIR TRAINING COURSE.
SO DON'T TRY ANYTHING FUNNY.
......
OF COURSE.
THE GREAT SHIRAKAWA-SAN IS OUR DEPARTMENT'S STAR, AFTER ALL.
I'M COUNTING ON YOU, SENPAI!
AS MUCH AS I CAN, ANYWAY.
HMM...

AREN'T YOU MISS POPULAR?
HEH HEH HEH!
SHH! SHE'LL HEAR US!
OH, HI, MISS EAVESDROP 2.0.
WHAT KIND OF STUPID NICKNAME IS THAT?
AW, HAVE YOU BEEN LOOKING FOR ME, YOUR BELOVED KAYO-CHAN?
CUT THE CRAP!
GRIT
I CAME TO WARN YOU.
WARN ME?
ABOUT TODAY'S TRAINING FOR THE NEW HIRES.
YOU'VE LOOKED OVER THE MATERIALS TOO, RIGHT?

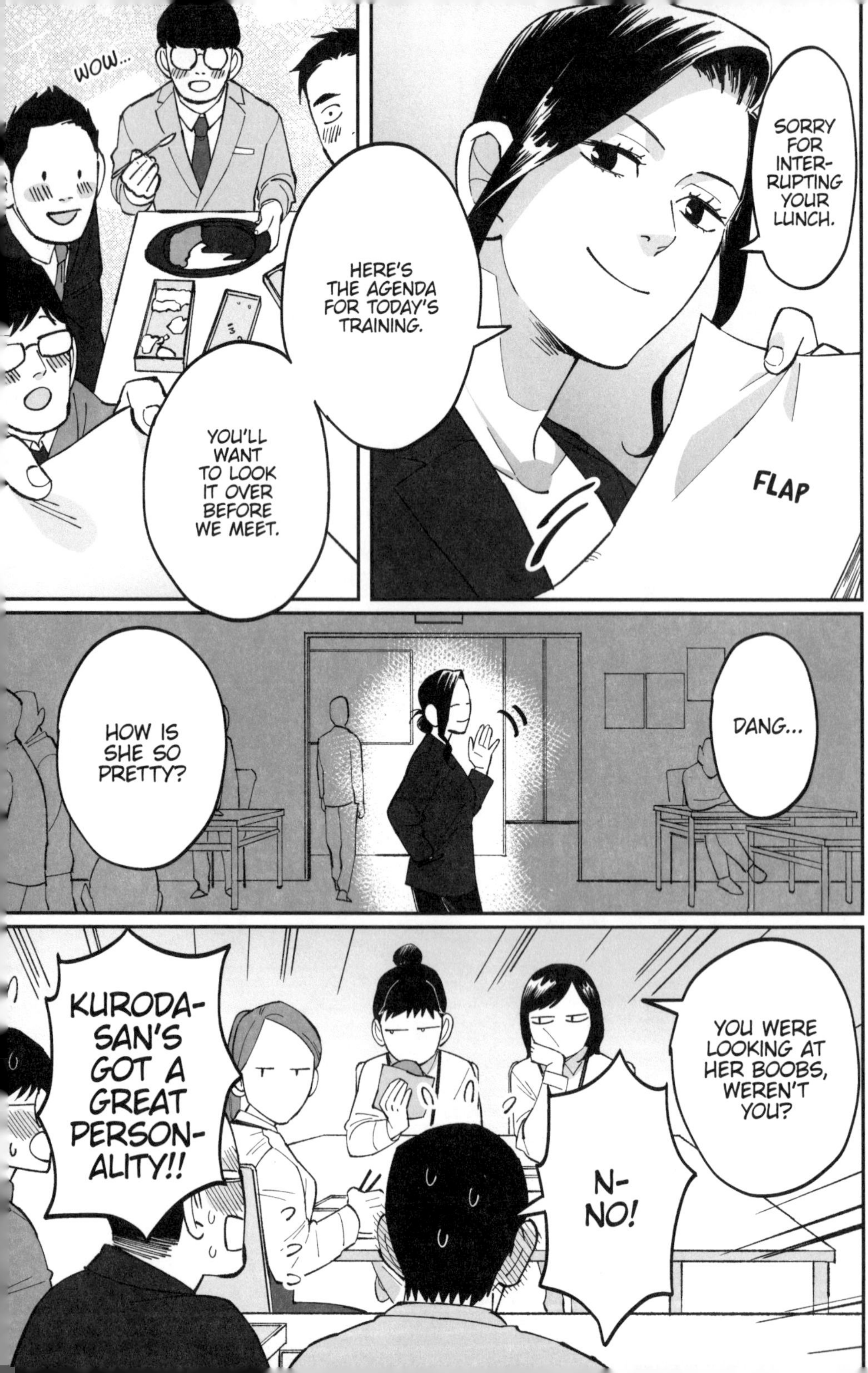
SORRY FOR INTER-RUPTING YOUR LUNCH.
HERE'S THE AGENDA FOR TODAY'S TRAINING.
FLAP
YOU'LL WANT TO LOOK IT OVER BEFORE WE MEET.
WOW...
DANG...
HOW IS SHE SO PRETTY?
YOU WERE LOOKING AT HER BOOBS, WEREN'T YOU?
N-NO!
KURODA-SAN'S GOT A GREAT PERSON-ALITY!!

REALLY?!

LUCKY! I WISH I HAD SHIRAKAWA-SAN, TOO!

I'VE ONLY TALKED TO HER ONCE, BUT...

DON'T YOU THINK SHE SMELLS AMAZING?

SHE DOES!

HER GLASSES HIDE IT, BUT...

SHE'S GORGEOUS.

FOR REAL?

I WANT TO MEET HER!

WE DO HAVE TRAINING TODAY...

ALL RIGHT!

POP

'SUP KIDS.

KURODA-SAN!

Chapter 5: Training

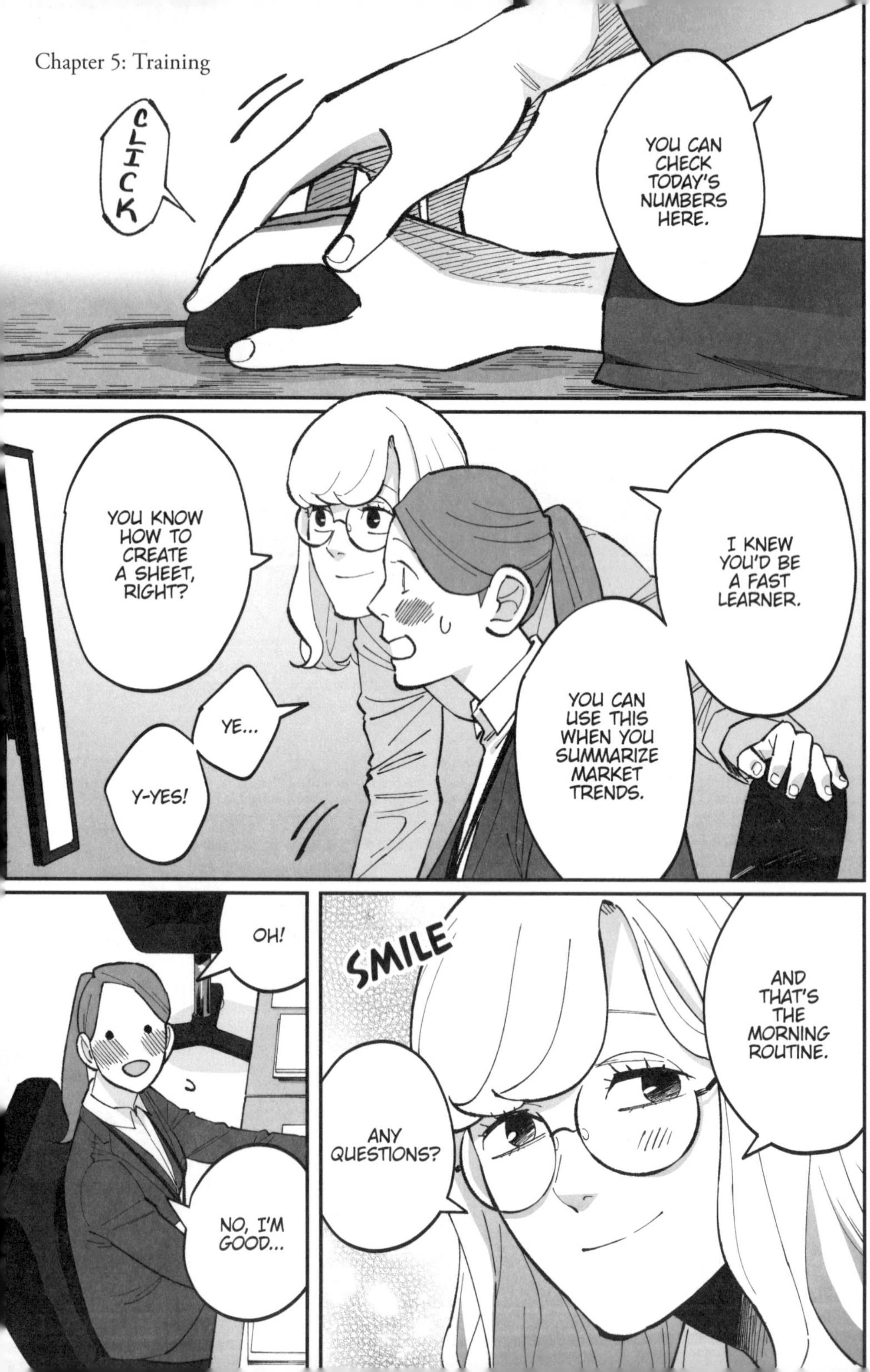

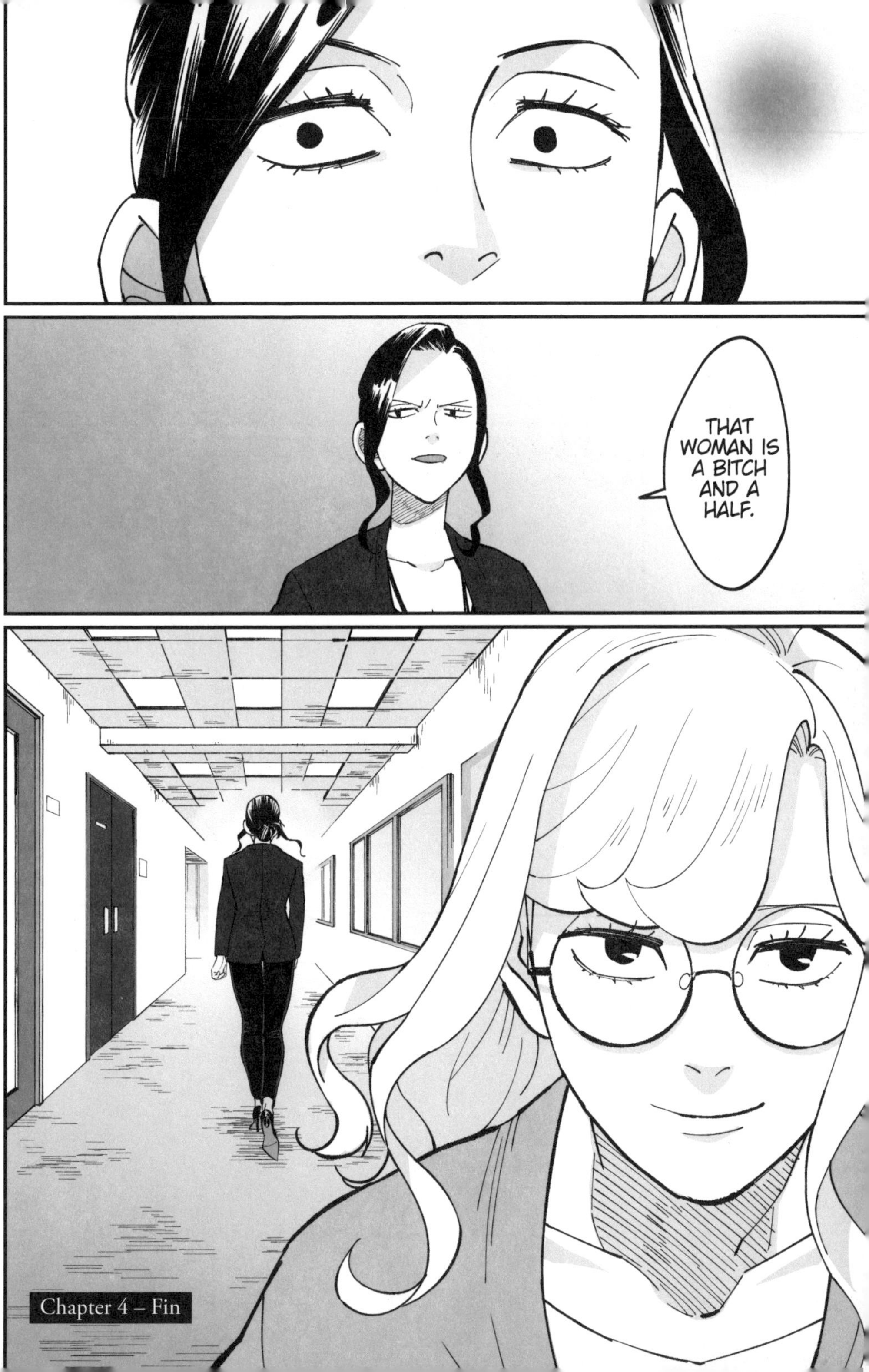
THAT WOMAN IS A BITCH AND A HALF.
Chapter 4 – Fin

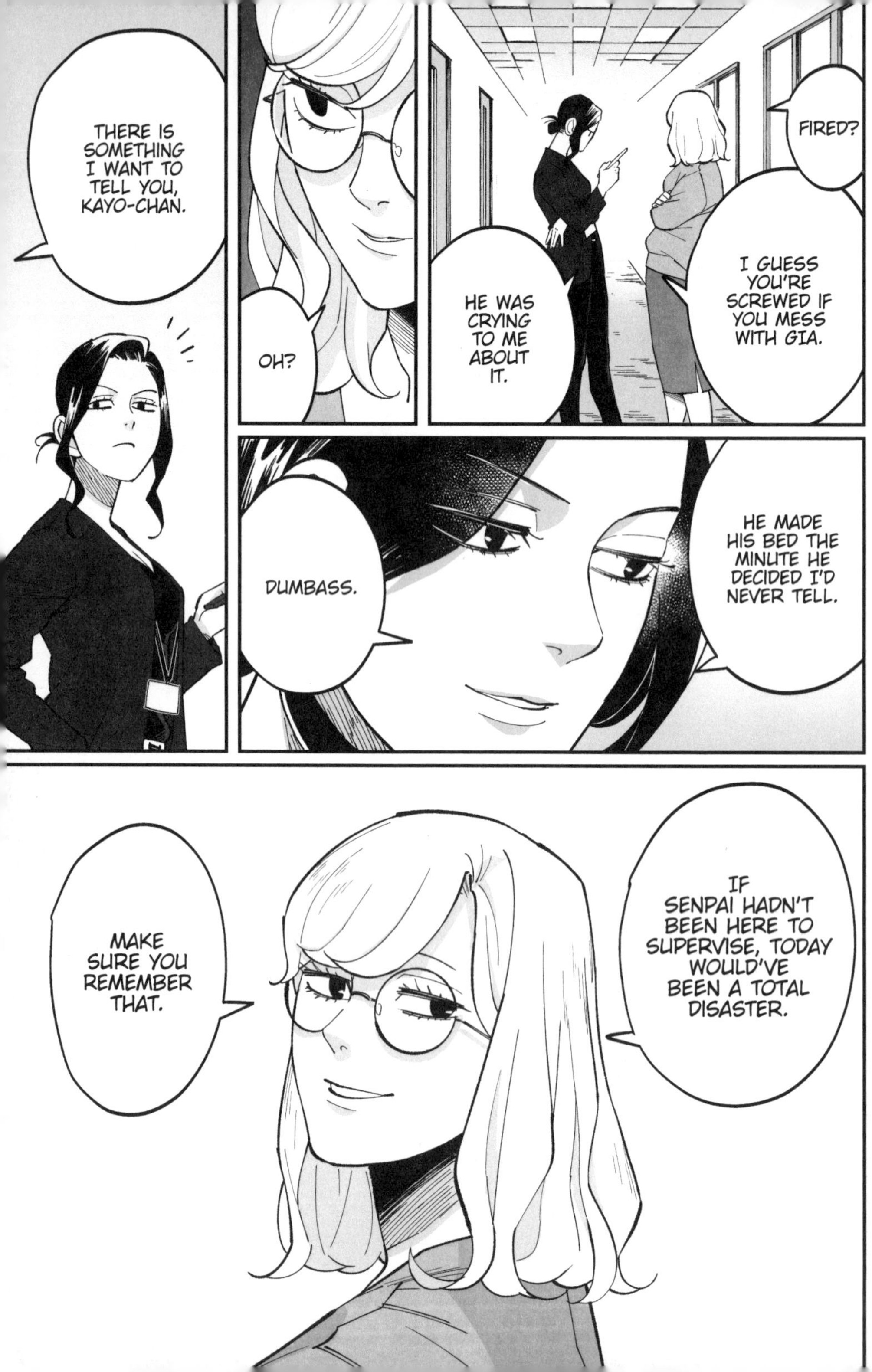
FIRED?
I GUESS YOU'RE SCREWED IF YOU MESS WITH GIA.
HE WAS CRYING TO ME ABOUT IT.
OH?
HE MADE HIS BED THE MINUTE HE DECIDED I'D NEVER TELL.
DUMBASS.
THERE IS SOMETHING I WANT TO TELL YOU, KAYO-CHAN.
IF SENPAI HADN'T BEEN HERE TO SUPERVISE, TODAY WOULD'VE BEEN A TOTAL DISASTER.
MAKE SURE YOU REMEMBER THAT.

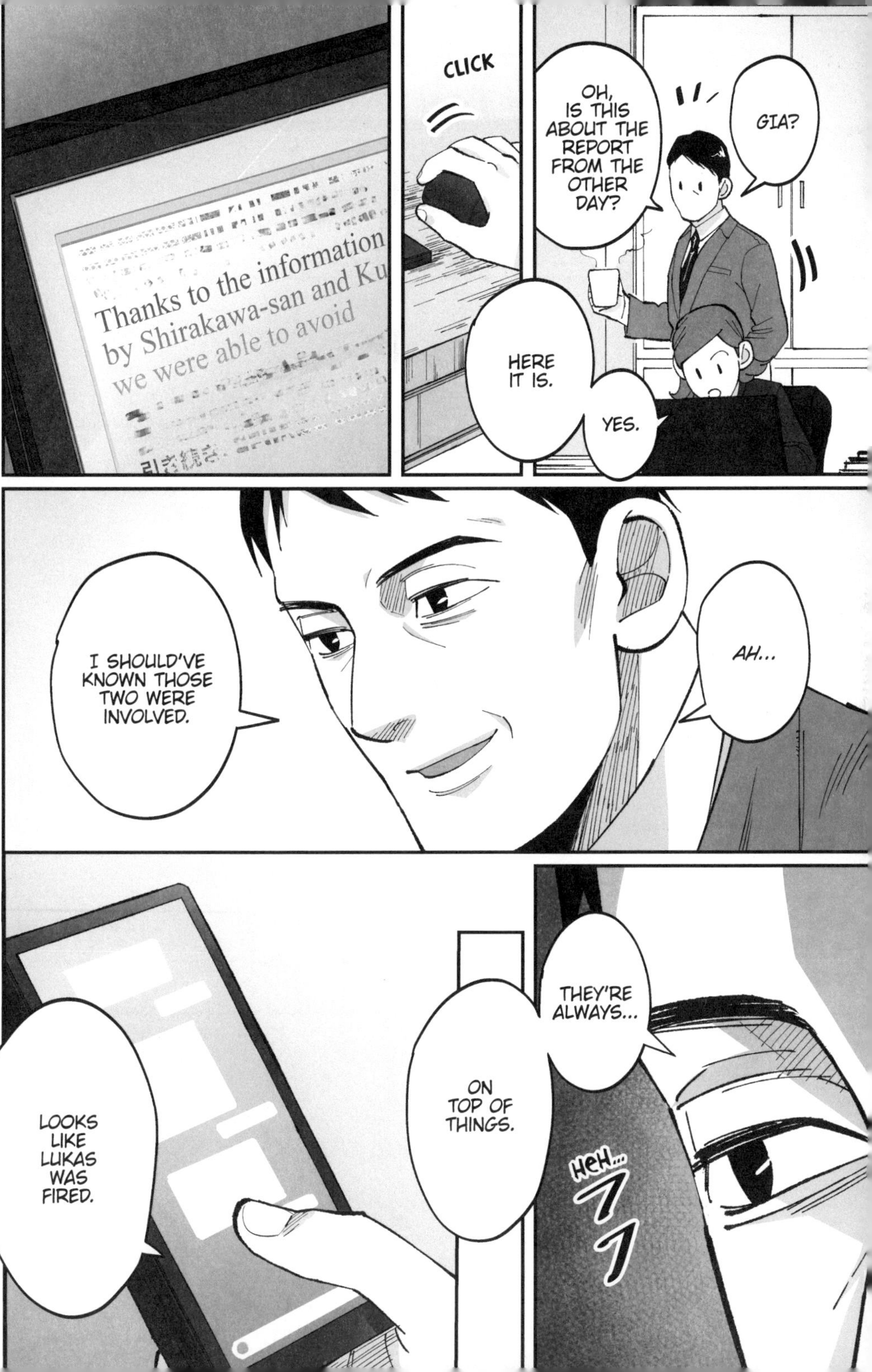
GIA?
OH, IS THIS ABOUT THE REPORT FROM THE OTHER DAY?
YES.
HERE IT IS.
CLICK
Thanks to the information
by Shirakawa-san and Ku
we were able to avoid
AH...
I SHOULD'VE KNOWN THOSE TWO WERE INVOLVED.
THEY'RE ALWAYS...
ON TOP OF THINGS.
HEH...
LOOKS LIKE LUKAS WAS FIRED.

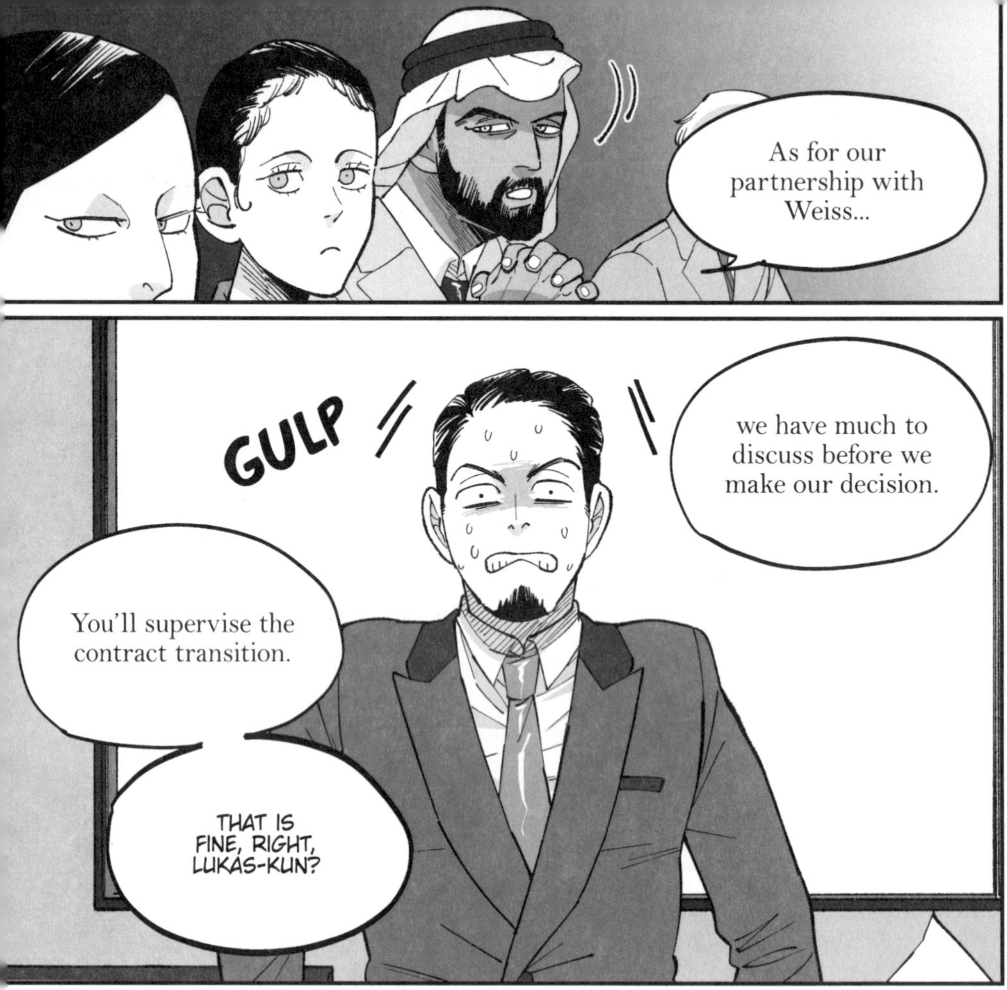
As for our partnership with Weiss...
GULP
we have much to discuss before we make our decision.
You'll supervise the contract transition.
THAT IS FINE, RIGHT, LUKAS-KUN?

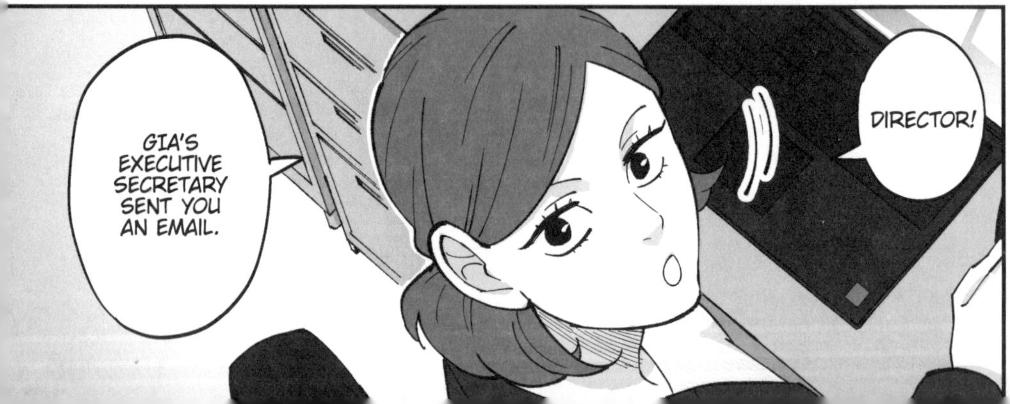
DIRECTOR!
GIA'S EXECUTIVE SECRETARY SENT YOU AN EMAIL.

......!
Like I said.
We want to renew our contract with KMBC.
However...
we'd also like to make it a direct contract.
To tell you the truth...
I came here intending to terminate our contract today.
HA HA HA!
T-TERMINATE?!
SHOCK
But then I thought it over.
I decided there's no better partner than KMBC.

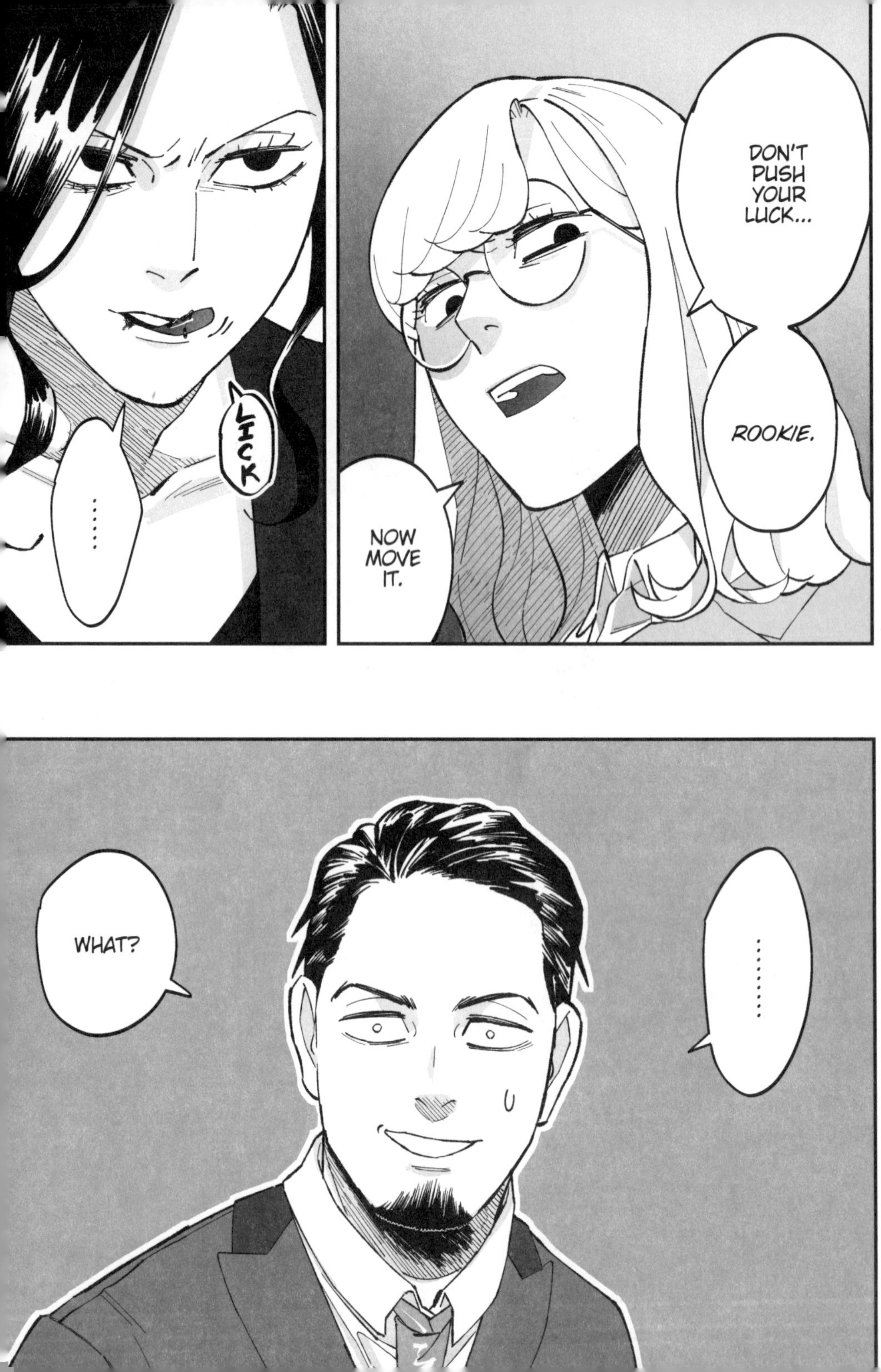
DON'T PUSH YOUR LUCK...
ROOKIE.
NOW MOVE IT.
LICK
......
....
WHAT?

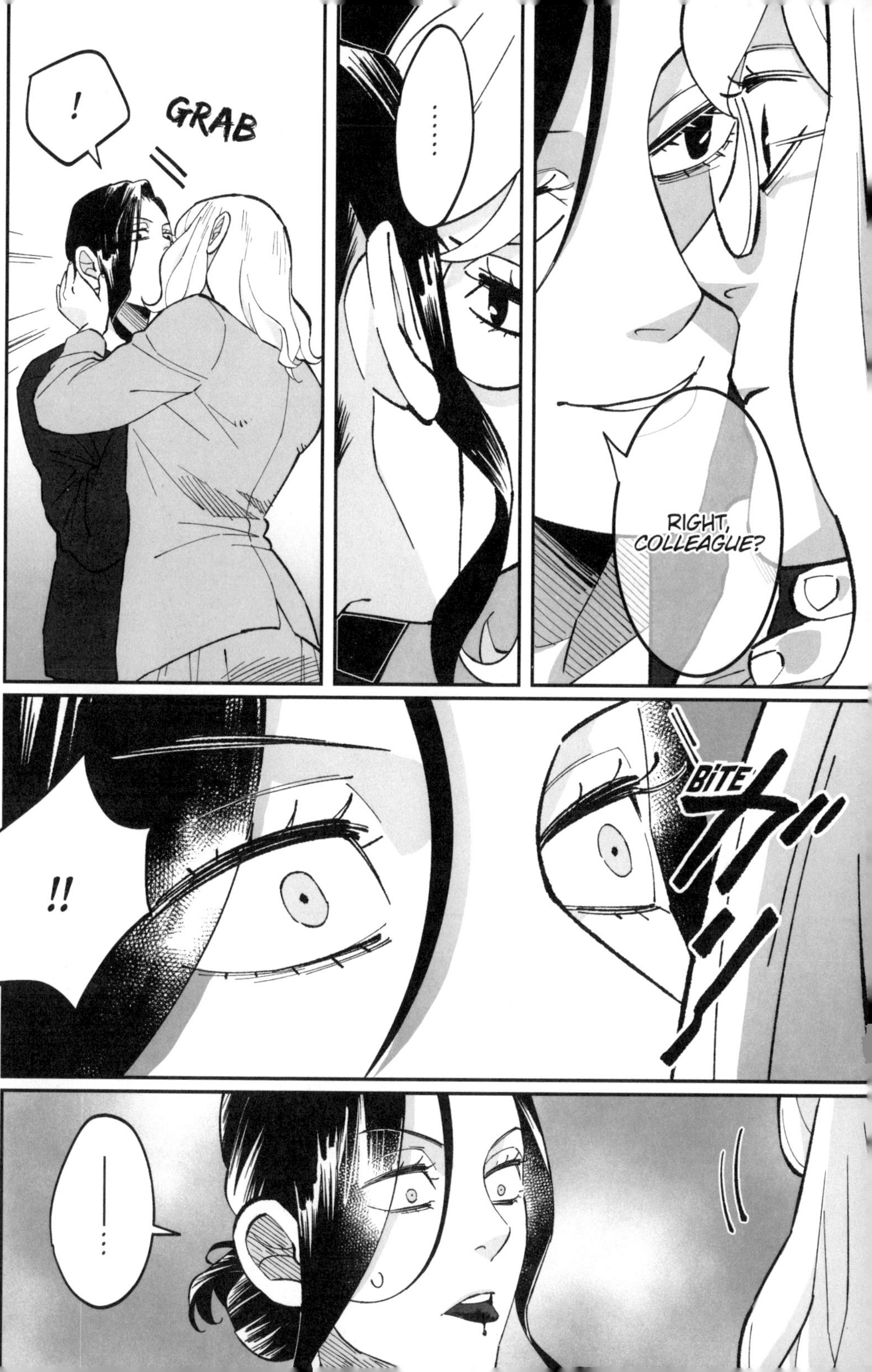
RIGHT, COLLEAGUE?
......
!
GRAB
BITE
!!
—......

WHAT DO YOU MEAN BY "CONTACT"?
SHE'S THE MVP AT THEIR LOCAL OFFICE.
HMM...
SHE'S MORE A *FRIEND*, THEN?
COULD YOU NOT SAY IT LIKE THAT?
SHE'S A COLLEAGUE.
GRAB
WE'VE GOT SOMETHING IN COMMON, THEN.
TAP
TAP
TAP
LET'S GET BACK.
TAP

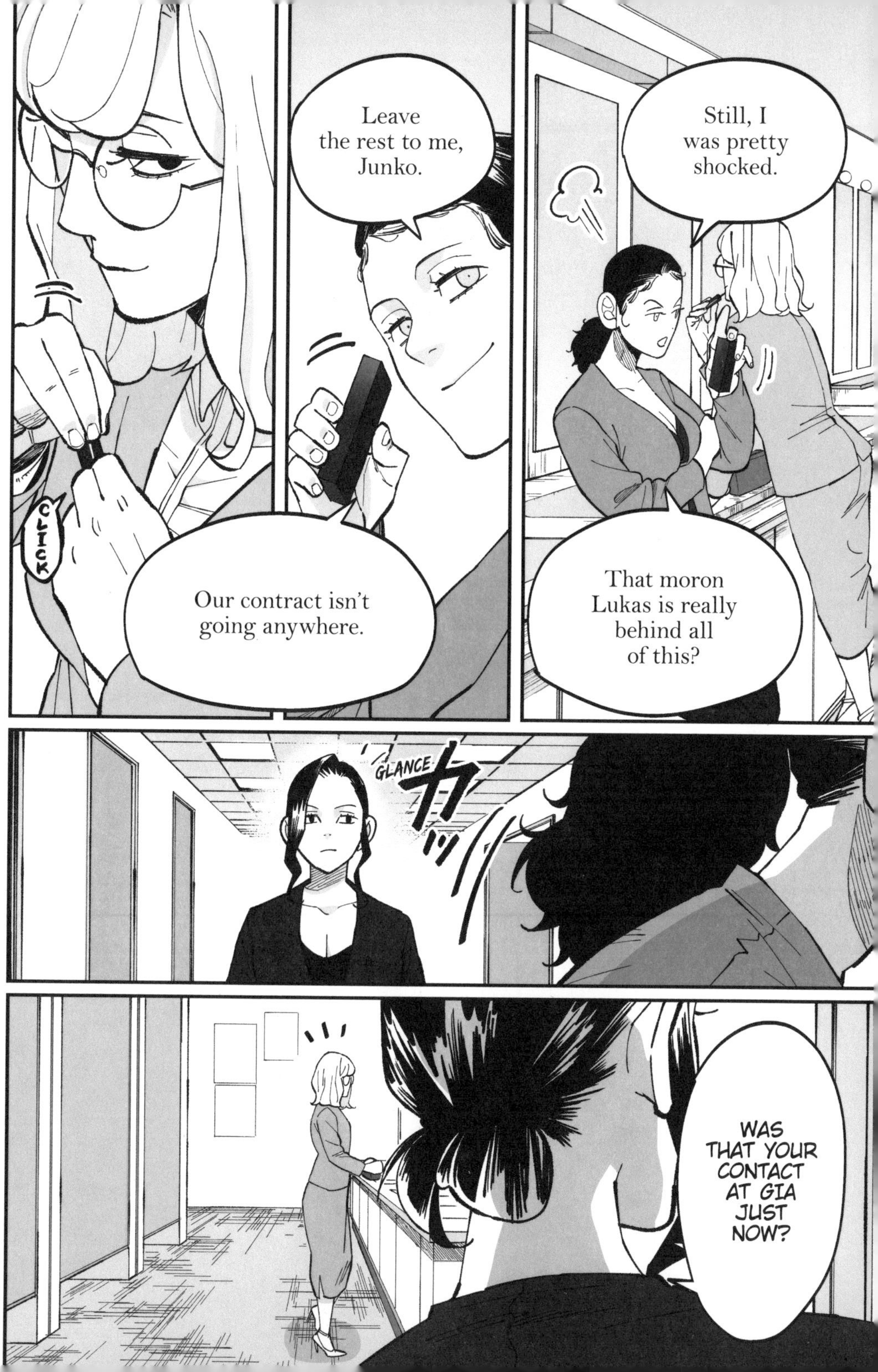
Still, I was pretty shocked.
That moron Lukas is really behind all of this?
Leave the rest to me, Junko.
Our contract isn't going anywhere.
CLICK
GLANCE
WAS THAT YOUR CONTACT AT GIA JUST NOW?

It's been a while since we last met.
I've been looking forward to this.
SMILE
Here's evidence regarding what we discussed.

—...
YOU'RE THE SORT OF FRIEND WHO KEEPS IT REAL.
HERE'S AN EDITED VERSION OF THE RECORDING.
GRAB
PASS
I CUT THE PARTS THAT MENTIONED MY NAME AND DEPARTMENT.
IT'S ALL YOURS.
CLACK ガチャ
SLAM
ALL MINE?
DOES THIS MEAN SHE TRUSTS ME?
......
HE'S HERE!
AH!
His Excellence, Abdul.

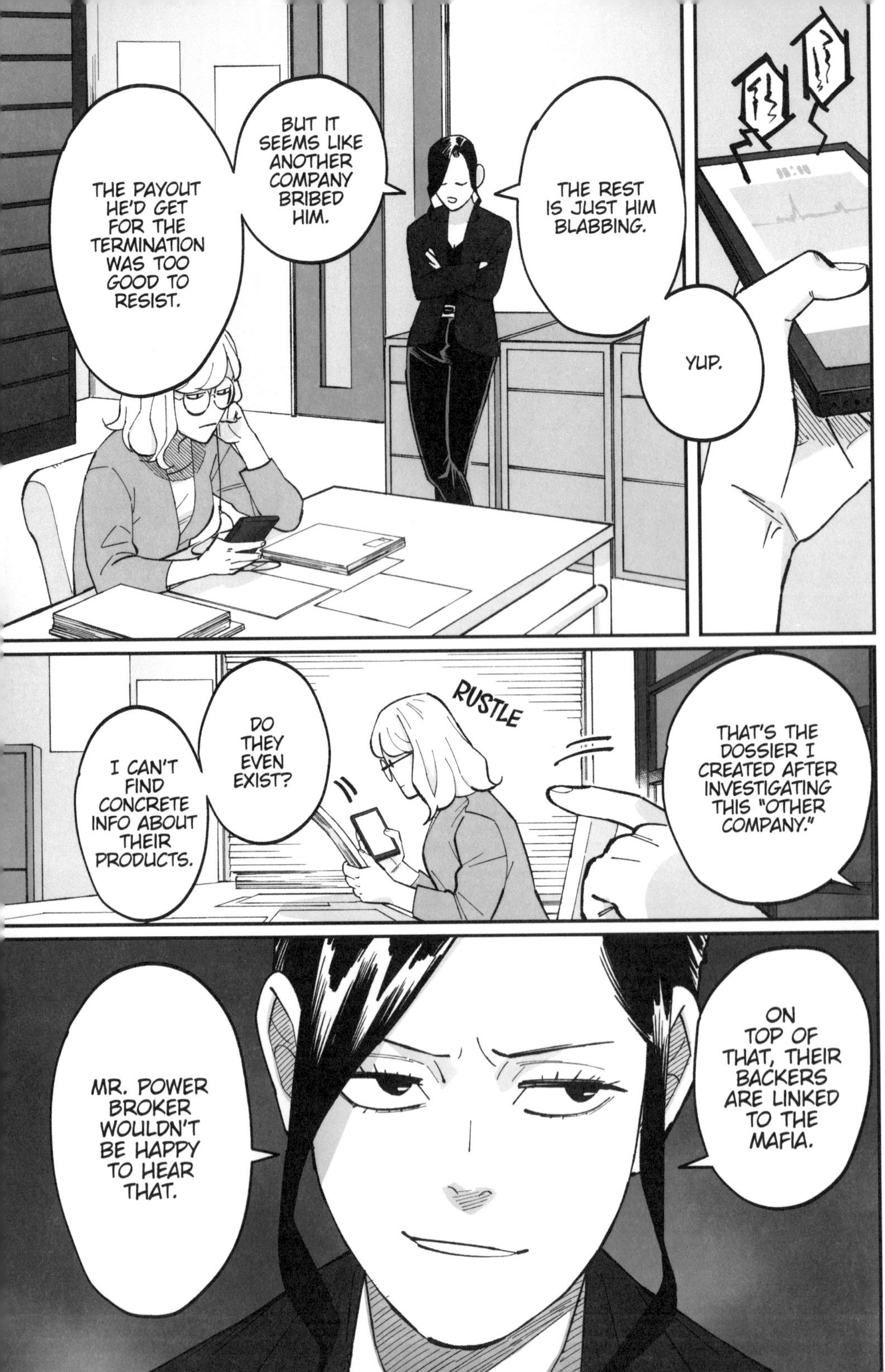
YUP.
THE REST IS JUST HIM BLABBING.
BUT IT SEEMS LIKE ANOTHER COMPANY BRIBED HIM.
THE PAYOUT HE'D GET FOR THE TERMINATION WAS TOO GOOD TO RESIST.
THAT'S THE DOSSIER I CREATED AFTER INVESTIGATING THIS "OTHER COMPANY."
RUSTLE
DO THEY EVEN EXIST?
I CAN'T FIND CONCRETE INFO ABOUT THEIR PRODUCTS.
ON TOP OF THAT, THEIR BACKERS ARE LINKED TO THE MAFIA.
MR. POWER BROKER WOULDN'T BE HAPPY TO HEAR THAT.

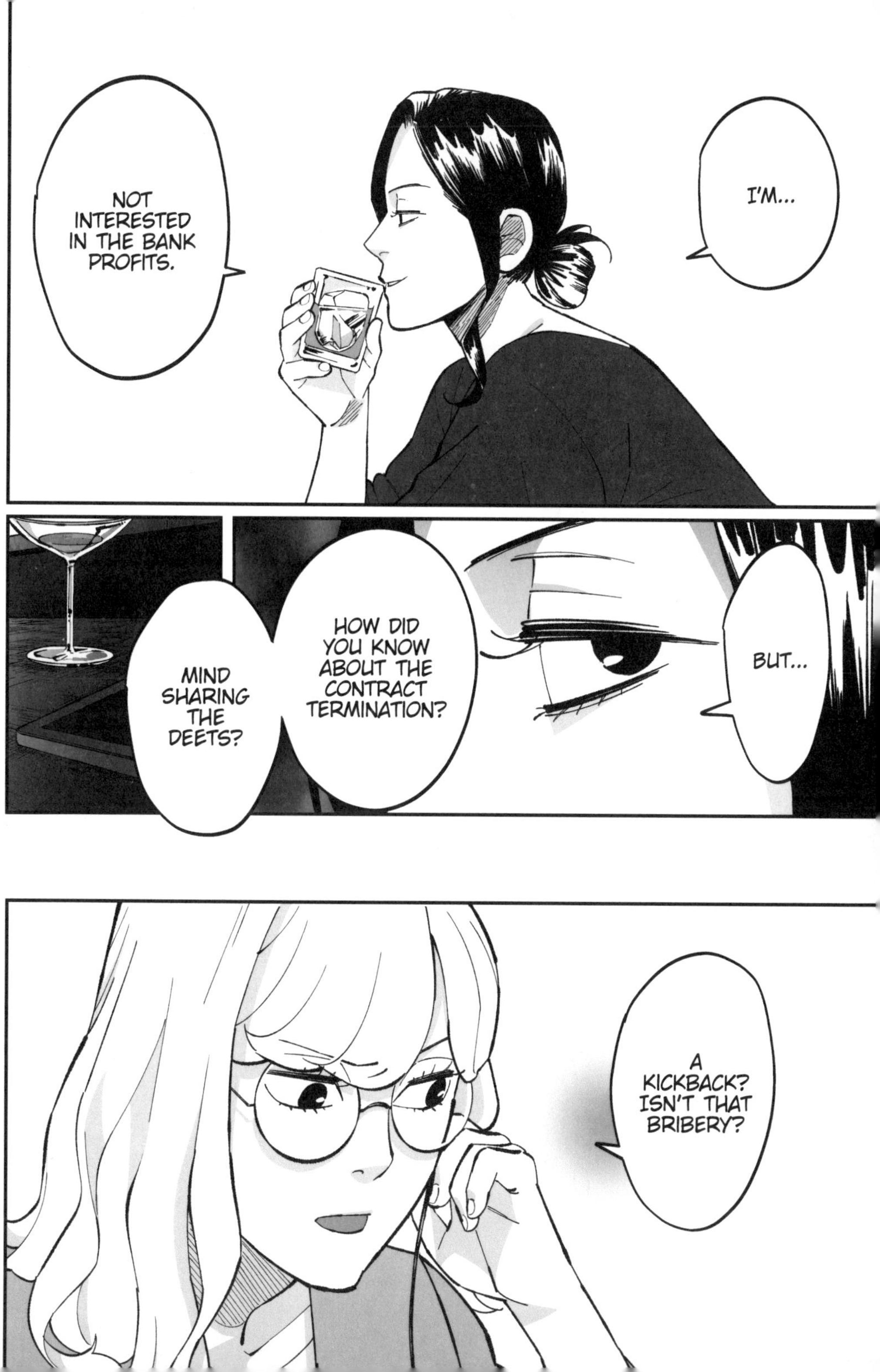
I'M...
NOT INTERESTED IN THE BANK PROFITS.
BUT...
HOW DID YOU KNOW ABOUT THE CONTRACT TERMINATION?
MIND SHARING THE DEETS?
A KICKBACK? ISN'T THAT BRIBERY?

SINCE I'M NEW TO THE DEPARTMENT, I DIDN'T REALIZE THAT...
GIA WAS SUCH A BIG ORGANIZATION.
YOU'RE QUITE THE POWER BROKER.
GLEAM
WELL...
I GUESS I KINDA AM!
I SWOOPED IN AT THE RIGHT TIME, BUT...
UH-HUH.
THE FACT THAT I'M SOCIABLE AND CAN TALK THE TALK CERTAINLY HELPED!
THAT SAID...
IT LOOKS LIKE THE CONTRACT'S GOING IN THE TRASH.
SORRY...

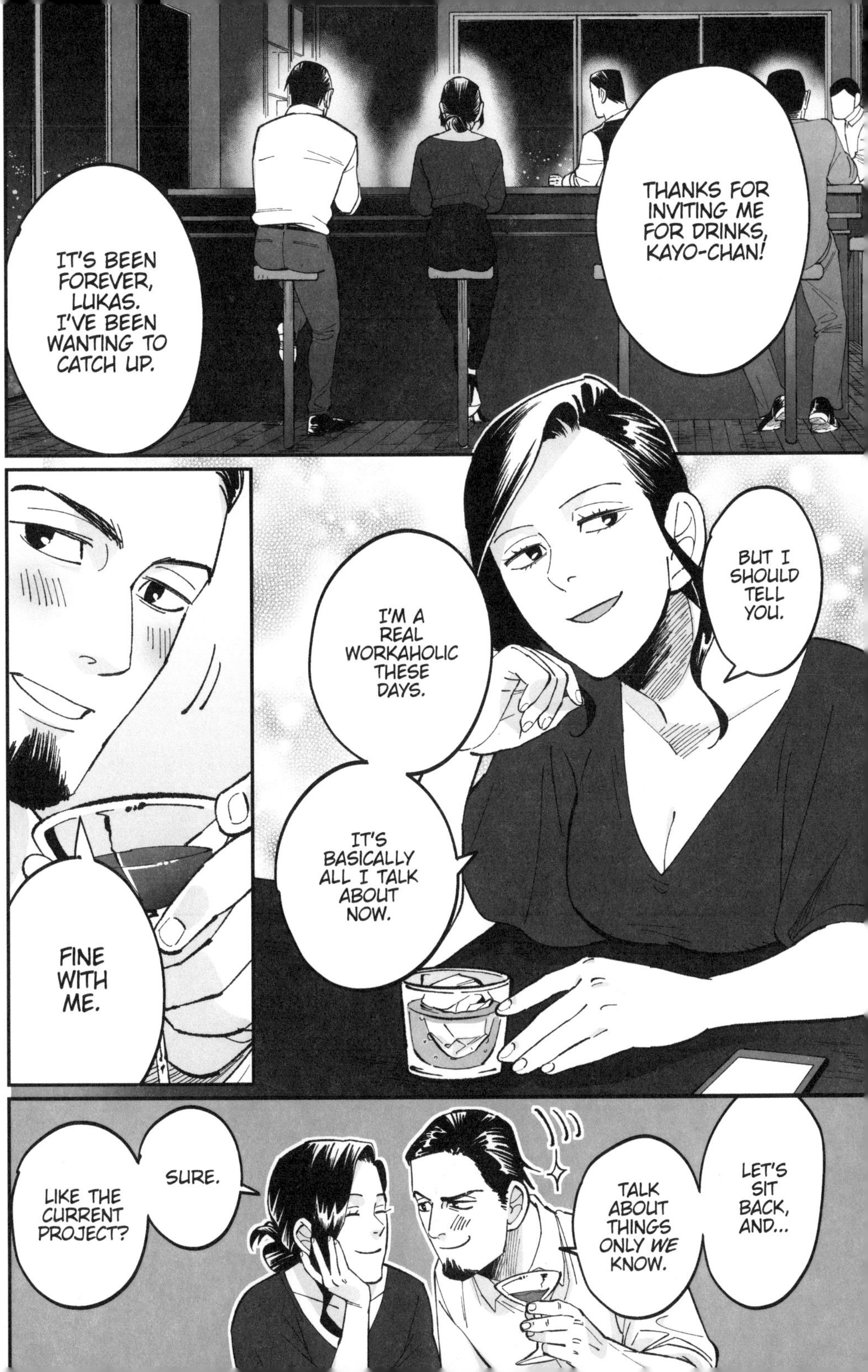
THANKS FOR INVITING ME FOR DRINKS, KAYO-CHAN!
IT'S BEEN FOREVER, LUKAS. I'VE BEEN WANTING TO CATCH UP.
BUT I SHOULD TELL YOU.
I'M A REAL WORKAHOLIC THESE DAYS.
IT'S BASICALLY ALL I TALK ABOUT NOW.
FINE WITH ME.
LET'S SIT BACK, AND...
TALK ABOUT THINGS ONLY *WE* KNOW.
SURE.
LIKE THE CURRENT PROJECT?

WHIRL

TAP

TAP

HMPH.

....

TAP

AS IF I'D WANT TO WORK WITH *YOU*.

MY REPUTATION WOULD BE ON THE LINE.

TAP

HEH.

TAP

TAP

TAP

I'M JUST SPITBALLING HERE, BUT...
IF WE MADE A MOVE...
DON'T YOU THINK WE COULD TURN THE TABLES ON THEM?
......
YOU MEAN...
ON TOP OF PREVENTING THE CONTRACT TERMINATION...
GIA
Delegate
Weiß
Contract
Us
Report
GIA
Contract
Us
Report
WE COULD ENTER A DIRECT AGREEMENT WITH GIA...
AND REMOVE WEISS AS THE MIDDLEMAN?
YOU'VE DEALT WITH GIA FOR YEARS NOW.
I CAN INVESTIGATE WEISS THROUGH LUKAS.
TOGETHER, WE CAN GET THIS DONE IN NO TIME.

NOT TELLING. ♡
LICK
UGH!
SHUDDER
BITCH!!
SWOOSH
JUST KIDDING.
I GOT THE INFO FROM WEISS.
YOU KNOW THE GUY IN CHARGE OF MANAGING THE DEAL, LUKAS HÖLTER?
HE'S A FRIEND OF MINE FROM BACK WHEN I LIVED IN ENGLAND.
....
SHE'S TELLING ME THE TRUTH.
DOES THIS MEAN SHE WANTS TO TEAM UP?

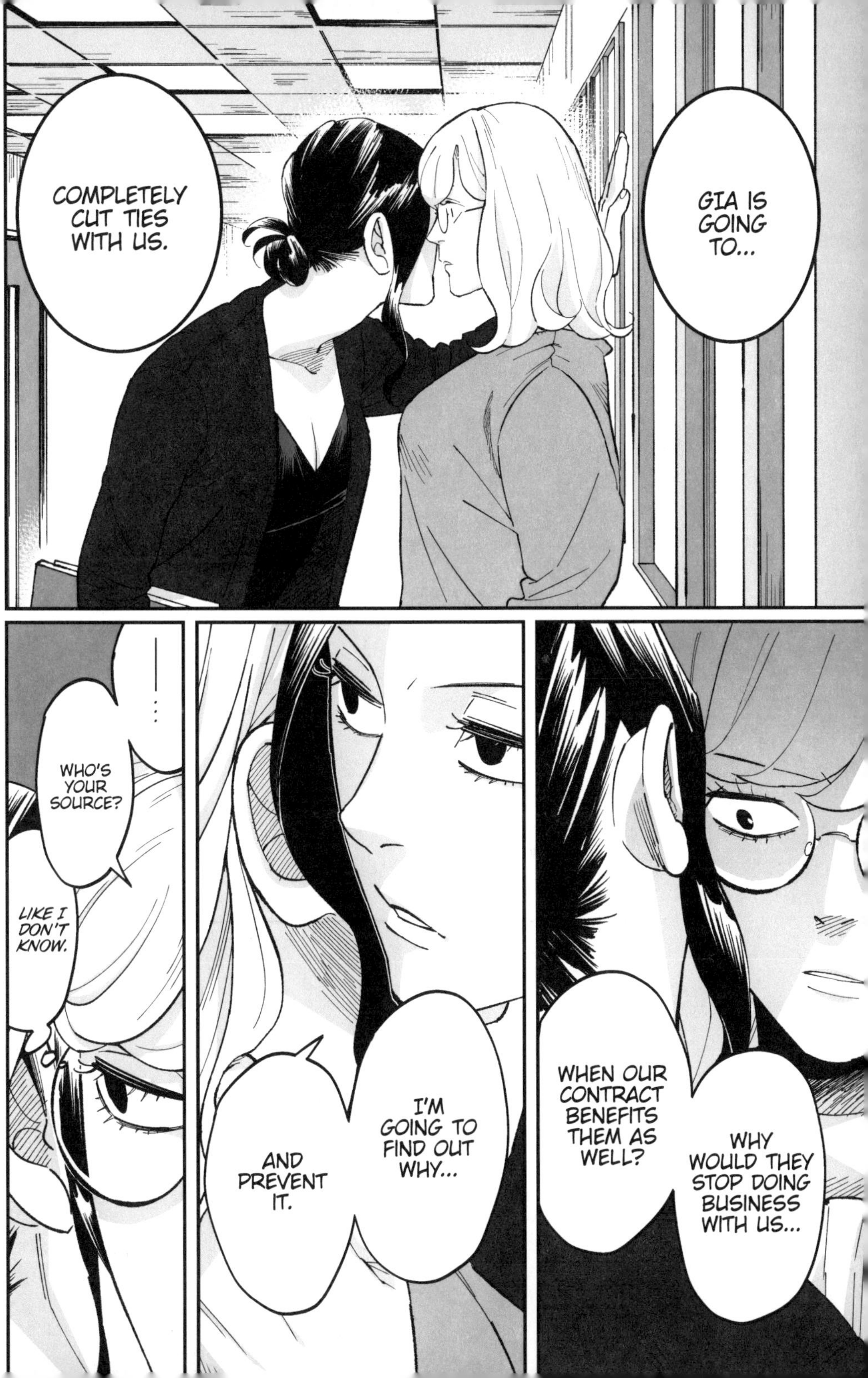
GIA IS GOING TO...
COMPLETELY CUT TIES WITH US.
WHY WOULD THEY STOP DOING BUSINESS WITH US...
WHEN OUR CONTRACT BENEFITS THEM AS WELL?
I'M GOING TO FIND OUT WHY...
AND PREVENT IT.
......
WHO'S YOUR SOURCE?
LIKE I DON'T KNOW.

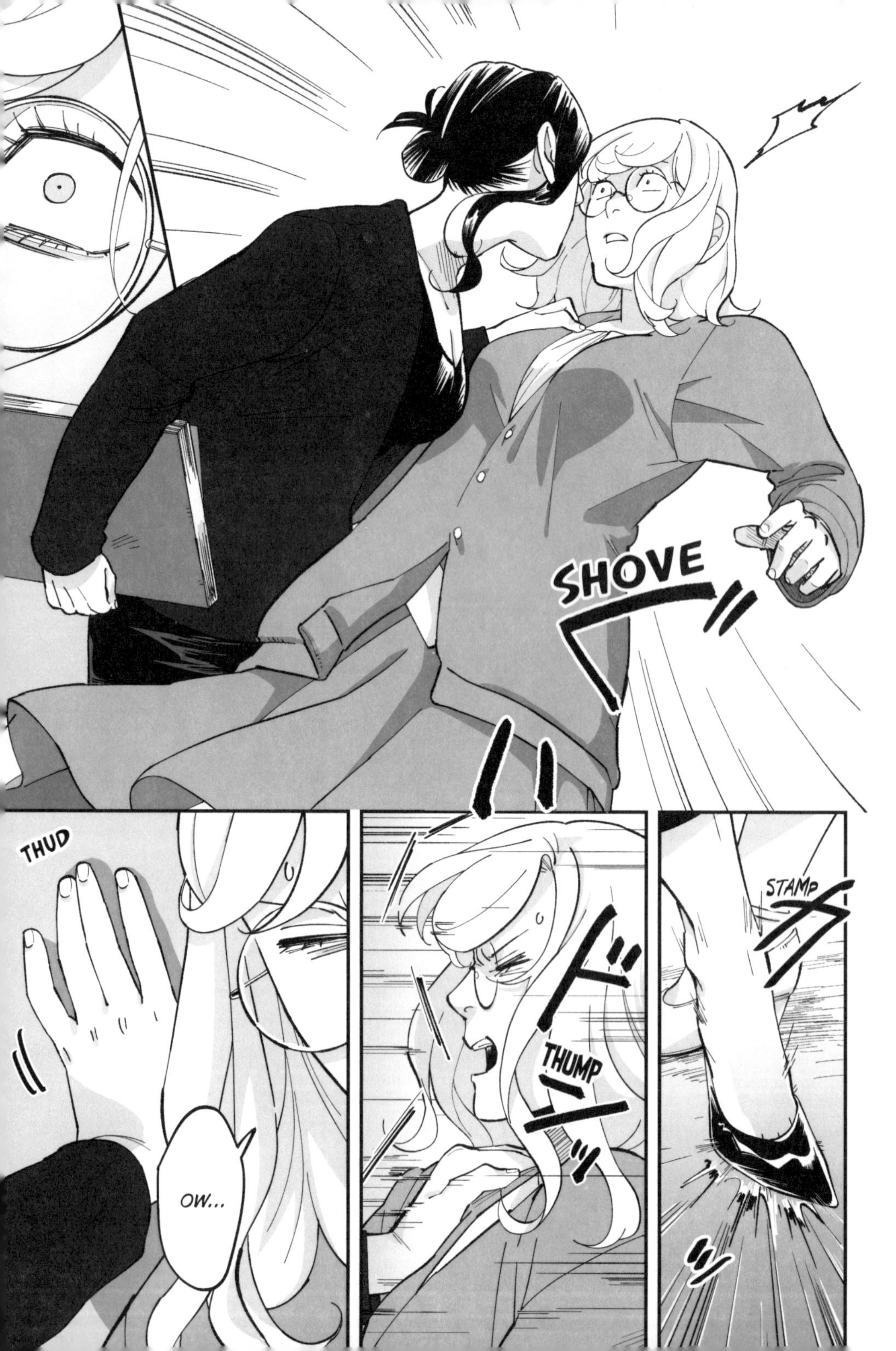
SHOVE
STAMP
ド
THUMP
THUD
OW...

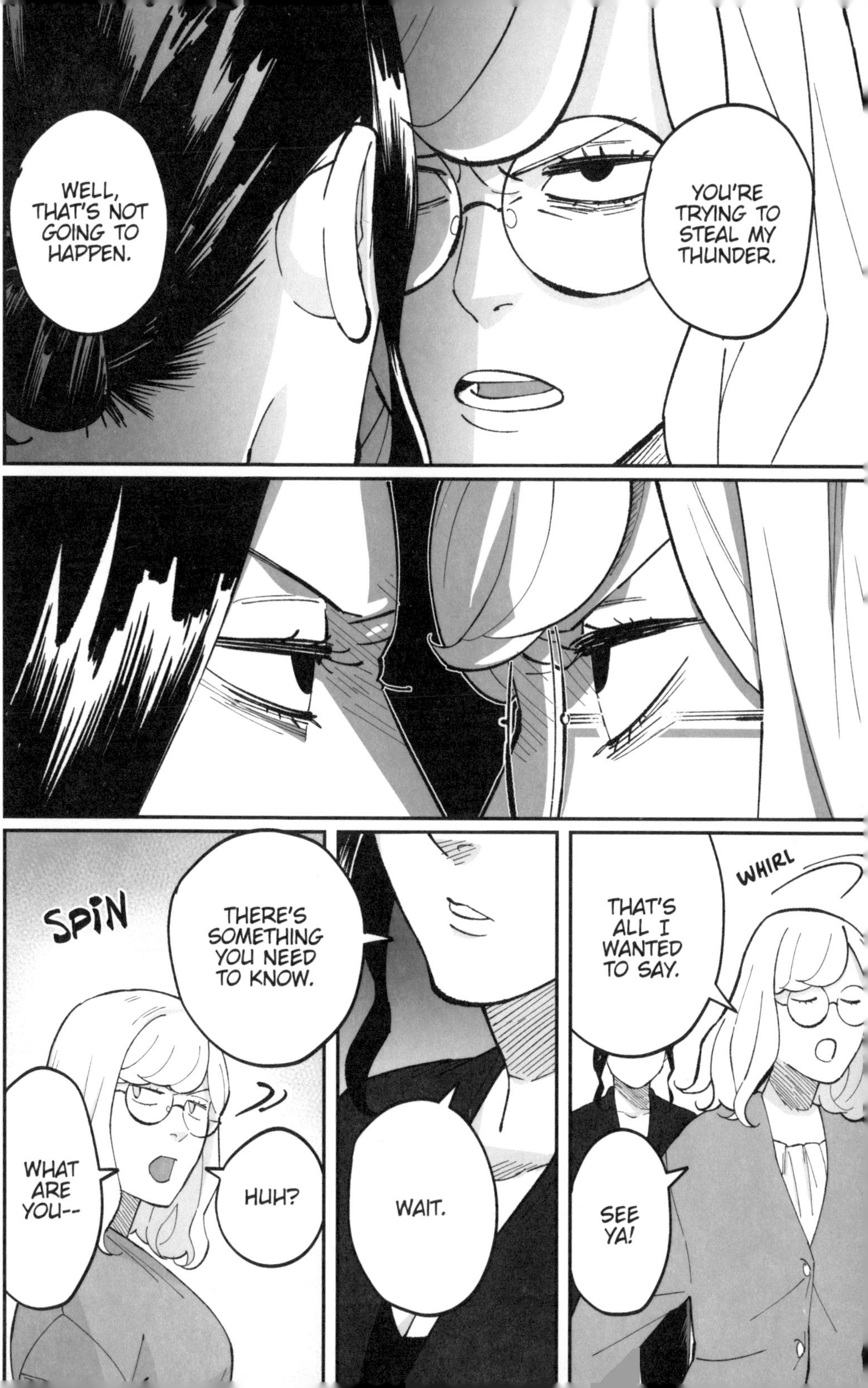
YOU'RE TRYING TO STEAL MY THUNDER.
WELL, THAT'S NOT GOING TO HAPPEN.
WHIRL
THAT'S ALL I WANTED TO SAY.
SEE YA!
WAIT.
SPIN
THERE'S SOMETHING YOU NEED TO KNOW.
HUH?
WHAT ARE YOU--

"YOU REALLY..."

"LOVE CHASING MY ASS, DON'T YOU?"

"JUNKO-CHAN."

KLOK

"YOU'VE KEPT QUIET ABOUT THE GIA SITUATION..."

"BUT YOU'RE PLANNING SOMETHING, AREN'T YOU?"

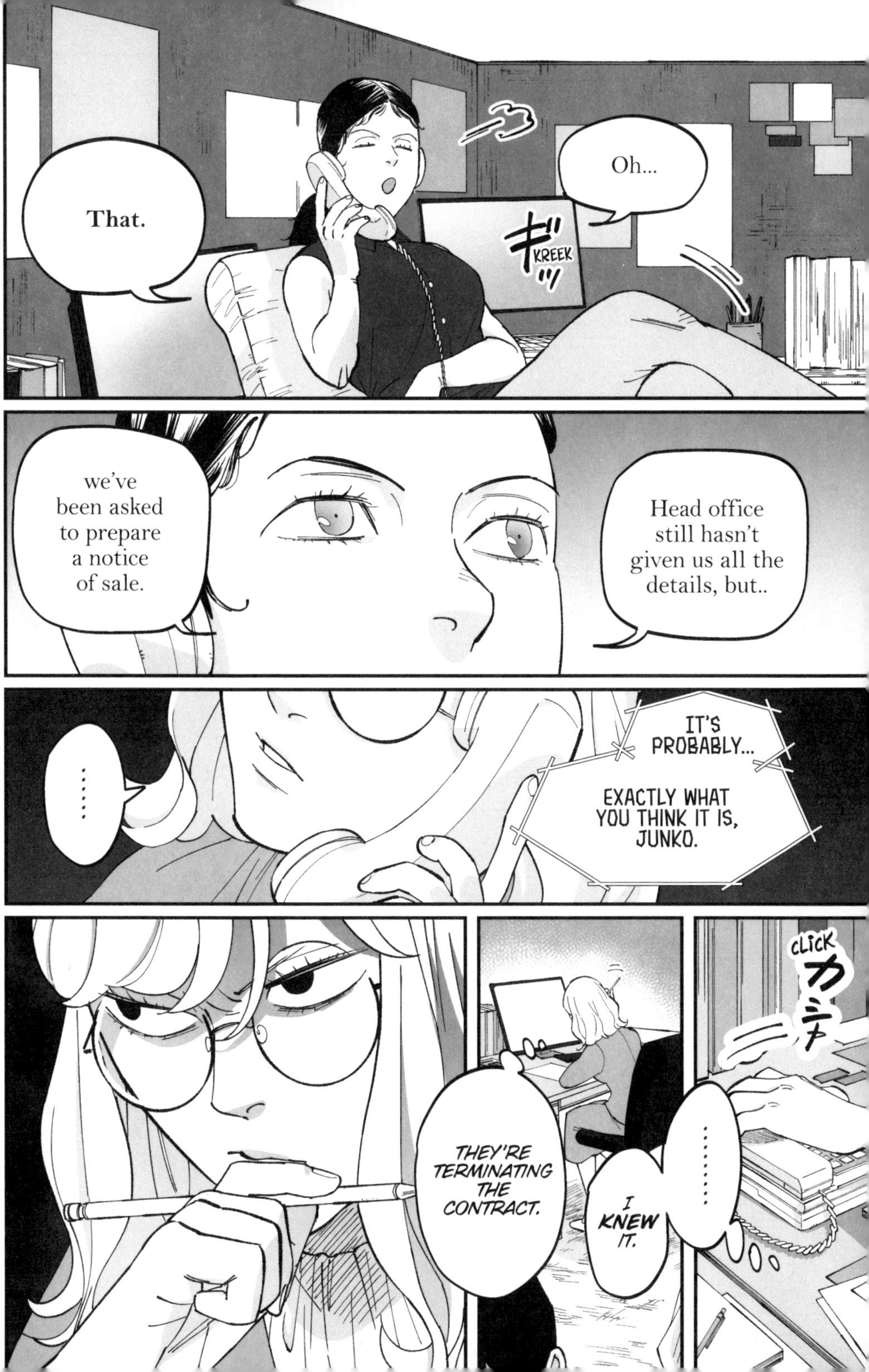

Oh...
ギッ KREEK
That.
Head office still hasn't given us all the details, but..
we've been asked to prepare a notice of sale.
IT'S PROBABLY...
EXACTLY WHAT YOU THINK IT IS, JUNKO.
......
CLICK カチャ
......
I KNEW IT.
THEY'RE TERMINATING THE CONTRACT.

Hi, Junko!
It's been a while. How've you been, Emma?
Happy to hear from you!
I didn't expect you'd be calling.
Oh!
The report's due today, right?
Word is there's going to be a big change.
For the Weiss Capital project?

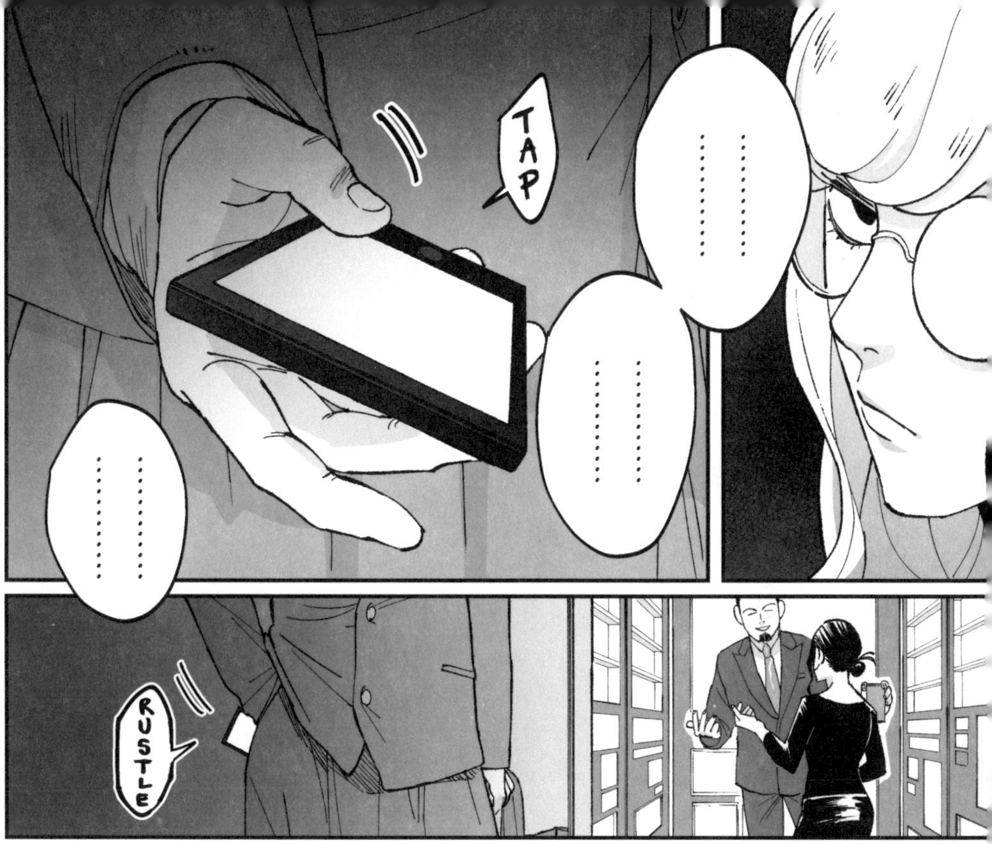
......
......
TAP
......
RUSTLE

Chapter 4: United Front (Part 2)

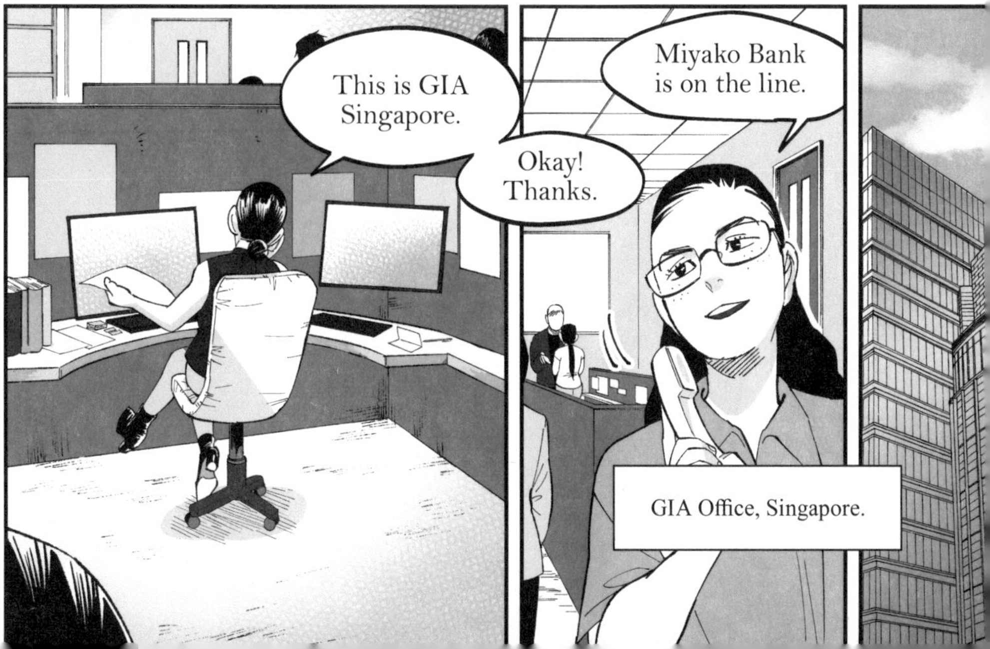
GIA Office, Singapore.
Miyako Bank is on the line.
Okay! Thanks.
This is GIA Singapore.

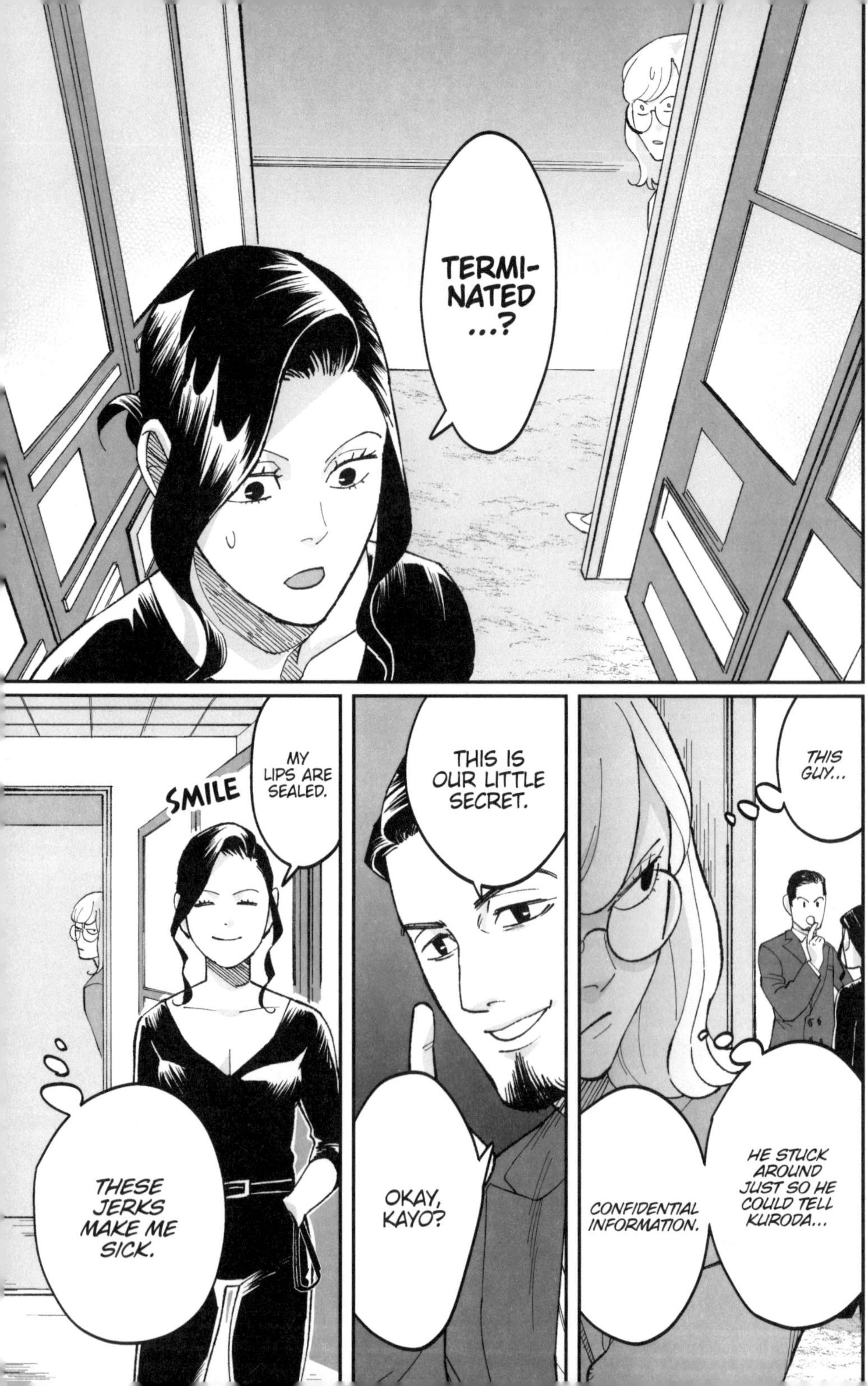
TERMI-NATED...?
THIS GUY...
HE STUCK AROUND JUST SO HE COULD TELL KURODA...
CONFIDENTIAL INFORMATION.
THIS IS OUR LITTLE SECRET.
OKAY, KAYO?
MY LIPS ARE SEALED.
SMILE
THESE JERKS MAKE ME SICK.

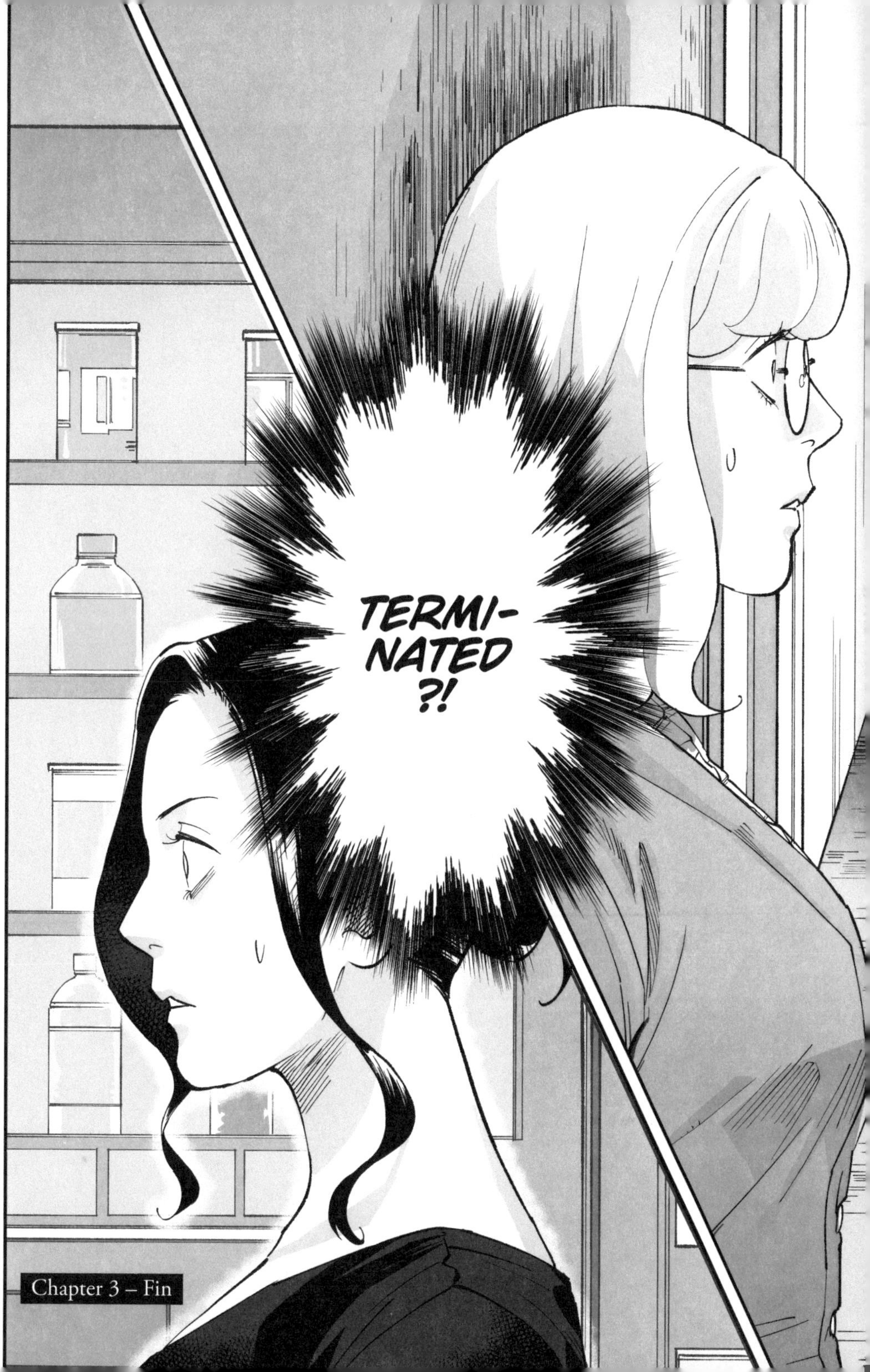
TERMI-
NATED
?!
Chapter 3 – Fin

IT'S ALMOST CERTAIN THAT...
THE CONTRACT WILL BE TERMINATED.
WHAT?
WHY...?

YEAH.
I TRANSFERRED TO THE OVERSEAS INVESTOR DEPARTMENT RECENTLY.
SO YOU FINALLY GET TO SHOW OFF YOUR LANGUAGE SKILLS!
MAYBE THEY'RE OLD FRIENDS?
OR COLLEAGUES FROM CORPORATE?
OR THEY MET OVERSEAS?
HELPING EXPLAIN THINGS, HUH? YOU'VE ALWAYS ACED PRESENTATIONS.
WELL...
IT'S JUST THAT, FOR THIS PROJECT...
IT SEEMS LIKE THE OTHER PARTY ALREADY MADE UP THEIR MINDS.
MADE UP THEIR MINDS?
I'M ONLY TELLING YOU THIS BECAUSE I TRUST YOU...
PI
LET'S KEEP IT BETWEEN US, OKAY?

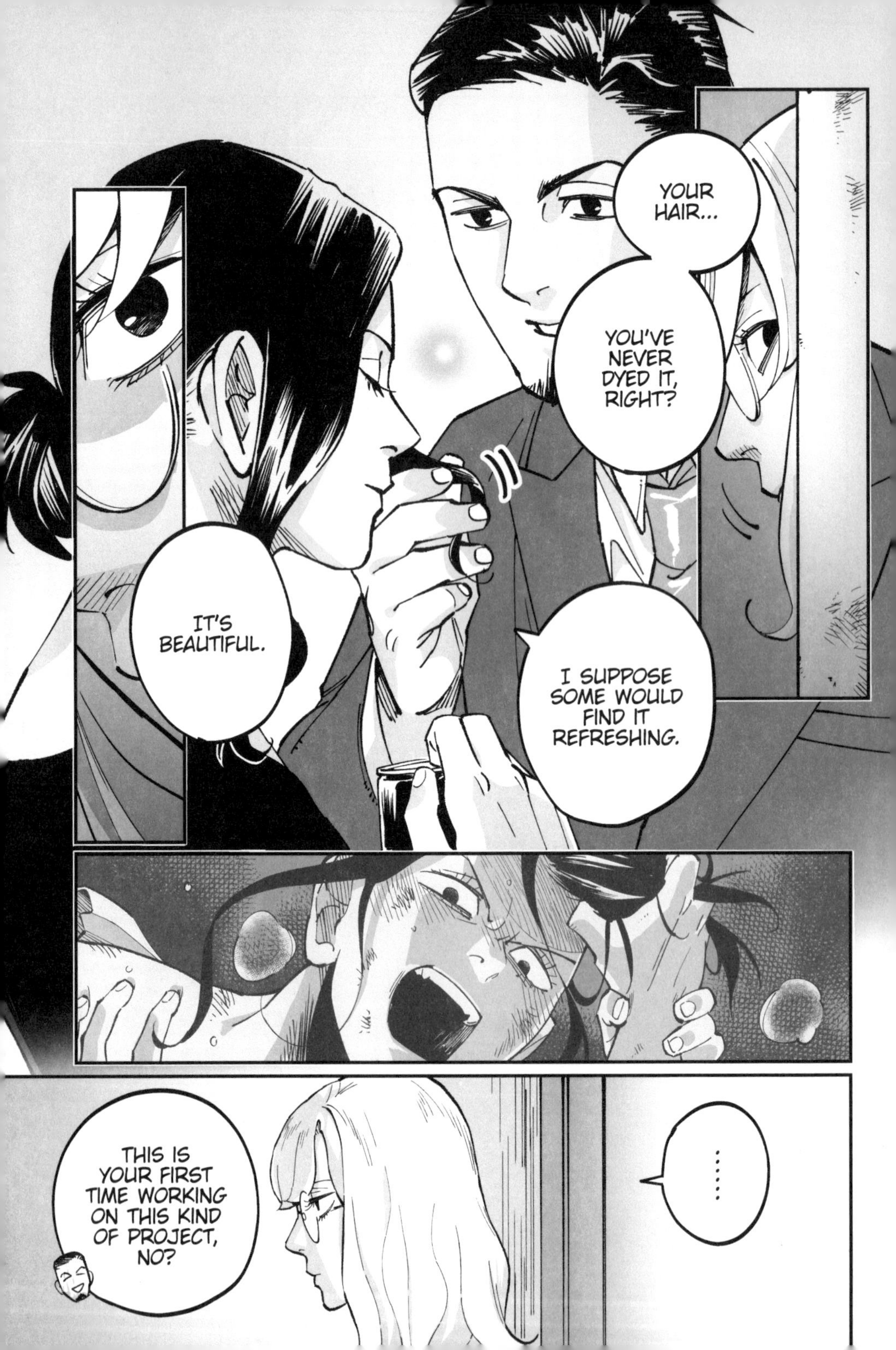
YOUR HAIR...
YOU'VE NEVER DYED IT, RIGHT?
IT'S BEAUTIFUL.
I SUPPOSE SOME WOULD FIND IT REFRESHING.
......
THIS IS YOUR FIRST TIME WORKING ON THIS KIND OF PROJECT, NO?

SLIP
BLACK, NOT TOO SWEET, RIGHT, KAYO?
YOU REMEMBERED!
OF COURSE.
HOW COULD I FORGET?
BINGO.
THEY DO KNOW EACH OTHER.
THEY DIDN'T EXCHANGE BUSINESS CARDS DESPITE THIS BEING THEIR FIRST MEETING.
AND SHE KNEW HE WAS LATINO.
I KNEW SOMETHING WAS UP.
SIGH
YOU'VE GOTTEN EVEN PRETTIER, KAYO!
NO NEED TO FLATTER ME.
THANKS.

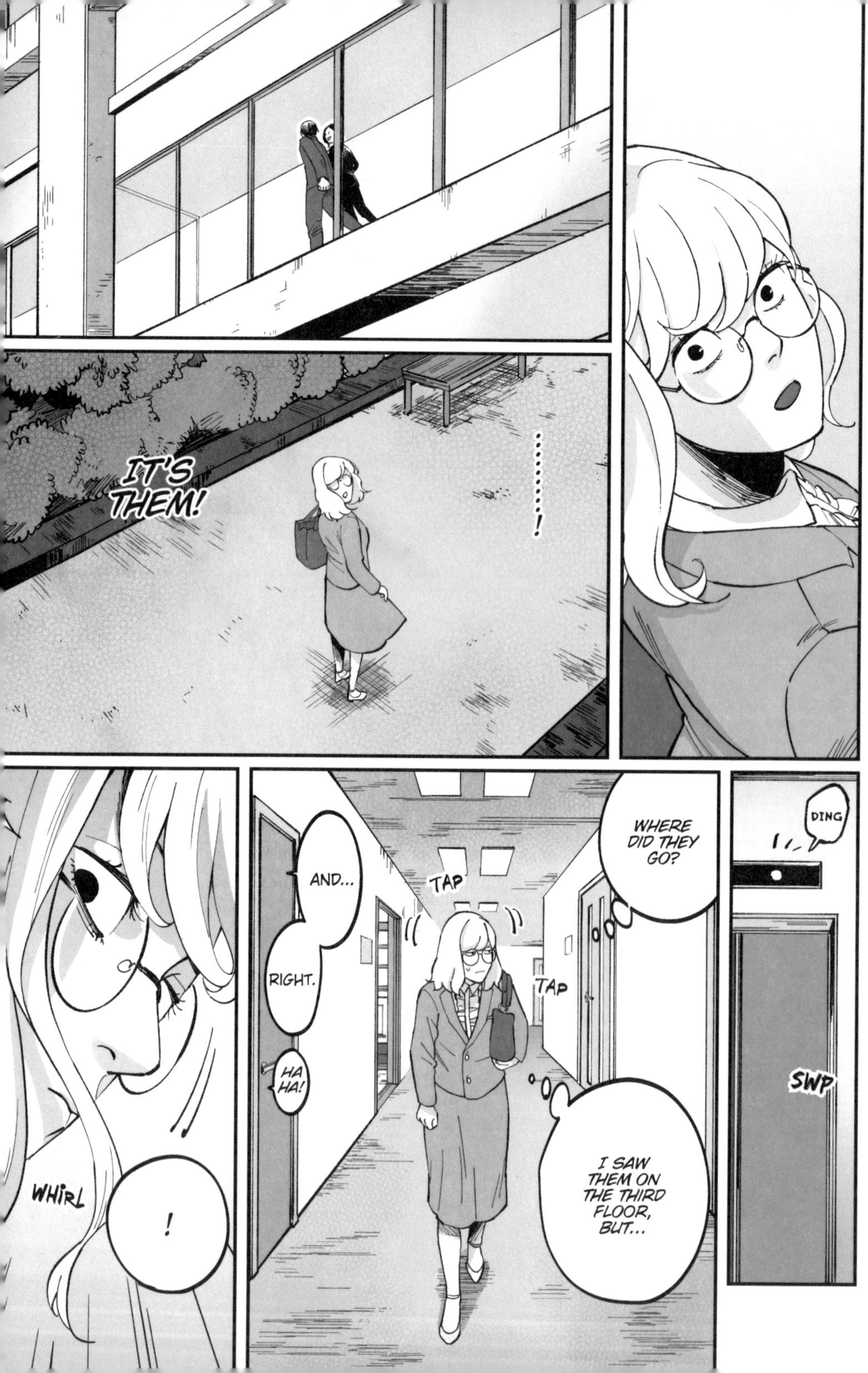
......!
IT'S THEM!
DING
SWP
WHERE DID THEY GO?
TAP
AND...
TAP
RIGHT.
I SAW THEM ON THE THIRD FLOOR, BUT...
HA HA!
!
WHIRL

BEFORE SHE GETS THE BETTER OF ME.

I NEED TO FIGURE OUT THEIR RELATIONSHIP...

STILL HERE?

SHE'S...

HM?

BETTER HEAD HOME.

SHE WORKS FAST, BUT...

SHE WORRIES OVER THE TINIEST DETAIL.

SHE STICKS AROUND LONGER THAN EVERYONE ELSE.

"THIS PROJECT IS ONGOING, BUT..."

"THEY DEFINITELY DIDN'T ACT LIKE IT."

"BUT IF THEY DO KNOW EACH OTHER..."

"IT'S VALUED AT TWO BILLION YEN."

"THEY PRETENDED, TO HAVE AN EXCUSE TO EXCHANGE INFO."

"CAUSE SHIRAKAWA-SAN MORE TROUBLE."

"I'D HATE TO..."

"IF SHE CAN SECRETLY OBTAIN INFO ABOUT THE OTHER PARTIES..."

"THAT'LL GIVE HER A HUGE ADVANTAGE."

"WE'RE NOT A TEAM."

"YOU'RE DAMN RIGHT."

"NOT ONLY THAT, BUT..."

FLIP

Weiß Capital   Lukas Hölter

That's weird...

How did she know he was Latino?

They've met before.

You can't tell from his name.

Plus, look at his card.

His company is German...

And his Japanese is native level.

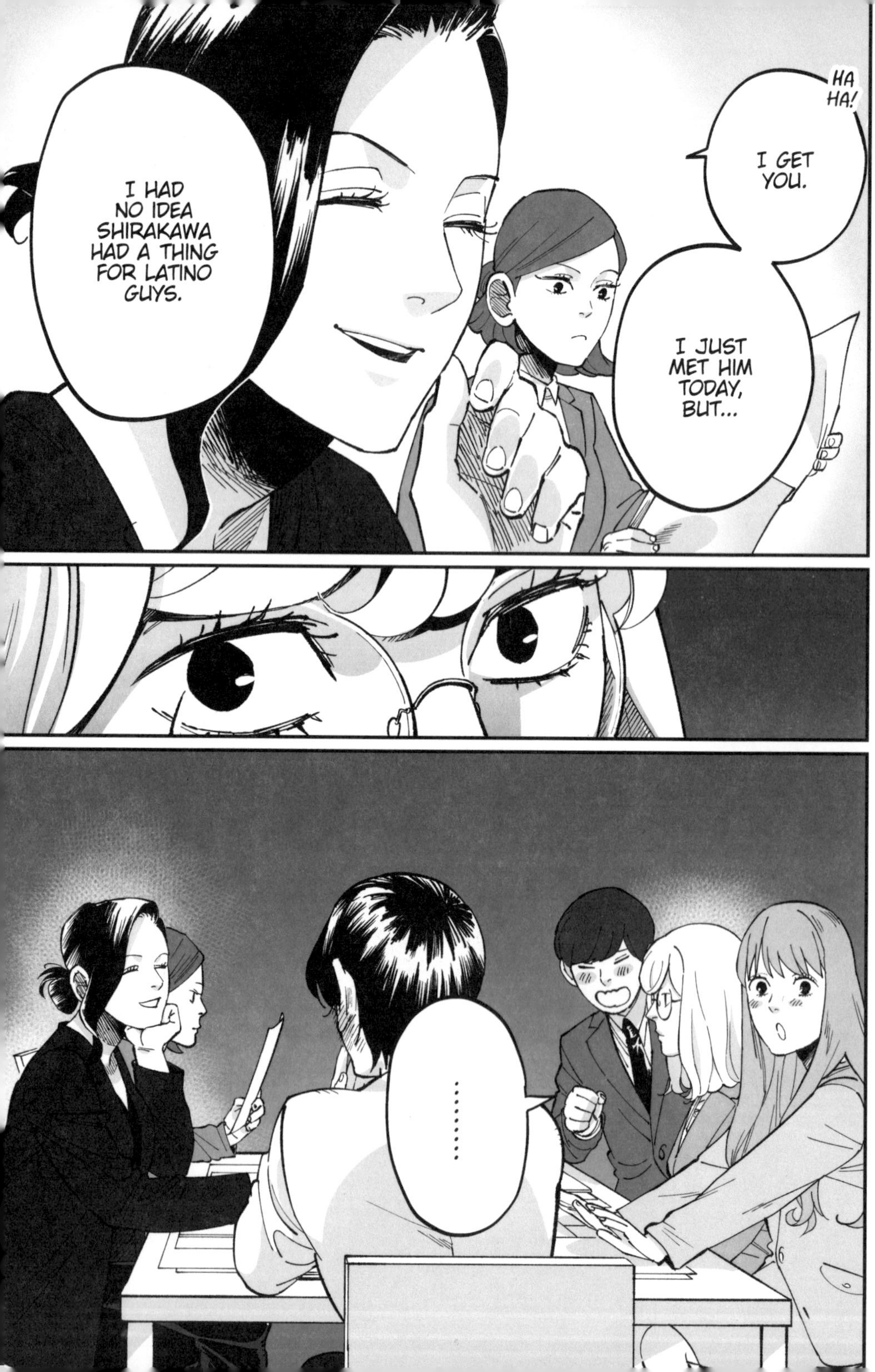
HA HA!
I GET YOU.
I JUST MET HIM TODAY, BUT...
I HAD NO IDEA SHIRAKAWA HAD A THING FOR LATINO GUYS.
....

THIS IS SUCH A WASTE OF TIME.
I DON'T WANT TO BE KNOWN FOR MY LOVE LIFE.
THAT KIND OF PERSON DOESN'T MOVE UP THE CORPORATE LADDER.
LET'S GET BACK TO WORK ALREADY...
C'MON, GUYS.
TALKING ABOUT BOYS IS FUN, BUT...
WE SHOULD GET BACK ON TRACK, UNLESS YOU WANNA WORK OVERTIME.
AH!
SHE'S RIGHT, IT'S ALREADY 5:30!
......
AWW, BUT I STILL HAVE STUFF I WANTED TO ASK JUNKO-SENPAI...

SO HE IS YOUR TYPE!!
NO WAY!
AH... NO...
THEY CAN'T BE SERIOUS ABOUT THIS CRAP...
RIGHT?
I WANT TO SEE THIS GUY FOR MYSELF!
ME TOO!
WHAT DOES HE LOOK LIKE?
FROM WHAT I SAW...
TALL AND LEAN BUT MUSCULAR, AND HAD AN UNDERCUT.
TALL?!
TALLER THAN ME?!
YOU'RE NOT THAT TALL, NOGIWA-KUN.
HEY, WADA-CHAN IS TALL, TOO!
SI GH

WHO'S "HE"?
THE GUY WHO CAME TO THE MEETING TODAY.
THE TALL HOT ONE WITH THE GOATEE!
OH!
DO YOU MEAN LUKAS-SAN?
I'M NOT SURE ABOUT THAT.
LUKAS?! HE'S MIXED?
BUT WITH A FACE LIKE THAT, HE COULD BE. HE'S CERTAINLY HANDSOME.
YOU TWO SEEMED SUPER COMPATIBLE, SENPAI!
WHAT?!
WHO IS THIS GUY?!

...?

JUNKO-SENPAI?

WAIT A SEC. IS HE YOUR TYPE...

SHWP

DO YOU KNOW EACH OTHER?
YES!
WE WORKED ON A PROJECT TOGETHER TWO YEARS AGO.
WOW!
I DIDN'T GET A CHANCE TO DO MUCH OF AN INTRODUCTION.
HERE'S MY CARD.
I'M LUKAS HÖLTER OF WEISS CAPITAL.
Weiß Capital
Lukas Hölter
THANK YOU!
I'M NISHIO FROM KOYO MIYAKO BANK.
THANK YOU.
I'M...

SHIRAKAWA-SAN!
LUKAS-SAN!
LONG TIME NO SEE!
I THINK IT'S BEEN TWO YEARS SINCE WE SAW EACH OTHER LAST.
HOW HAVE YOU BEEN?
I'M DOING GREAT!
GLAD TO SEE YOU'RE DOING WELL, TOO.
WELL THEN...
BOW
BOW
THANK YOU ALL FOR YOUR TIME!

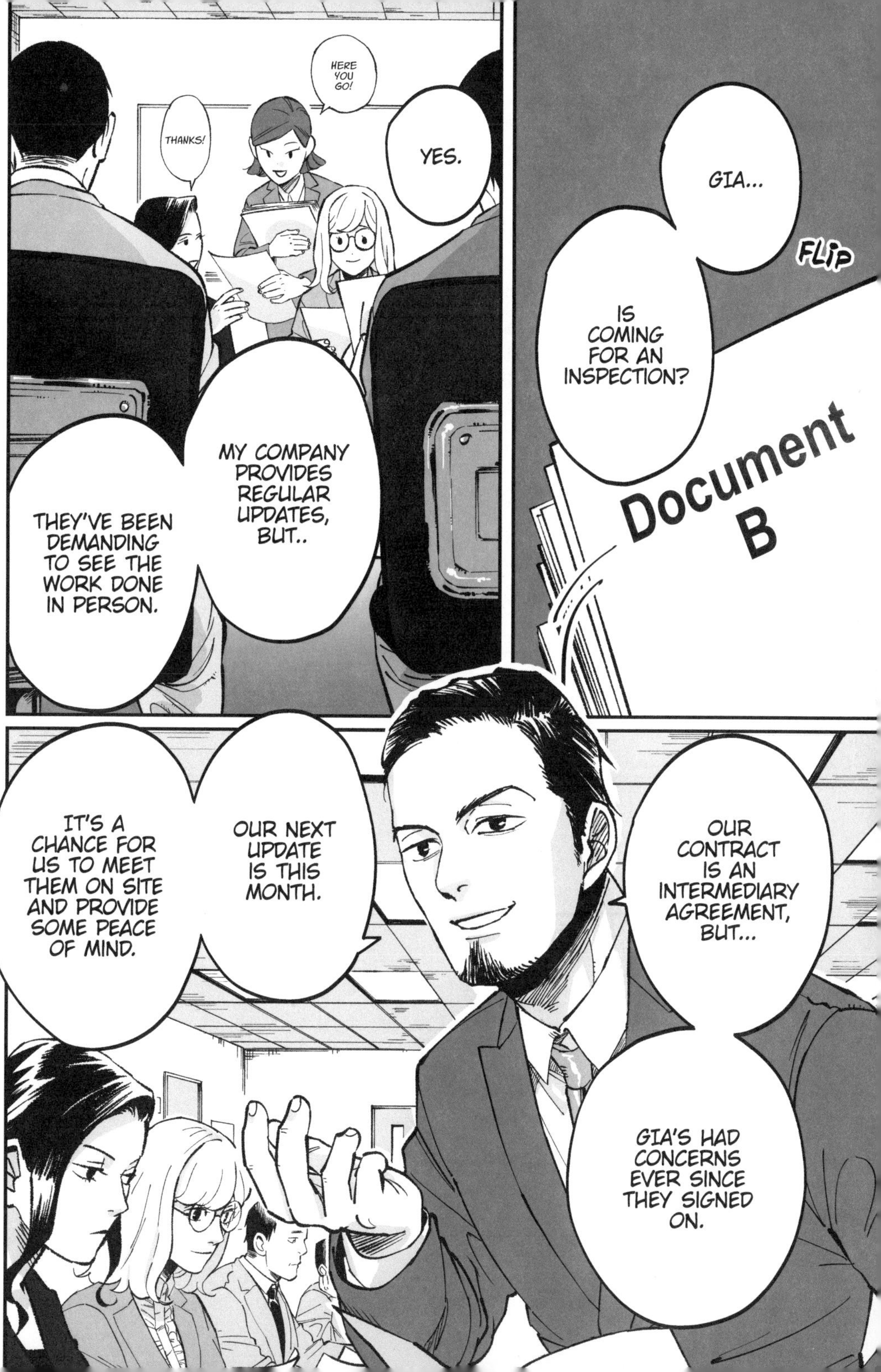
GIA...
IS COMING FOR AN INSPECTION?
FLIP
Document B
YES.
HERE YOU GO!
THANKS!
MY COMPANY PROVIDES REGULAR UPDATES, BUT..
THEY'VE BEEN DEMANDING TO SEE THE WORK DONE IN PERSON.
OUR CONTRACT IS AN INTERMEDIARY AGREEMENT, BUT...
GIA'S HAD CONCERNS EVER SINCE THEY SIGNED ON.
OUR NEXT UPDATE IS THIS MONTH.
IT'S A CHANCE FOR US TO MEET THEM ON SITE AND PROVIDE SOME PEACE OF MIND.

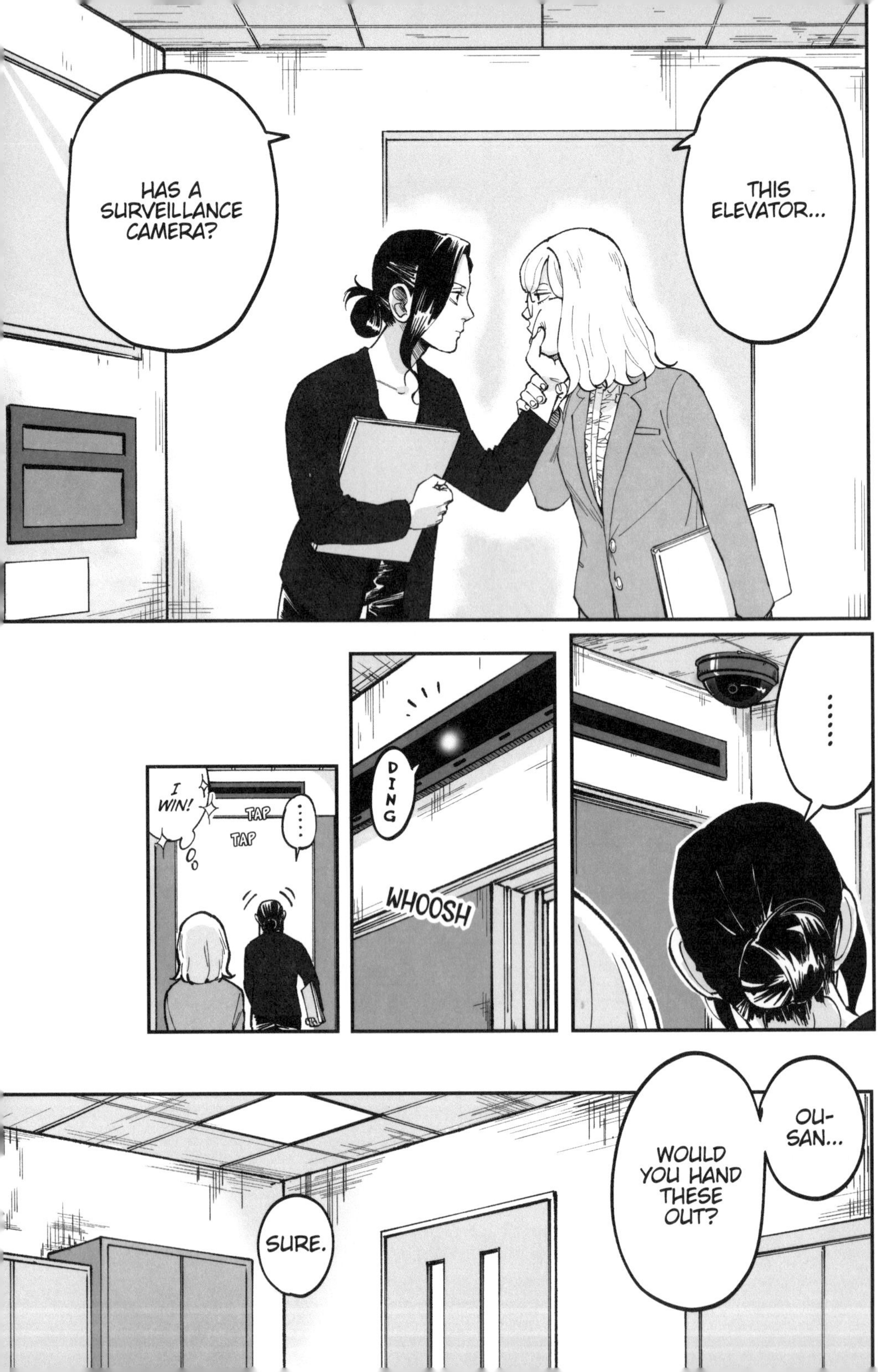
THIS ELEVATOR...
HAS A SURVEILLANCE CAMERA?
......
DING
WHOOSH
I WIN!
TAP
TAP
......
OU-SAN...
WOULD YOU HAND THESE OUT?
SURE.

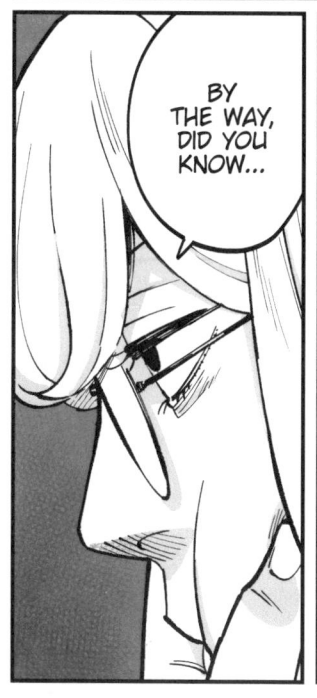

"WE."

"ARE. NOT. A. TEAM. GOT IT?"

"BY THE WAY, DID YOU KNOW..."

"THAT'S MY LINE. THE IDEA OF JOINING FORCES MAKES ME SICK."

"......"

……
I MEAN, THEY HAVE A POINT.
AWW...
YOU SAY THE *CUTEST* THINGS.
DING
IN CASE YOU FORGOT...
WHAT HAPPENED THE OTHER DAY WAS NOT US *GETTING ALONG.*
GRR
TWIST
YOU...
GRAB

> WELL... WE'LL SEE YOU AT THE MEETING AT FOUR.

> SEE YOU THEN.

> GREAT WORK!

> SAME TO YOU!

> "HMM"?

> I JUST HAD TO LAUGH...

SNICKER

> AT THE IDEA OF US "GETTING ALONG."

> HMM...

SHP

OH-SO-INNOCENT AS ALWAYS.

YOU'RE TOO MODEST.

ISN'T SHE?

JUST LOOKING OUT FOR HERSELF.

I'M JUST TRYING TO LEARN FROM HER EXAMPLE.

ONLY THANKS TO SHIRAKAWA-SAN.

ARE YOU SURE?

YOU'RE ALREADY AHEAD OF THE GAME.

SHE ONLY WANTS HIGH-PROFILE PROJECTS THAT'LL BOOST HER REPUTATION.

I KNOW WHAT SHE'S THINKING.

I HATE TO ADMIT IT, BUT...

WE *DO* THINK ALIKE.

WELL, YOU WON'T CATCH ME SHARING CREDIT. NOT IF IT COSTS ME A PROMOTION.

KURODA-SAN DOESN'T NEED ANY MORE TRAINING...
AND IT'D BE NICE TO HAVE YOU TWO COLLAB ON OTHER PROJECTS.
YEAH!
THEY GET ALONG GREAT.
FOR NEW IDEAS...
WOMEN HAVE US BEAT.
I'M NOT QUITE THERE YET.
AND I'D HATE TO CAUSE SHIRAKAWA-SAN MORE TROUBLE.
I'LL NEED TWO MORE WEEKS OF TRAINING AT THE VERY LEAST...
......
"GET ALONG GREAT."
THESE GEEZERS HAVE NO CLUE.

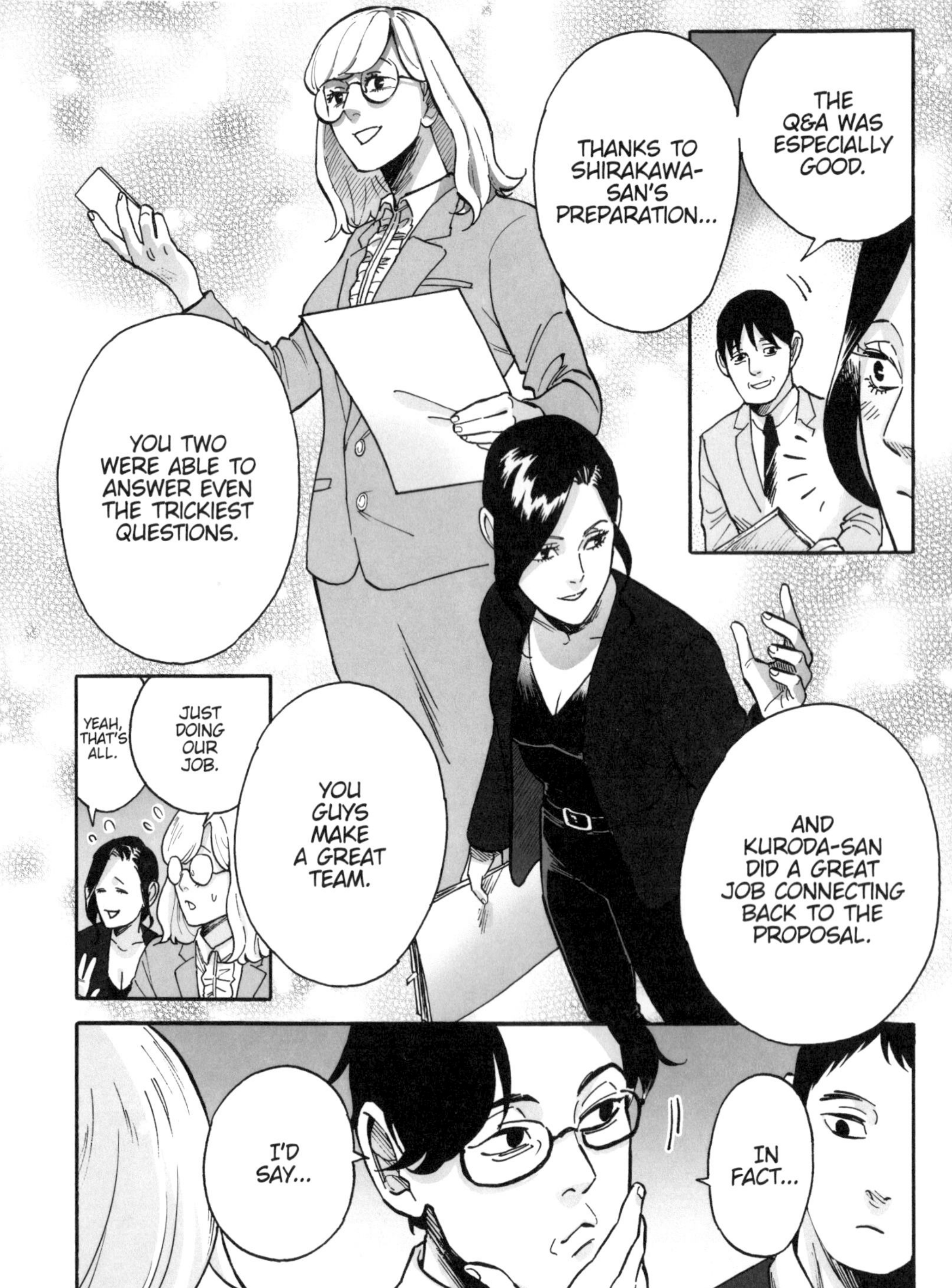
THE Q&A WAS ESPECIALLY GOOD.
THANKS TO SHIRAKAWA-SAN'S PREPARATION...
YOU TWO WERE ABLE TO ANSWER EVEN THE TRICKIEST QUESTIONS.
AND KURODA-SAN DID A GREAT JOB CONNECTING BACK TO THE PROPOSAL.
YOU GUYS MAKE A GREAT TEAM.
JUST DOING OUR JOB.
YEAH, THAT'S ALL.
IN FACT...
I'D SAY...

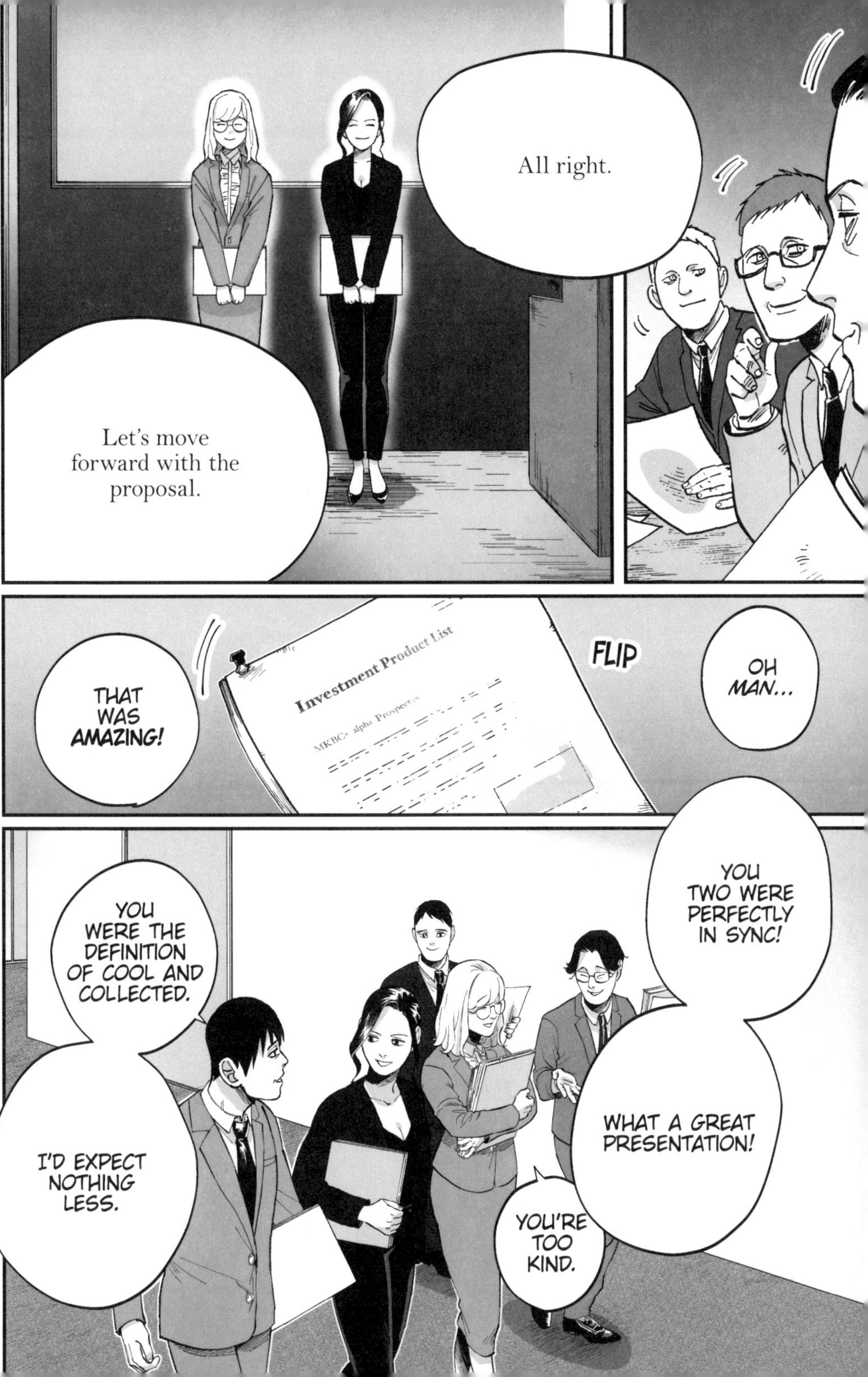
All right.
Let's move forward with the proposal.
OH MAN...
FLIP
Investment Product List
MKBC+ alpha Prospectus
THAT WAS AMAZING!
YOU TWO WERE PERFECTLY IN SYNC!
YOU WERE THE DEFINITION OF COOL AND COLLECTED.
WHAT A GREAT PRESENTATION!
I'D EXPECT NOTHING LESS.
YOU'RE TOO KIND.

As you can see...
CLINK
our premier institutional fund, the KMBC+ alpha...
has beaten the market average since its inception.
I see.
Hmm.
In addition, we are prepared to lower fees...
for ongoing investments...
if you invest in KMBC+ alpha.

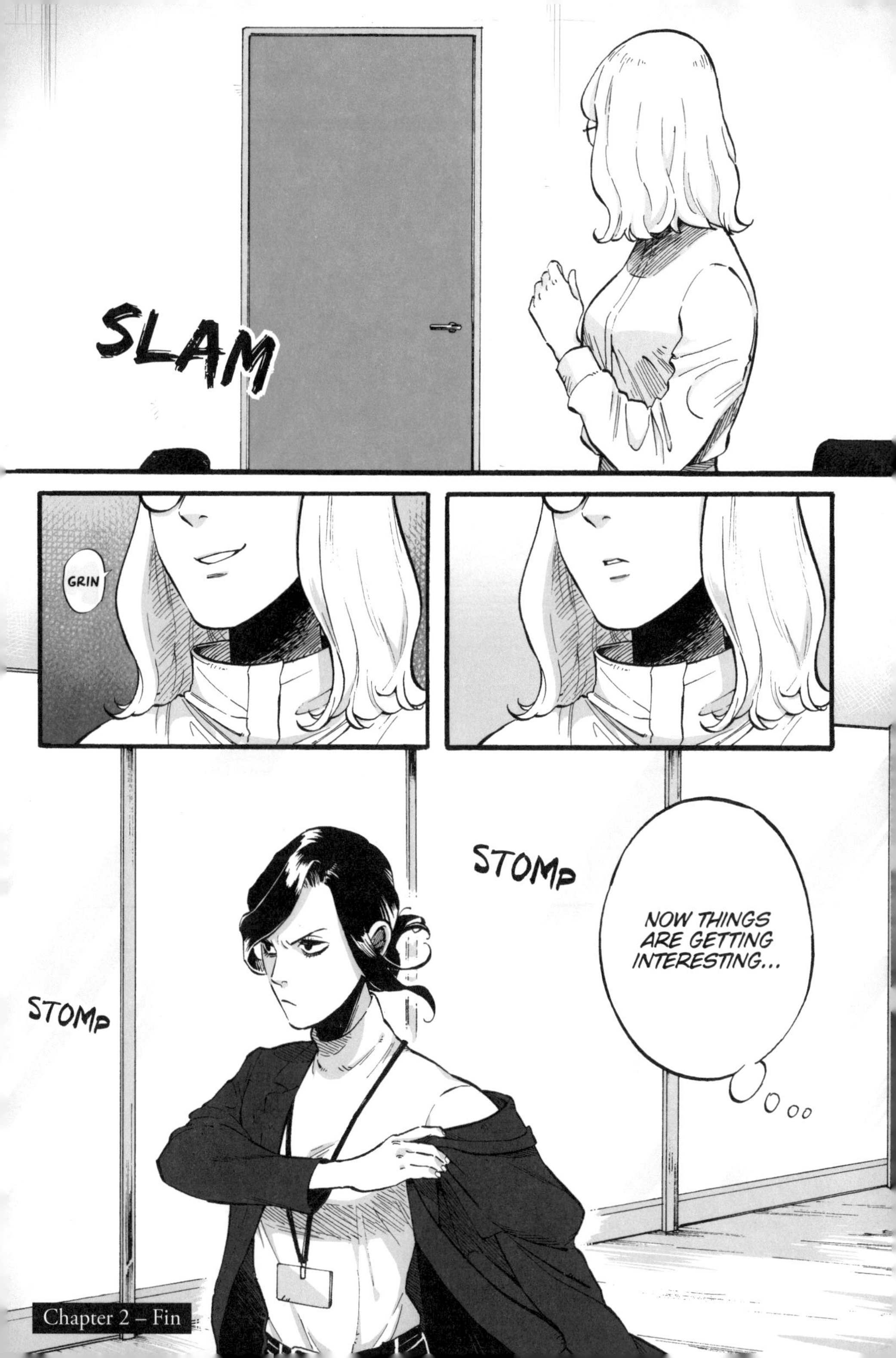
SLAM
GRIN
NOW THINGS ARE GETTING INTERESTING...
STOMP
STOMP
Chapter 2 – Fin

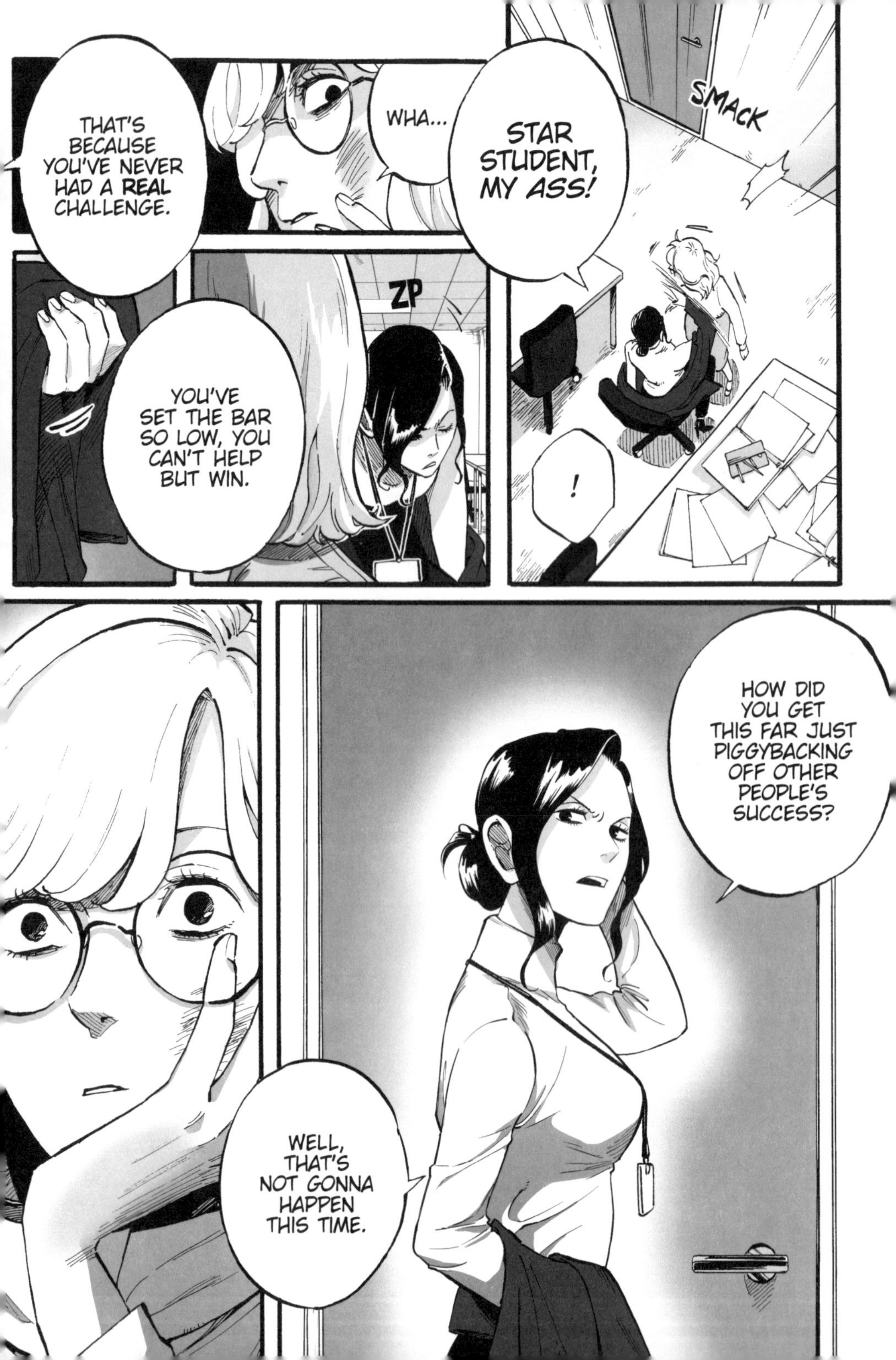
SMACK
STAR STUDENT, MY ASS!
!
WHA...
THAT'S BECAUSE YOU'VE NEVER HAD A **REAL** CHALLENGE.
ZP
YOU'VE SET THE BAR SO LOW, YOU CAN'T HELP BUT WIN.
HOW DID YOU GET THIS FAR JUST PIGGYBACKING OFF OTHER PEOPLE'S SUCCESS?
WELL, THAT'S NOT GONNA HAPPEN THIS TIME.

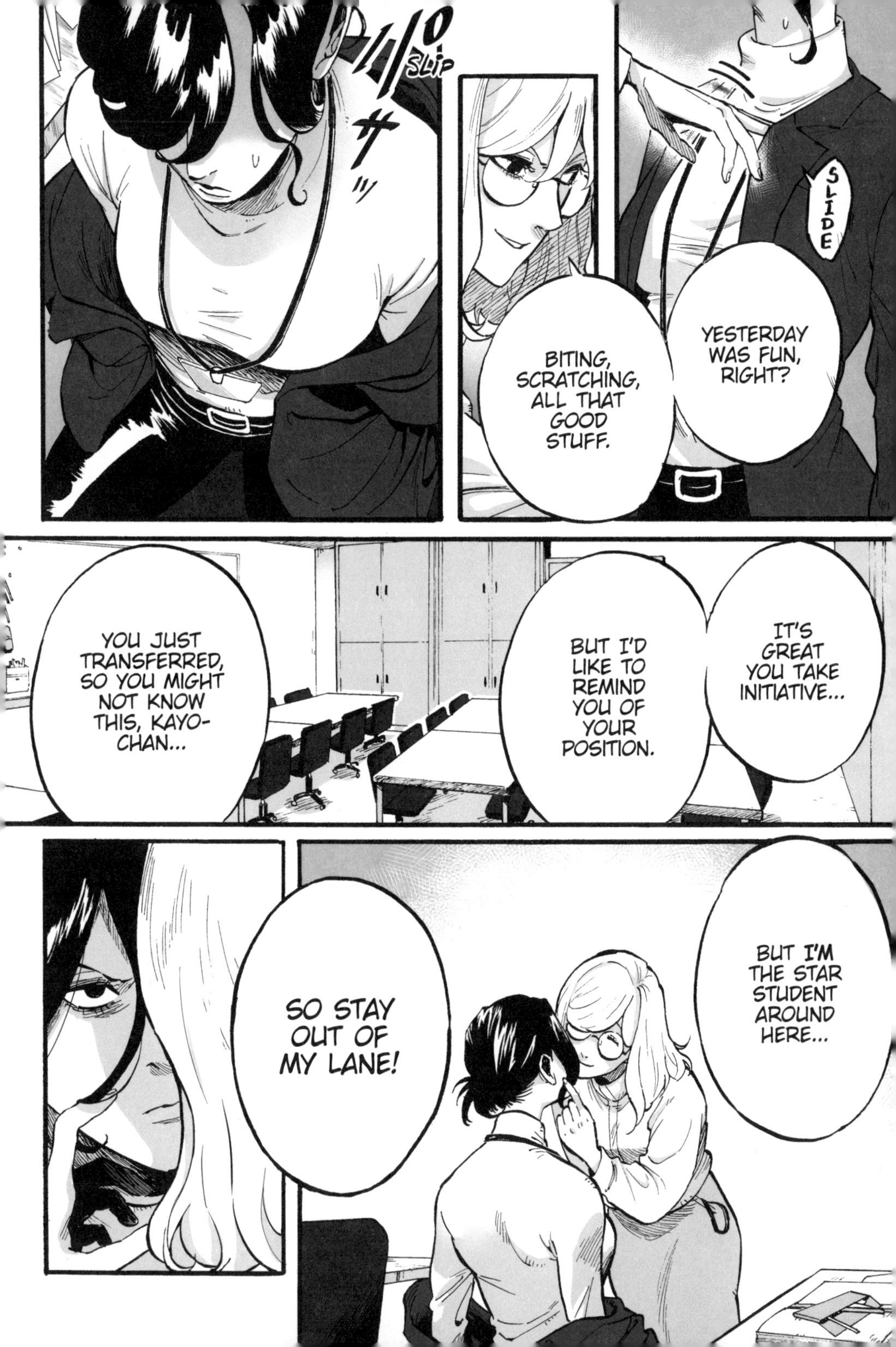
SLIDE
YESTERDAY WAS FUN, RIGHT?
BITING, SCRATCHING, ALL THAT GOOD STUFF.
SLIP
IT'S GREAT YOU TAKE INITIATIVE...
BUT I'D LIKE TO REMIND YOU OF YOUR POSITION.
YOU JUST TRANSFERRED, SO YOU MIGHT NOT KNOW THIS, KAYO-CHAN...
BUT I'M THE STAR STUDENT AROUND HERE...
SO STAY OUT OF MY LANE!

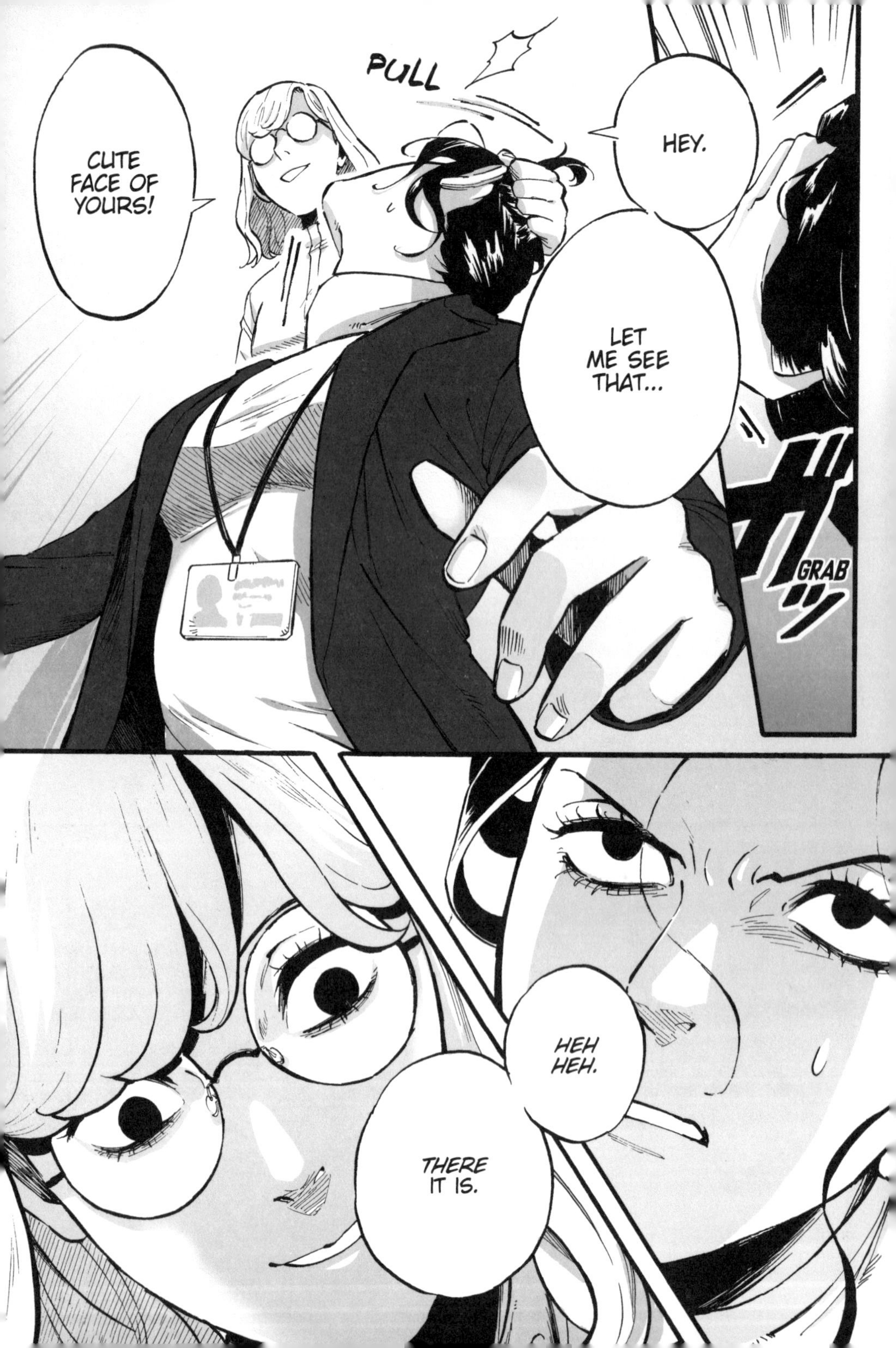
HEY.
PULL
LET ME SEE THAT...
GRAB
CUTE FACE OF YOURS!
HEH HEH.
THERE IT IS.

......
WHAT, WAS IT ON YOUR MIND TOO?
GLARE
YOU HAD ME WORRIED, Y'KNOW.
TAP
TAP
I WAS AFRAID I HURT YOUR FEELINGS...
AND YOU'D WRITTEN ME OFF.
RIGHT?
......
IT WAS ONLY YESTERDAY, AFTER ALL.
YOU SEEMED SO *CALM* THIS MORNING.
I WAS AFRAID YOU'D ALREADY FORGOTTEN.
HOW COULD I *FORGET?*

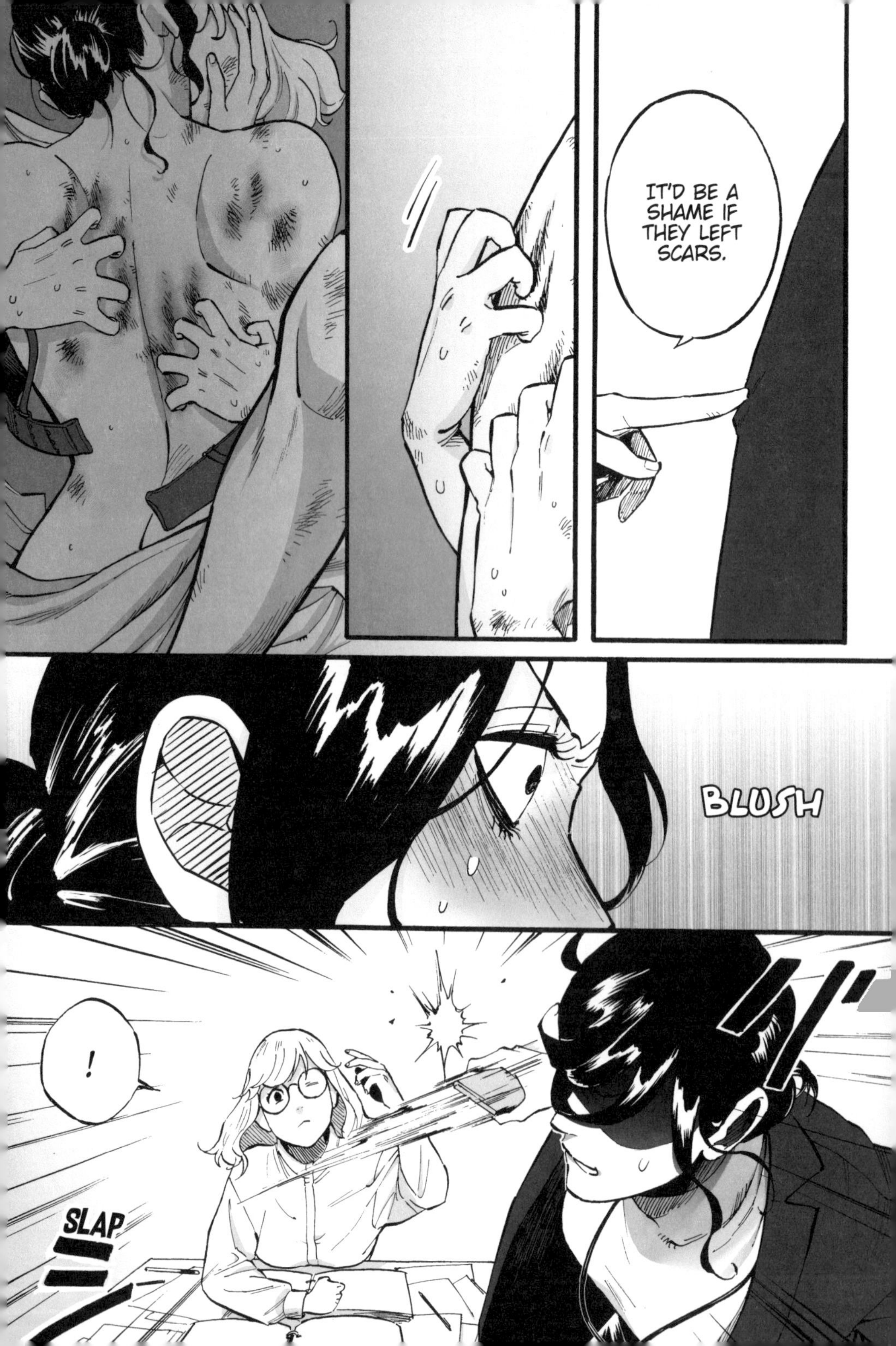
IT'D BE A SHAME IF THEY LEFT SCARS.
BLUSH
!
SLAP

JOLT

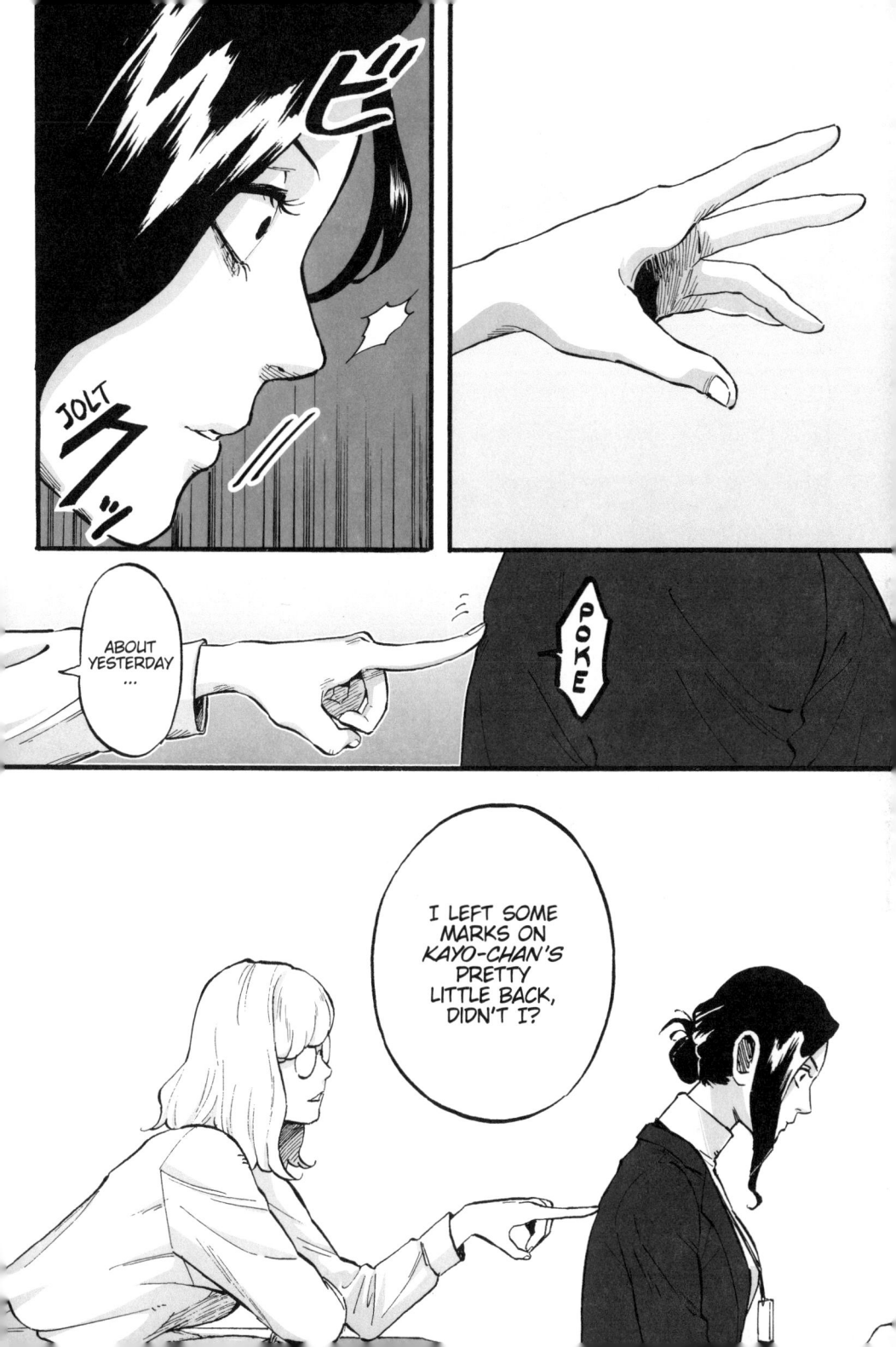

ABOUT YESTERDAY...

POKE

I LEFT SOME MARKS ON *KAYO-CHAN'S* PRETTY LITTLE BACK, DIDN'T I?

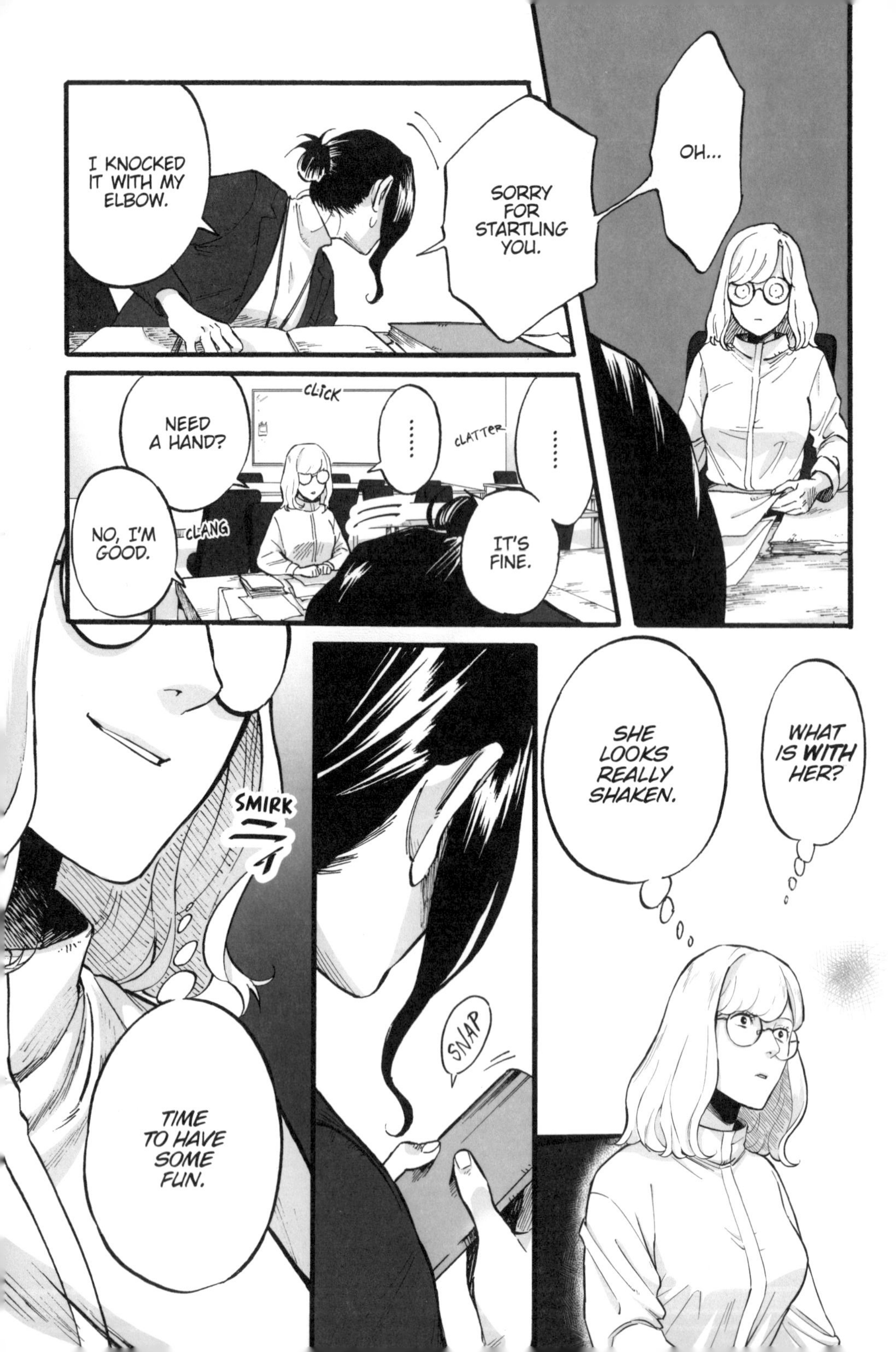
OH...
SORRY FOR STARTLING YOU.
I KNOCKED IT WITH MY ELBOW.
......
IT'S FINE.
CLATTER
......
CLICK
NEED A HAND?
CLANG
NO, I'M GOOD.
WHAT IS WITH HER?
SHE LOOKS REALLY SHAKEN.
SNAP
SMIRK
ニィ
TIME TO HAVE SOME FUN.

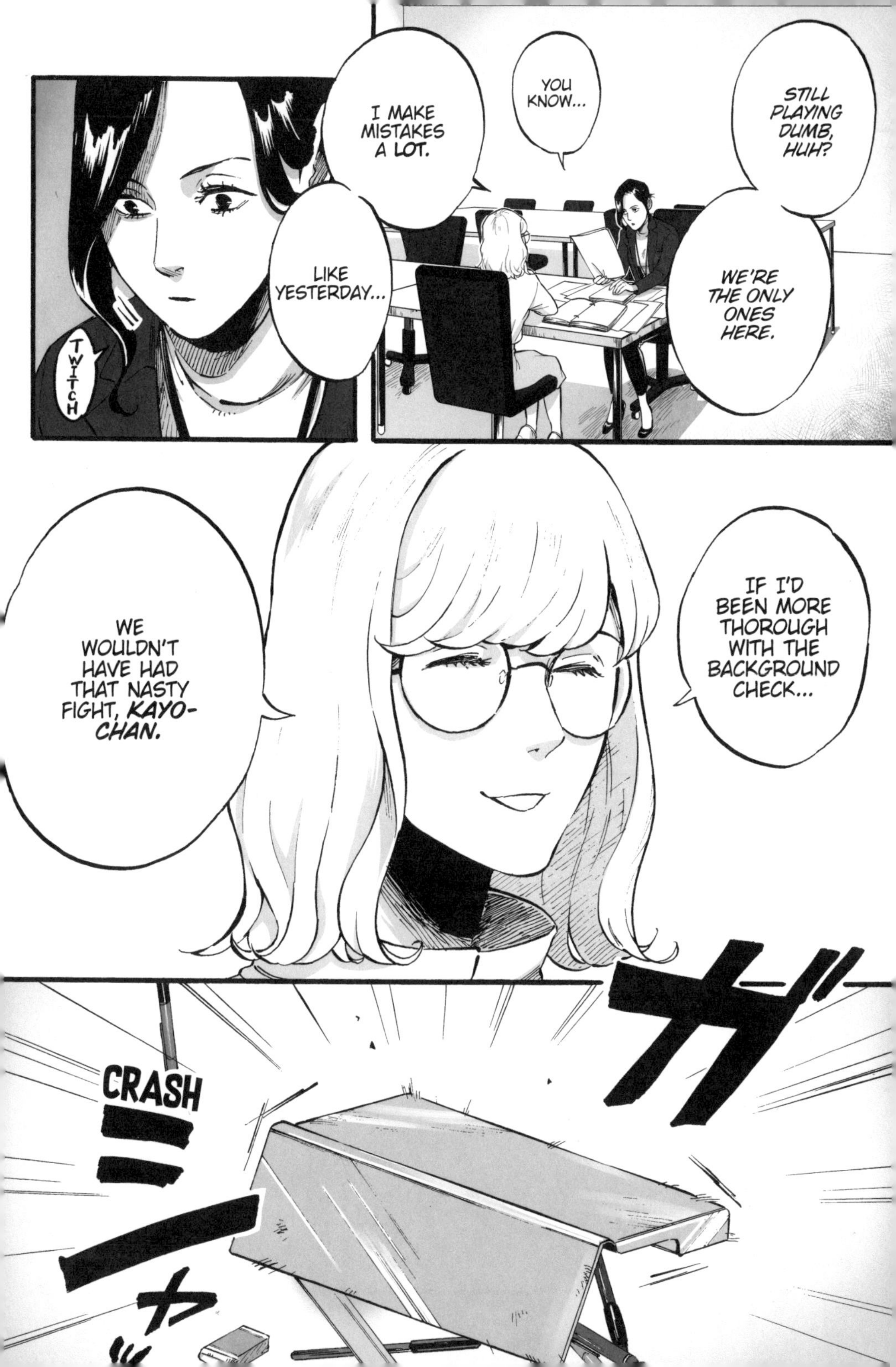
STILL PLAYING DUMB, HUH?
WE'RE THE ONLY ONES HERE.
YOU KNOW...
I MAKE MISTAKES A LOT.
LIKE YESTERDAY...
TWITCH
IF I'D BEEN MORE THOROUGH WITH THE BACKGROUND CHECK...
WE WOULDN'T HAVE HAD THAT NASTY FIGHT, *KAYO-CHAN.*
CRASH

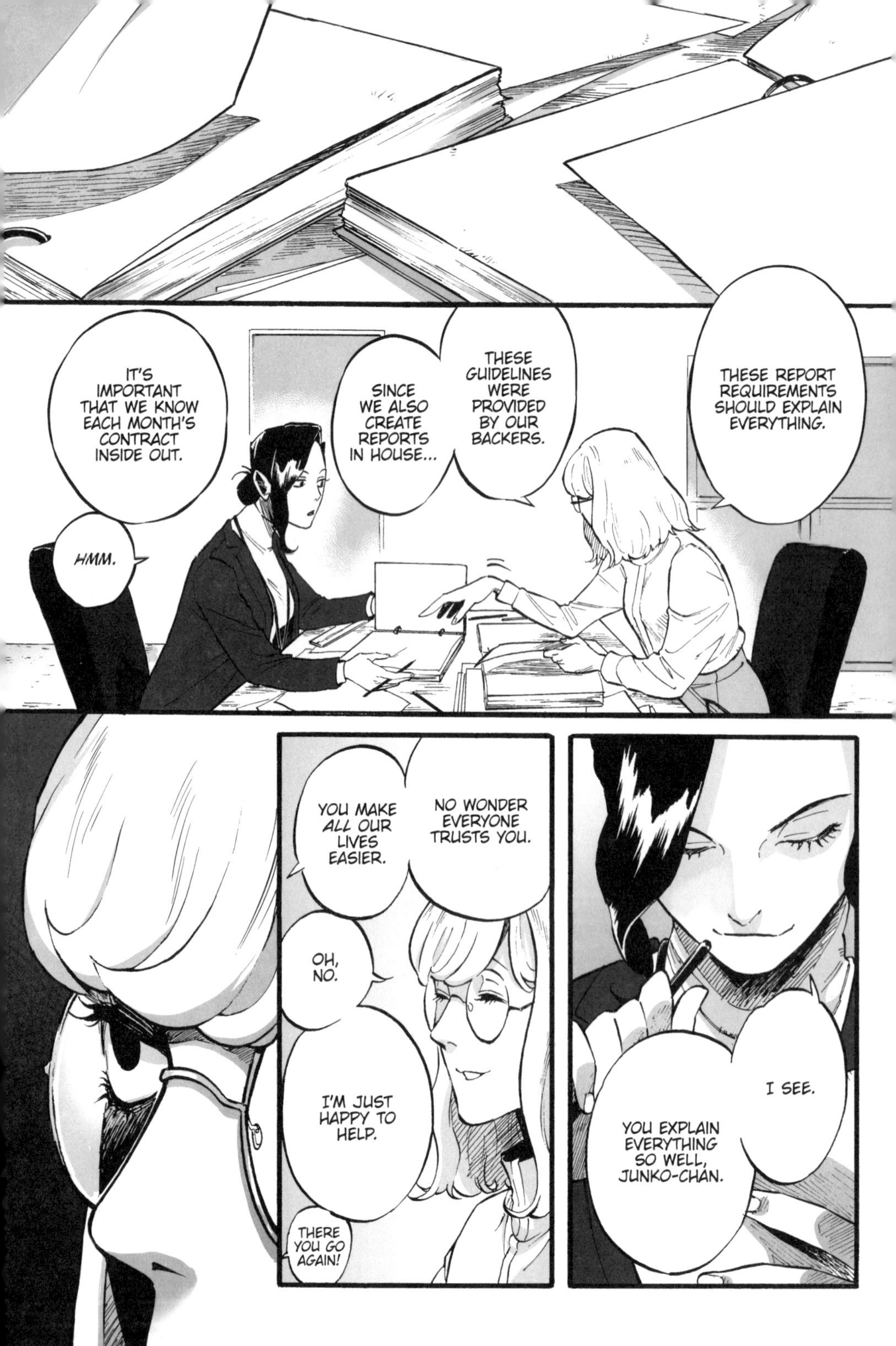
THESE REPORT REQUIREMENTS SHOULD EXPLAIN EVERYTHING.
THESE GUIDELINES WERE PROVIDED BY OUR BACKERS.
SINCE WE ALSO CREATE REPORTS IN HOUSE...
IT'S IMPORTANT THAT WE KNOW EACH MONTH'S CONTRACT INSIDE OUT.
HMM.
I SEE.
YOU EXPLAIN EVERYTHING SO WELL, JUNKO-CHAN.
NO WONDER EVERYONE TRUSTS YOU.
YOU MAKE *ALL* OUR LIVES EASIER.
OH, NO.
I'M JUST HAPPY TO HELP.
THERE YOU GO AGAIN!

SEEMS LIKE YOU TWO ARE GETTING ALONG.
THE TRAINING'S GOING WELL, I TAKE IT?
DEPUTY DIRECTOR HIGA-SHINO!
WHAT BRINGS YOU HERE?
IT'S GREAT.
KURODA-SAN IS A FAST LEARNER.
SHE SHOULD BE ALL CAUGHT UP BY NEXT MONTH.
GRIN
GLAD TO HEAR IT!
CAN YOU ORGANIZE THIS CLIENT FILE?
I THINK GETTING TO KNOW OUR HISTORY...
WOULD BE GOOD FOR KURODA-SAN.
ABSOLUTELY.
YOU CAN USE THE CONFERENCE ROOM.
WILL DO!
IF YOU FEEL LOST AT ANY POINT, KURODA-SAN...
SHIRAKAWA-SAN WILL FILL YOU IN.
GRIN
OKAY!

HOW DID I END UP WORKING WITH...
THIS STUCK-UP BITCH?
OH!
SLIDE
I JUST GOT THIS FROM THE MANAGER.
BUT IT LOOKS LIKE THERE ARE SOME FILES MISSING.
AH...
THIS FILE ONLY CONTAINS LAST YEAR'S SECTION.
OH?
YOU CAN GO AHEAD AND RESUBMIT IT.
GOT IT, THANKS!
WELL THEN!

HOW ABOUT YOU GIVE ME A HAND?
SENPAI.
UNLIKE YOU, I HAVEN'T PLAYED ALL MY CARDS YET.
SLAP
JEEZ...
AND HOW WOULD I KNOW THAT?
THUD
UGH!
WELL...
GRRR...
AGAIN WITH THE "SENPAI"!

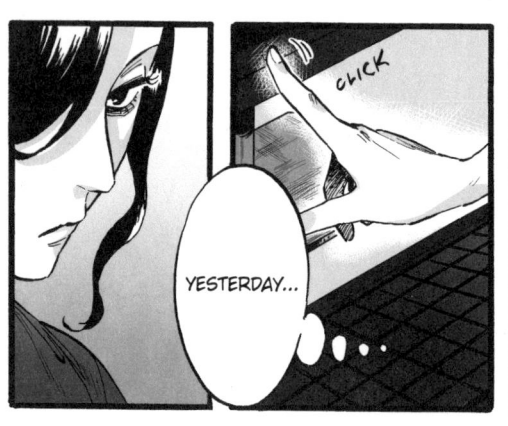

YESTERDAY... *CLICK* ...

NOT TO MENTION CALLING ME BY MY FIRST NAME.

LIKE WE'RE BFFS. WHAT NERVE!

HOW ABOUT YOU FINISH WHAT YOU STARTED?

IS THAT ALL YOU GOT?

SHUT UP!

THANKS, KAYO-CHAN.

DON'T MENTION IT!

OH REALLY...

I WAS JUST PRINTING SOME EMAILS FROM OUR PARTNERS.

OH! WELCOME BACK, JUNKO-CHAN.

SHE'S ACTING LIKE...

YESTERDAY NEVER HAPPENED.

OH, I WAS PLAYING WITH A DOG AND IT GOT ROUGH.
SHE LEFT A MARK.
OH NO!
THAT WOMAN IS ABSURDLY STRONG!
THERE'S NO WAY I CAN HIDE ALL OF THESE.
I DIDN'T NOTICE IT YESTERDAY, BUT...
I'M COVERED IN SCRATCHES AND BRUISES.
I CAN'T **BELIEVE** THIS.
IF ANY OF THE SENIOR STAFF NOTICE, I'M **DONE** FOR.
RUMMAGE
ACK!
HERE TOO?!
EEK!
THAT BITCH!

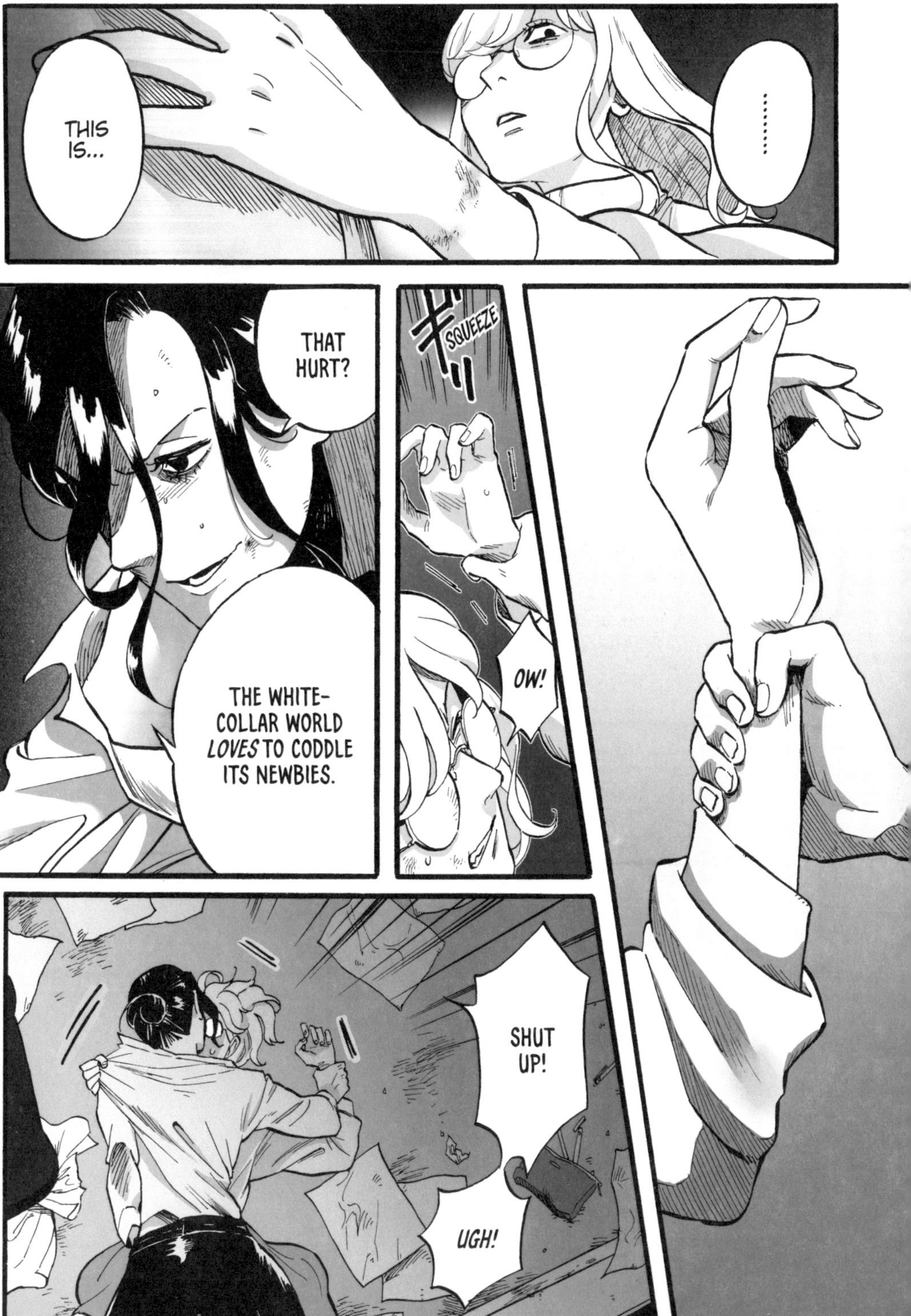
......
THIS IS...
SQUEEZE
OW!
THAT HURT?
THE WHITE-COLLAR WORLD *LOVES* TO CODDLE ITS NEWBIES.
SHUT UP!
UGH!

I HAD TIME SO I FIGURED I'D JUST DO IT.

JUNKO-SAN, YOU'RE SHREDDING DOCUMENTS?

WHAT?

I WAS SUPPOSED TO DO THAT!

DON'T WORRY ABOUT IT.

BUT I LET THEM PILE UP!

I'M SO SORRY!

THAT BRUISE ON YOUR WRIST...

Bow

IT'S FINE.

HUH?

WHAT HAPPENED?

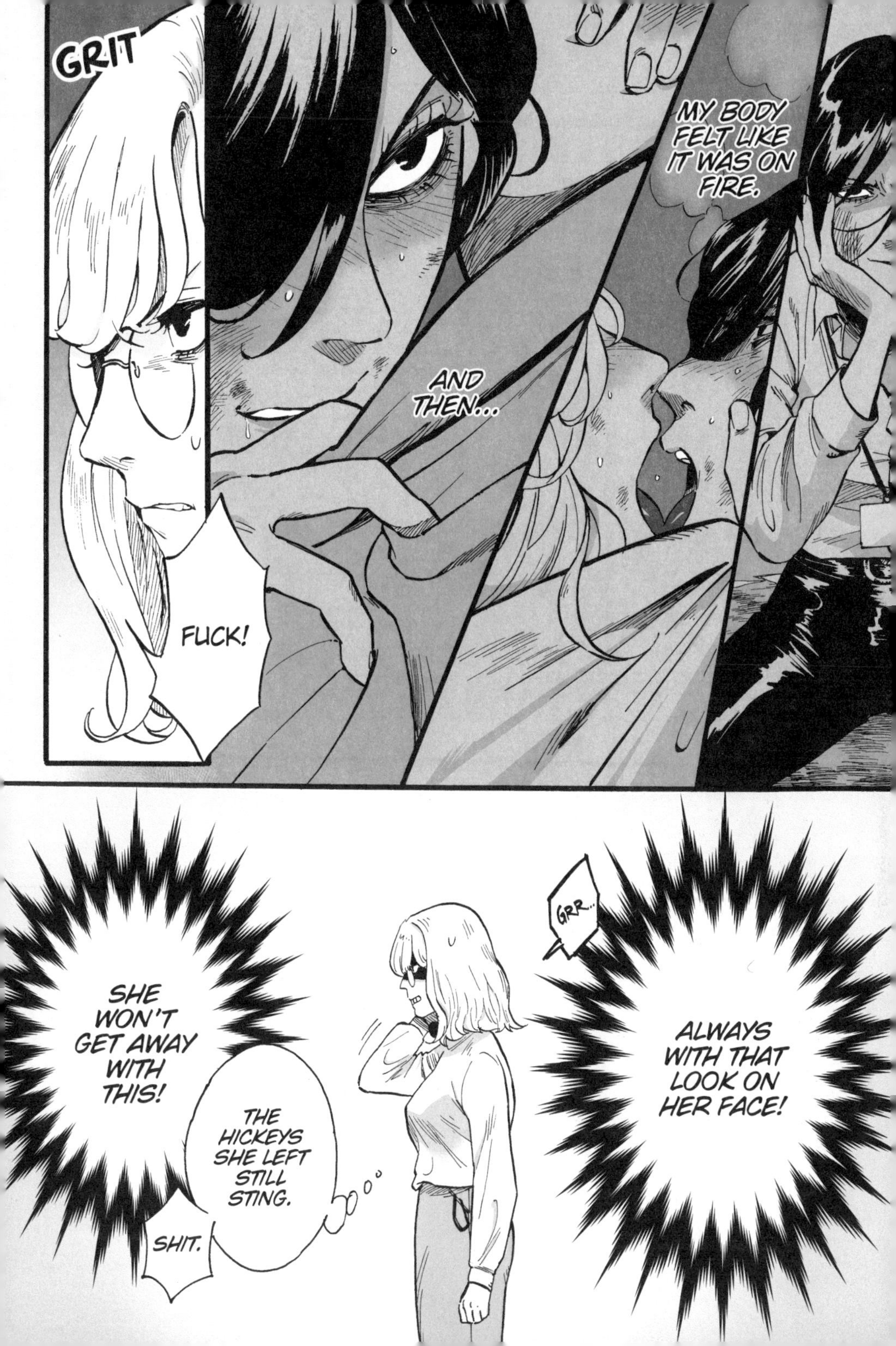
MY BODY FELT LIKE IT WAS ON FIRE.
AND THEN...
GRIT
FUCK!
GRR..
ALWAYS WITH THAT LOOK ON HER FACE!
SHE WON'T GET AWAY WITH THIS!
THE HICKEYS SHE LEFT STILL STING.
SHIT.

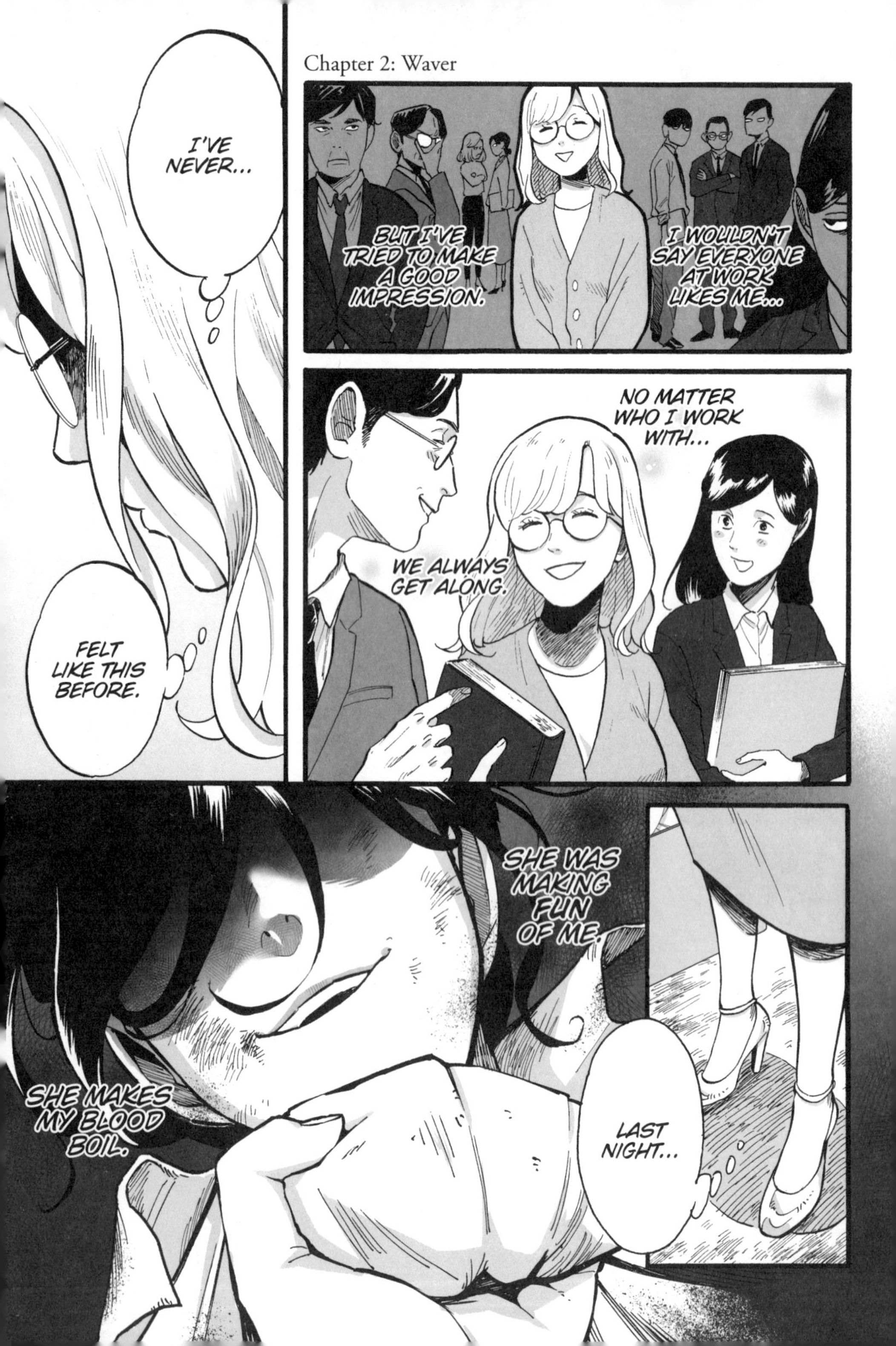
I WOULDN'T SAY EVERYONE AT WORK LIKES ME...
BUT I'VE TRIED TO MAKE A GOOD IMPRESSION.
NO MATTER WHO I WORK WITH...
WE ALWAYS GET ALONG.
I'VE NEVER...
FELT LIKE THIS BEFORE.
LAST NIGHT...
SHE WAS MAKING FUN OF ME.
SHE MAKES MY BLOOD BOIL.

......
WHAT HAVE I DONE?
AND AT WORK NO LESS. WHAT'S WRONG WITH ME?
I'VE DEALT WITH DIFFICULT NEWBIES...
BUT NEVER LIKE THIS.
BUZZ
HOW DID I GET SO WORKED UP OVER SOME CHILDISH TAUNTING?
IT'S HER FAULT.

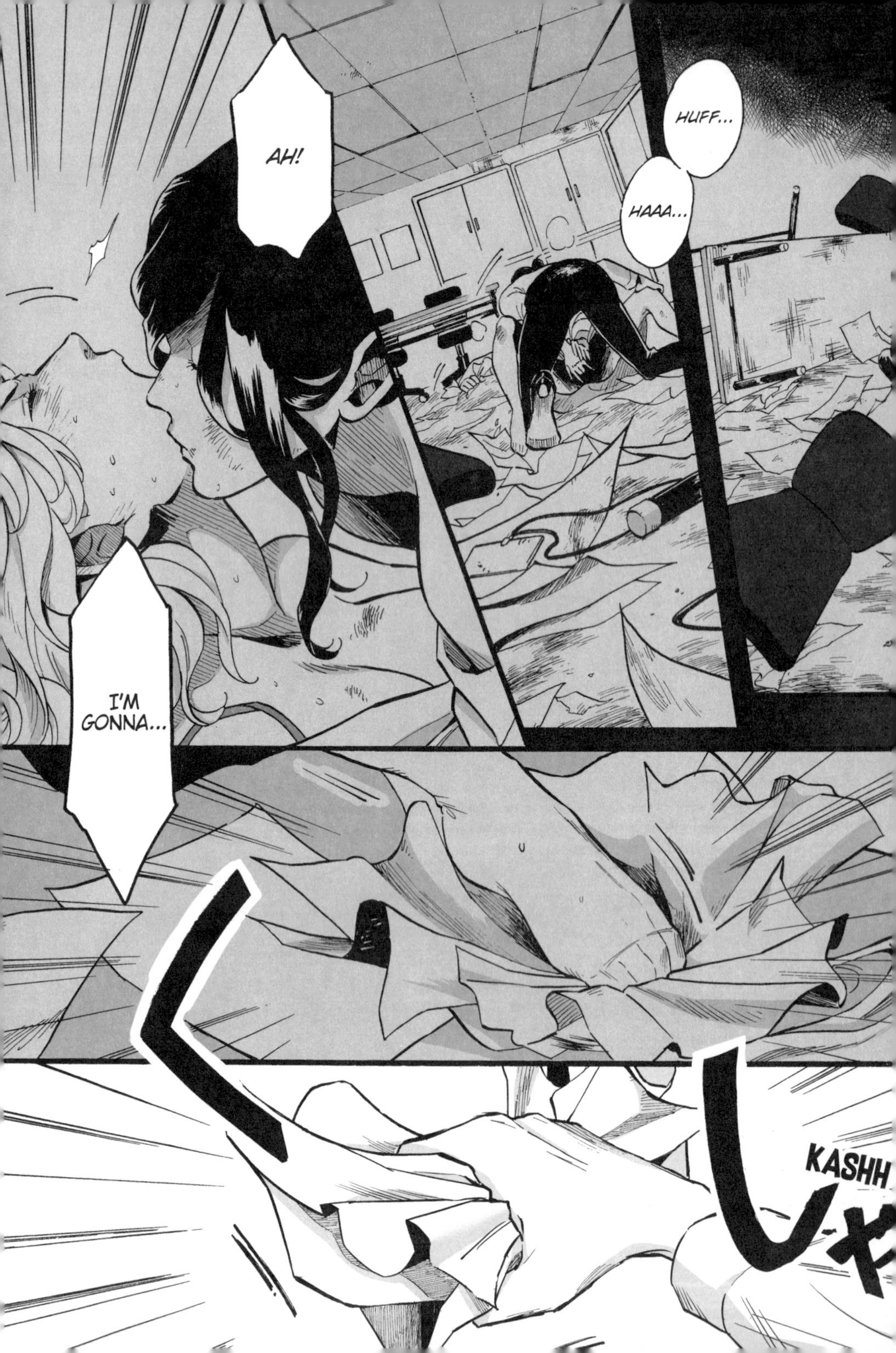
HUFF...
HAAA...
AH!
I'M GONNA...
KASHH

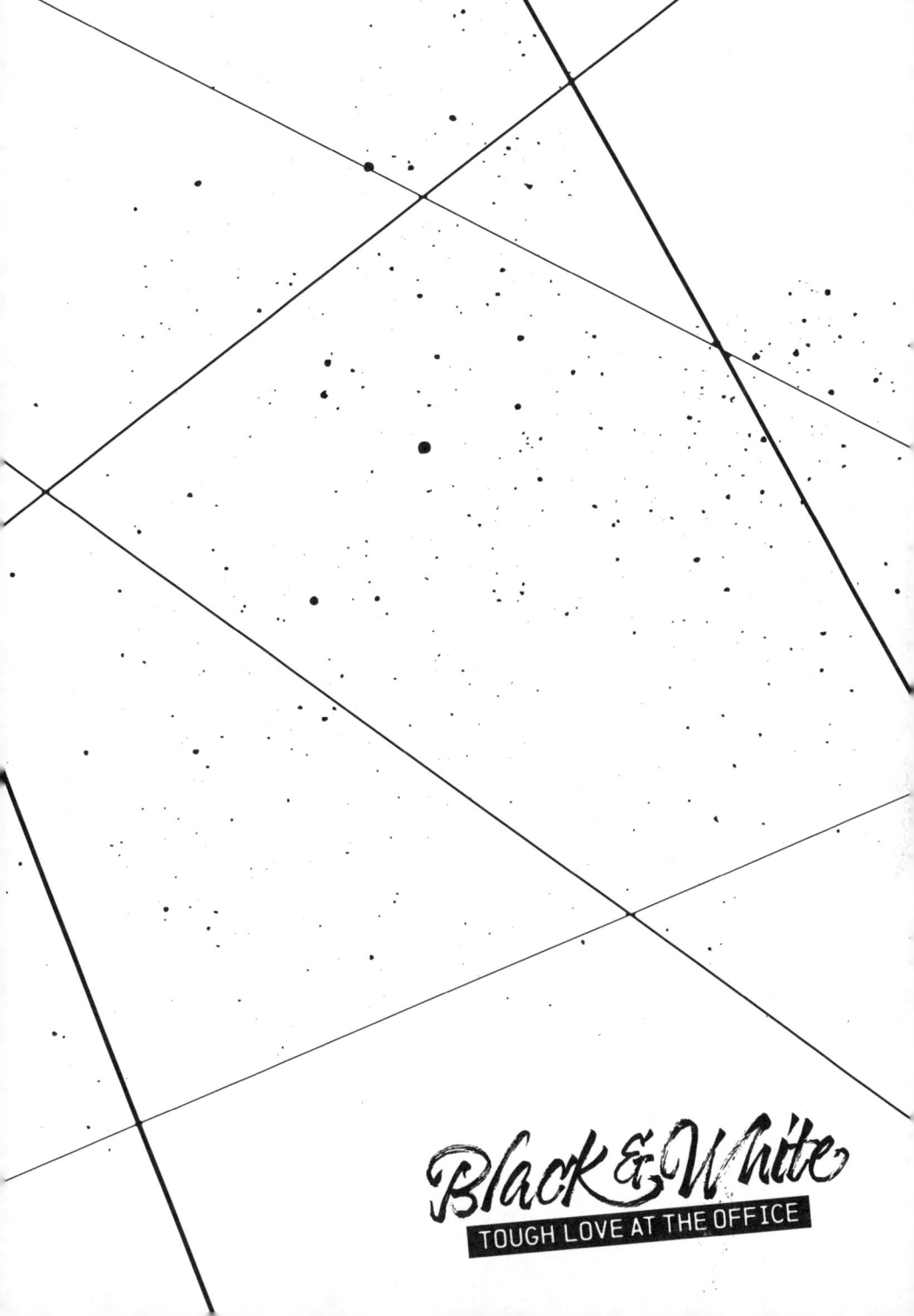

Black & White
TOUGH LOVE AT THE OFFICE

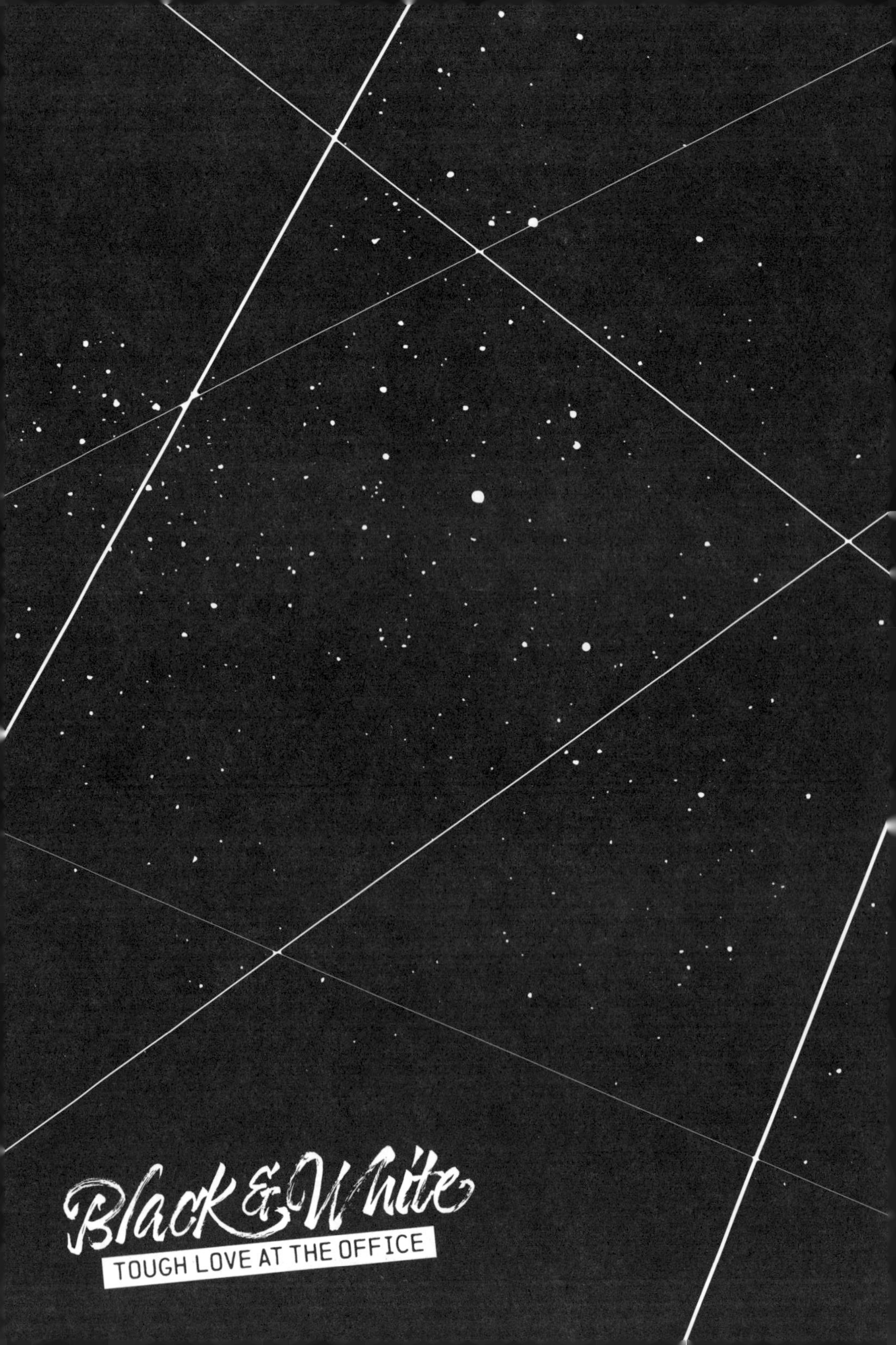
Black & White
TOUGH LOVE AT THE OFFICE

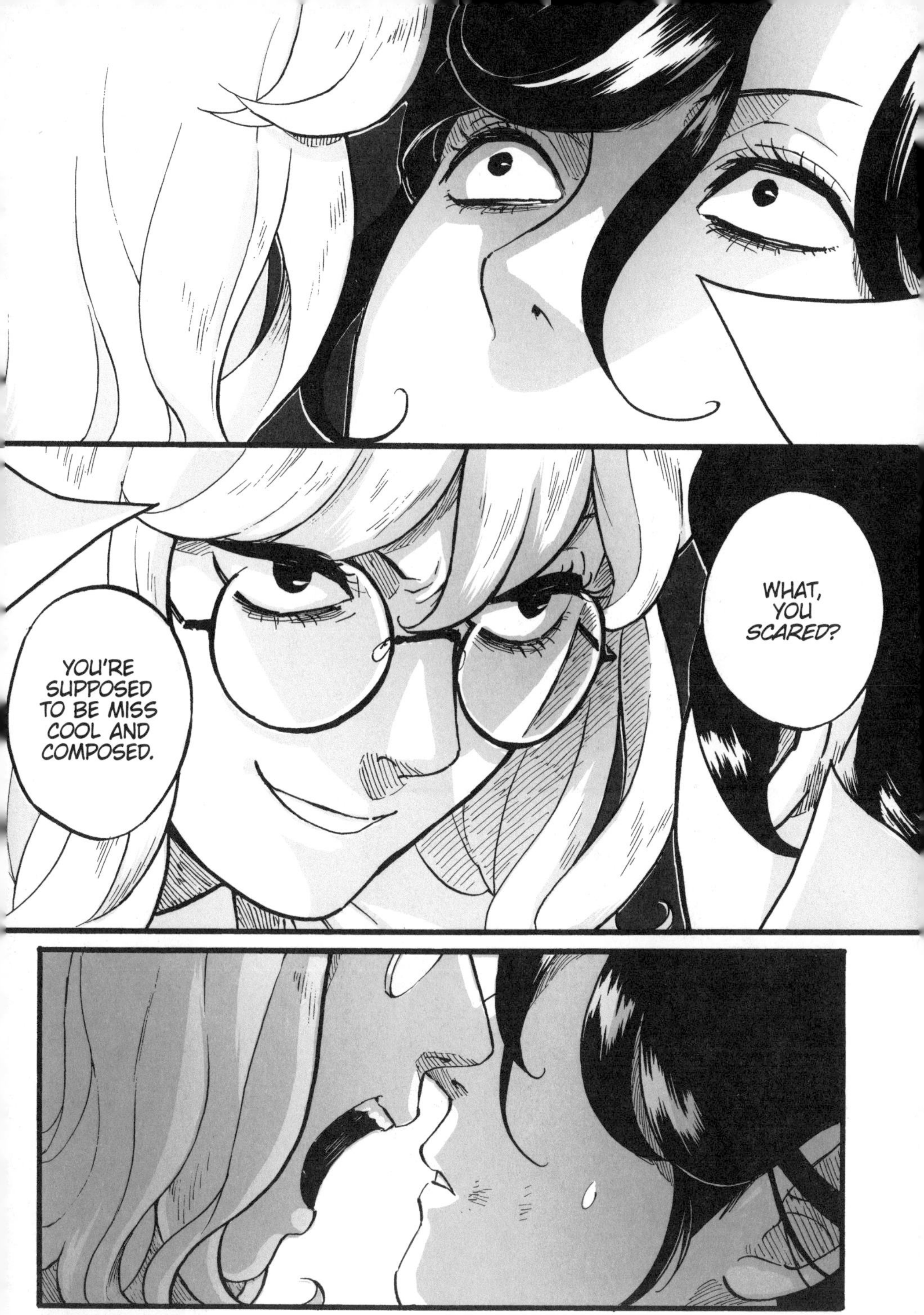

Chapter 1 – Fin

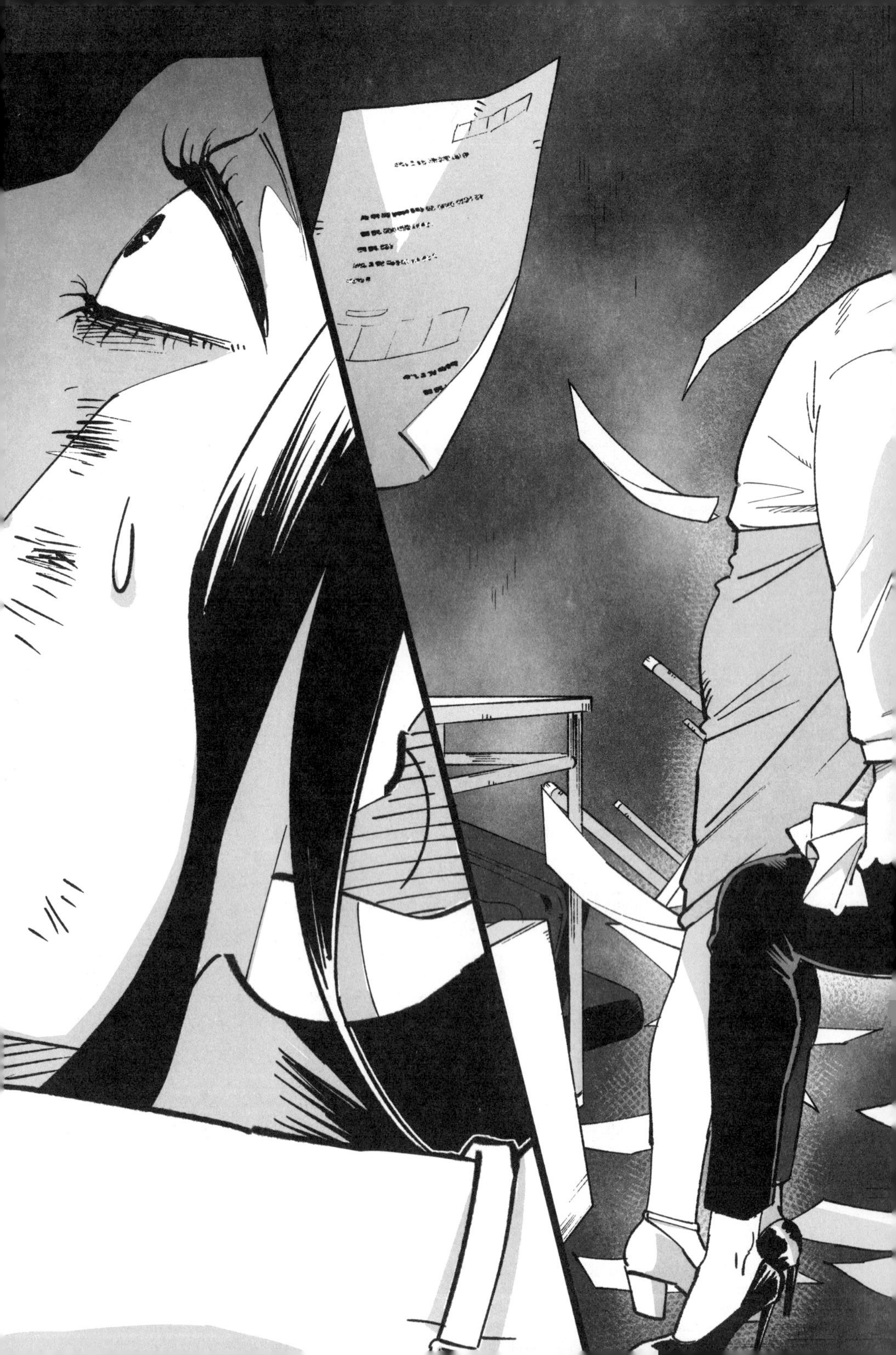

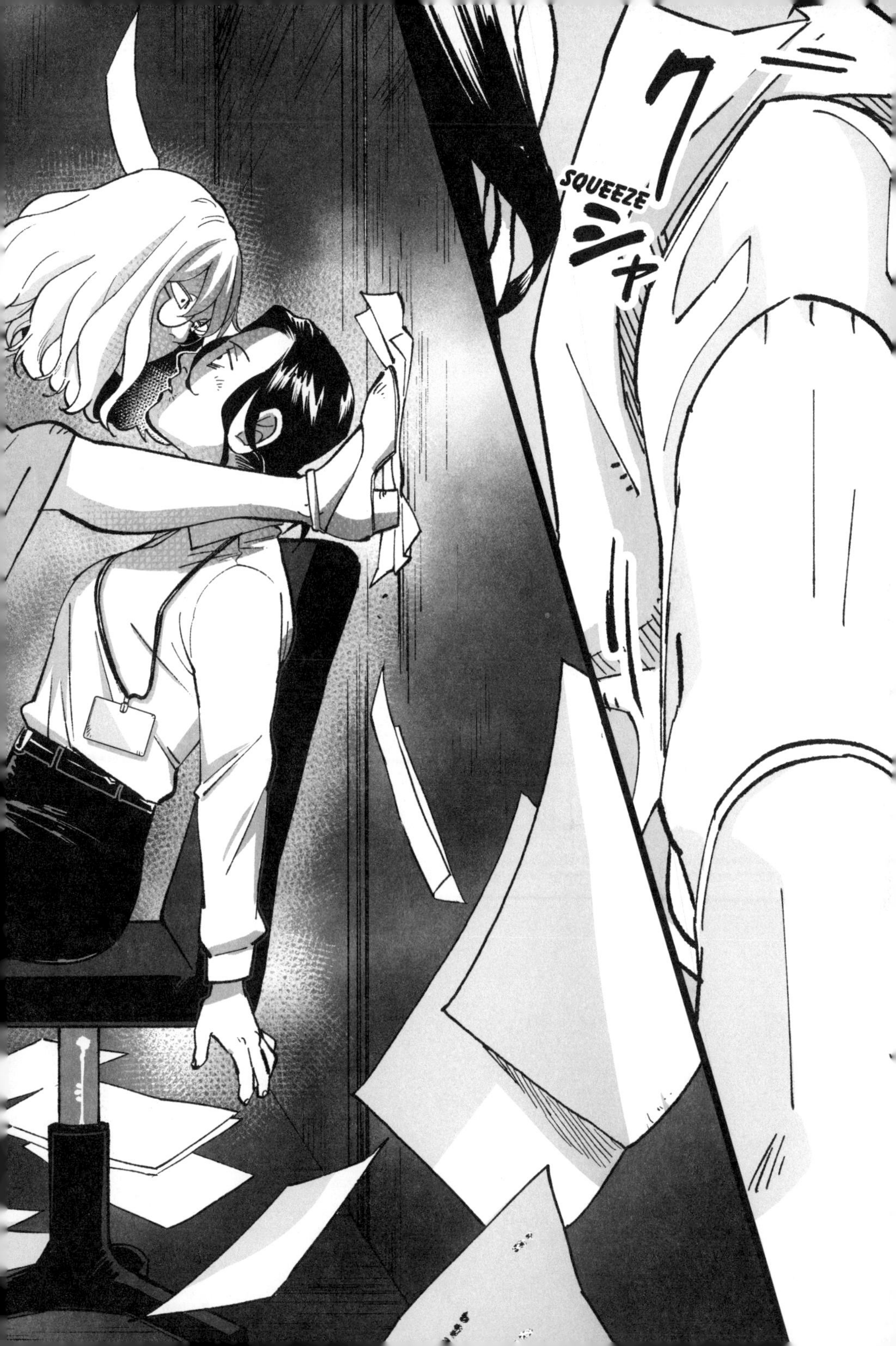
SQUEEZE
ク
シャ

YOU'VE BEEN PISSING ME OFF SINCE DAY ONE.
IF YOU STAYED PUT, I WOULDN'T BE IN THIS MESS!
CRUMPLe
ENOUGH WITH THE HYSTERICS.
FLUTTER
AH!
WAIT!
I WANT YOUR ASS OUT OF MY GODDAMN WAY!
SLAP
SLAM

—!
WHAT'S THE MATTER? NEVER BEEN KISSED?
BABY?
SMIRK
ギョッ
JOLT
ドスッ
THUD
RATTLE
SQUEAK
BANG
BITCH!
OW!

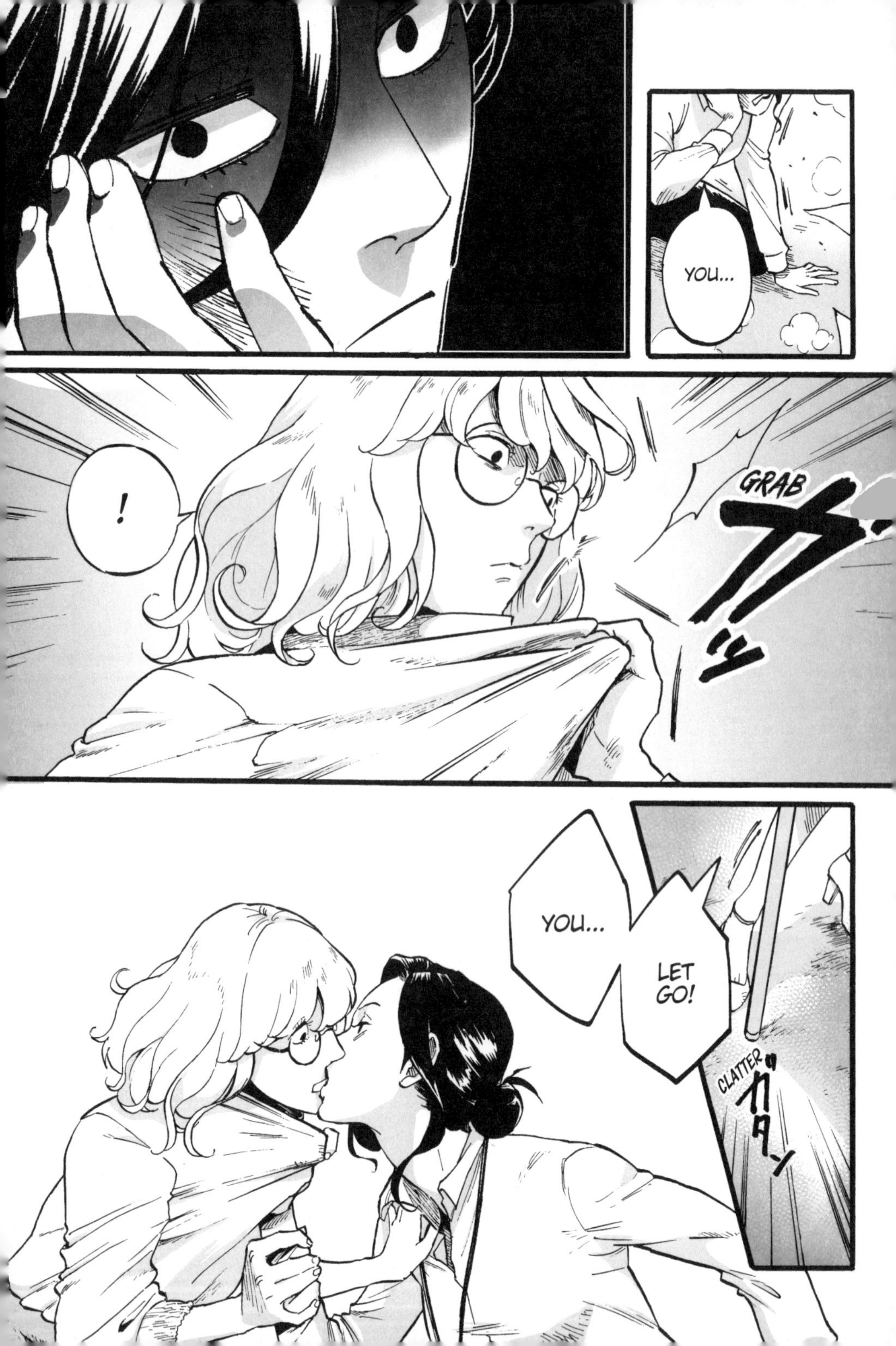
YOU...
!
GRAB
YOU...
LET GO!
CLATTER

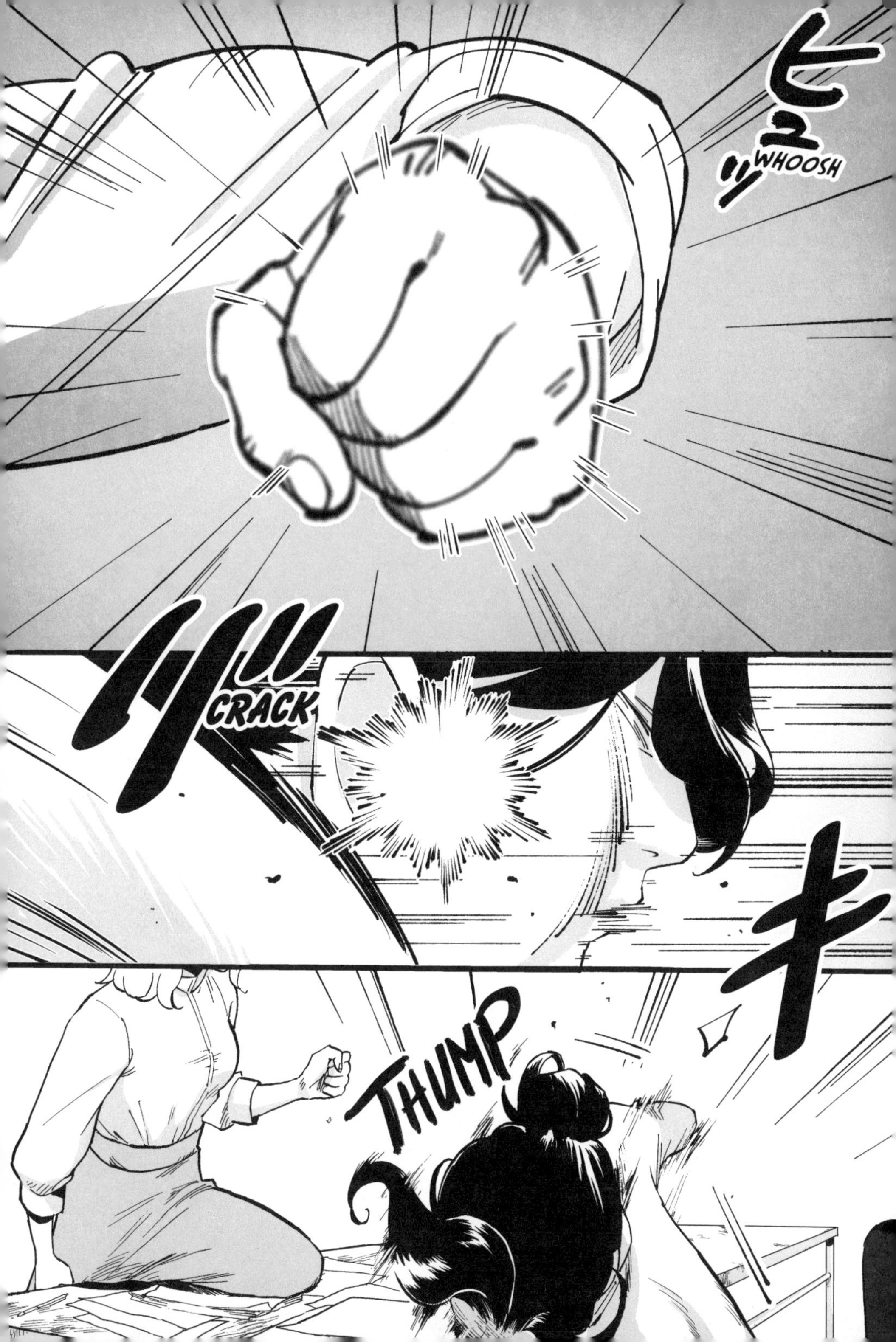
ヒュッ
WHOOSH
CRACK
THUMP

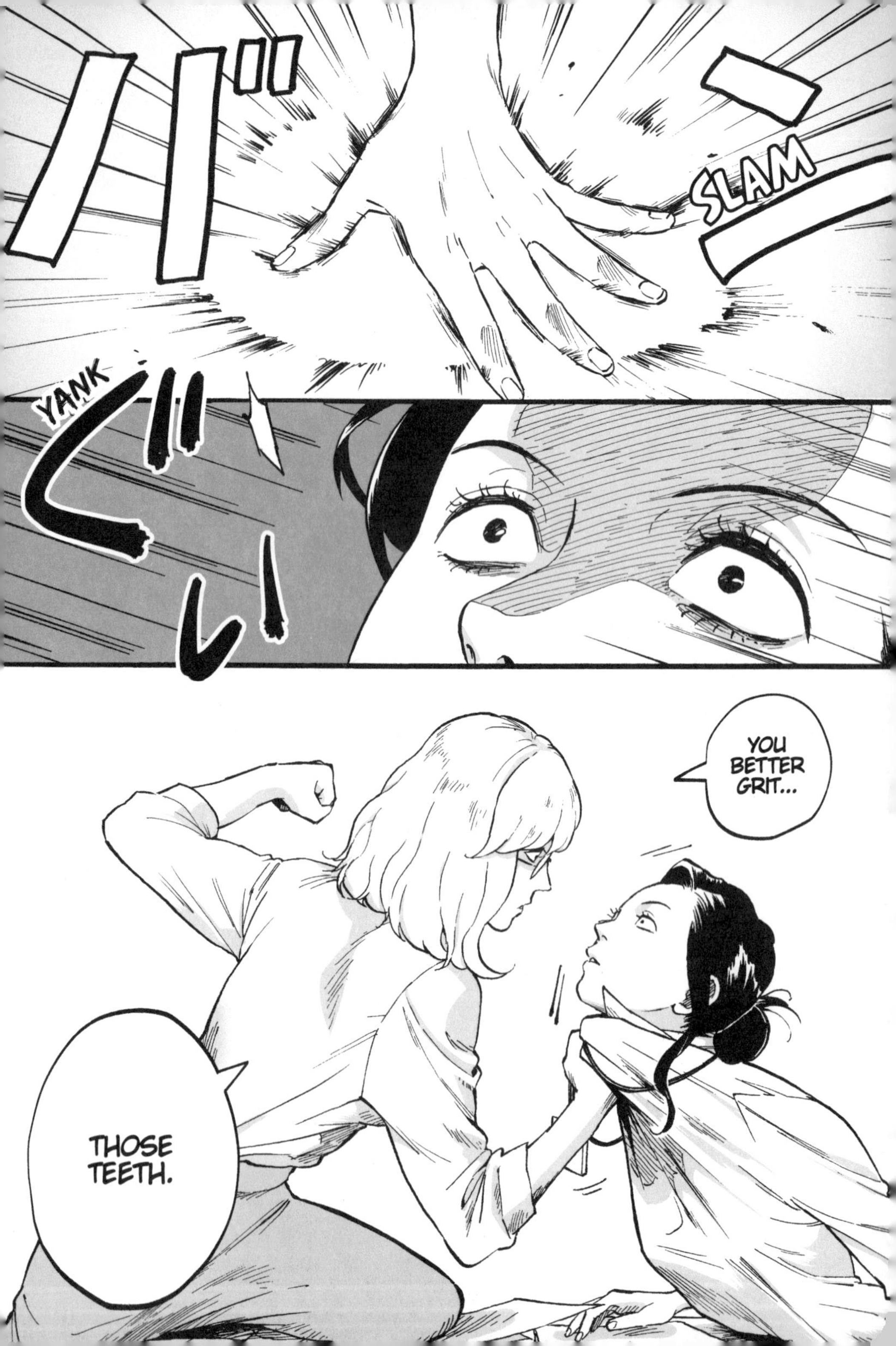
SLAM
YANK
YOU BETTER GRIT...
THOSE TEETH.

WHAT?
TAP
TAP
YOU THOUGHT I DIDN'T NOTICE?
REALLY?
ALL THAT HOVERING AND SNOOPING?
SENPAI.

WE WERE THE FIRST ONES TO CHECK IT, SO...	WE'LL HAVE TO GO OVER THE WHOLE THING.	SHIT HAPPENS.	WELL...

LET'S TRY OUR BEST.

RUSTLE

I HADN'T TRAINED YOU HOW TO DO IT YET, SO...

OH WELL. WHAT'S DONE IS DONE.

IT WOULD'VE BEEN NICE IF YOU BROUGHT THE SAME ENERGY TO THIS PROJECT.

WELL...

YOU CERTAINLY HAD ENOUGH TIME TO STICK YOUR NOSE IN MY BUSINESS.

FLAP

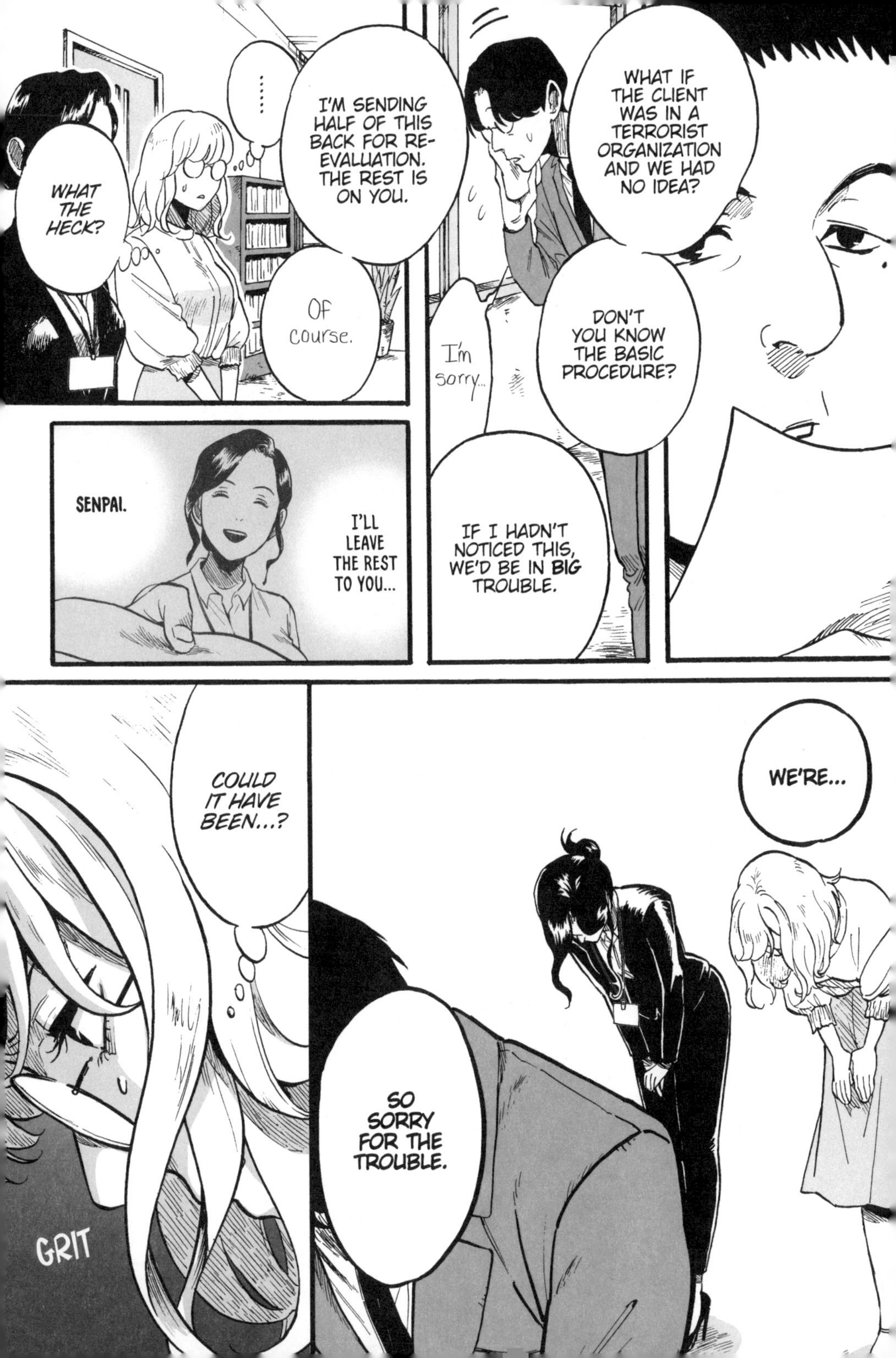
WHAT IF THE CLIENT WAS IN A TERRORIST ORGANIZATION AND WE HAD NO IDEA?
DON'T YOU KNOW THE BASIC PROCEDURE?
I'm sorry...
IF I HADN'T NOTICED THIS, WE'D BE IN BIG TROUBLE.
I'M SENDING HALF OF THIS BACK FOR RE-EVALUATION. THE REST IS ON YOU.
Of course.
......
WHAT THE HECK?
SENPAI.
I'LL LEAVE THE REST TO YOU...
WE'RE...
SO SORRY FOR THE TROUBLE.
COULD IT HAVE BEEN...?
GRIT

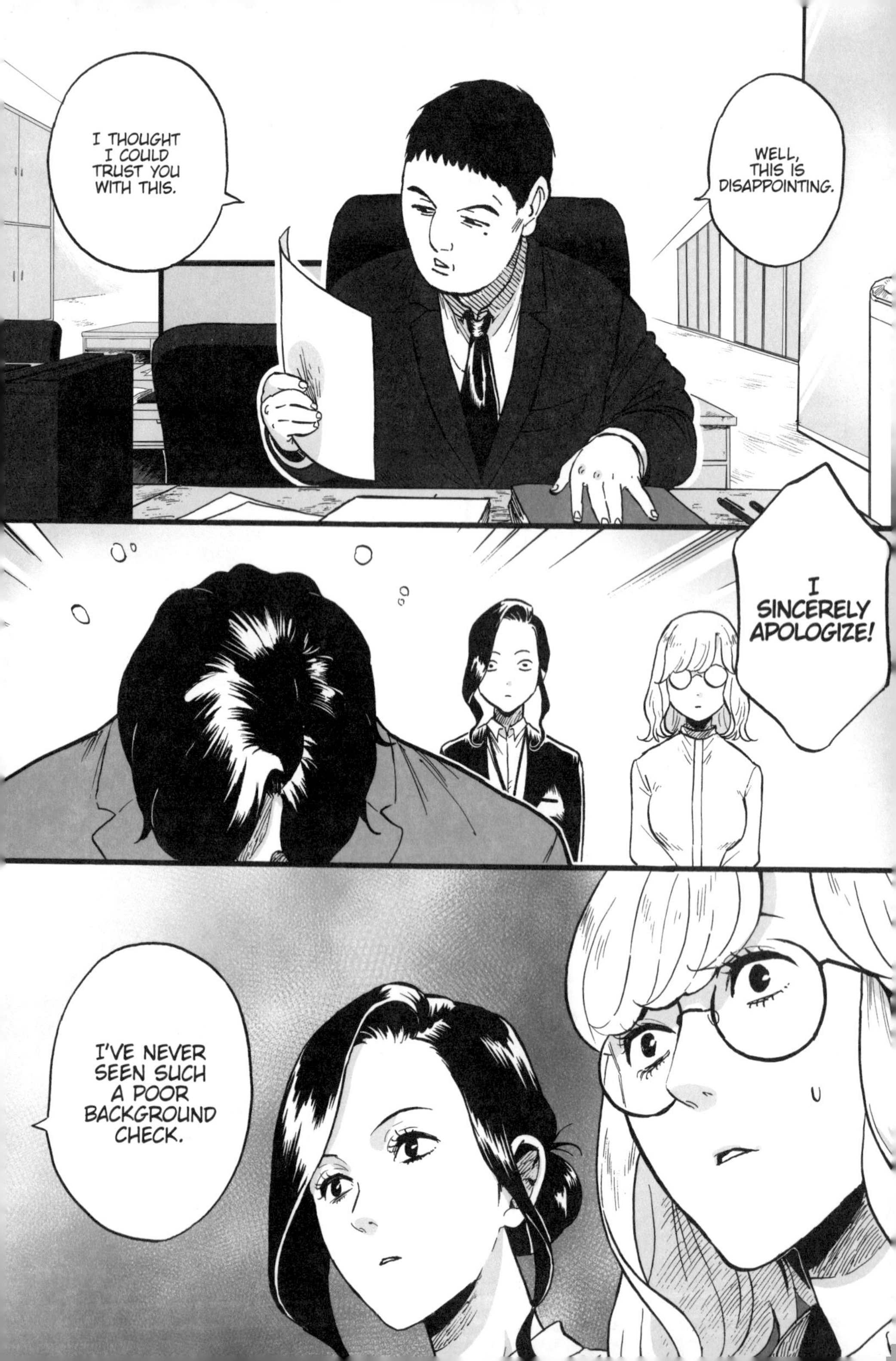
WELL, THIS IS DISAPPOINTING.
I THOUGHT I COULD TRUST YOU WITH THIS.
I SINCERELY APOLOGIZE!
I'VE NEVER SEEN SUCH A POOR BACKGROUND CHECK.

SCRITCH
SCRITCH
squeeze
OKAY!
I'M DONE FOR THE DAY.
STRETCH
THANKS FOR YOUR HARD WORK.
I KNOW THIS HASN'T BEEN THE EASIEST FIRST ASSIGNMENT, BUT YOU'VE DONE A GREAT JOB.
YOUR WORK HAS BEEN NEARLY FLAWLESS. IT'S IMPRESSIVE.
EVEN THE THINGS I HAVEN'T TAUGHT YOU YET WERE DONE PERFECTLY.
YOU'RE AMAZING.
SHF
FLIP
I WOULDN'T SAY THAT--
OH!
YOU DROPPED A PAGE.
HERE.
I'LL LEAVE THE REST TO YOU...
SENPAI.
THANKS.

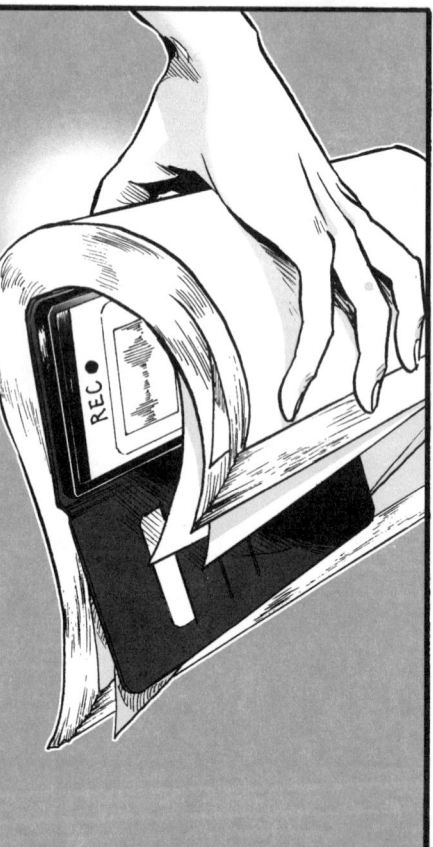

RUSTLE

AH!

I WAS, BUT...

ALL RIGHT.

GOT IT.

I LEFT THIS, AND THIS...

SORRY TO INTERRUPT!

THEN WE SHOULD SUBDIVIDE THE JURISDICTION AREAS.

RUSTLE

I DIDN'T NOTICE.

OOPS.

RUSTLE

OH. WERE YOU SITTING HERE?

I LEFT SOME DOCUMENTS BEHIND.

"DOCUMENTS."

REC ●

SORRY AGAIN FOR THE INTRUSION.

IT'S FINE.

RIGHT...

WAIT...

ISN'T THAT...?

THERE THEY ARE.

THE NICE GUYS FROM MANAGEMENT.

IT'S HER.

......

ISN'T THAT TANIGUCHI-SAN FROM HR?
PEEK
KURODA-SAN WORKED IN CORPORATE SALES.
WHERE DID THEY MEET?
KURODA-SAN, WE THOUGHT YOU'D BE WAY DIFFERENT.
I AM?
YOU BROUGHT YOUR BENTO TO WORK TODAY...
AND THEN YOU WENT OUT TO LUNCH.
YOU SEEMED LIKE SUCH A COOL GIRL...
BUT YOU'RE A TOTAL SPACE CADET!
OH MY GOD, I'M SO EMBAR-RASSED...
NO, IT WAS TOO CUTE! ♡♡
......
WAS THAT INTEN-TIONAL?

WHEW!
I NEVER THOUGHT I'D BE PUT IN CHARGE OF SOMETHING SO SOON.
THERE'S A LOT TO REMEMBER.
YOU'VE RAISED THE BAR. EXPECTATIONS ARE HIGH.
WELL, I'M LUCKY YOU'RE HERE, JUNKO-CHAN.
I'D BE LOST WITHOUT SUCH A GREAT TEACHER.
THANKS AGAIN.
HAPPY TO HELP.
THE EMPLOYEE LIST IS IN HER HISTORY...
......
OH, BY THE WAY...
CLICK
THAT GUY, THE ONE TWO YEARS BELOW US. I FORGOT HIS NAME...
TANAKA-SAN?
YEAH, HIM.
HE WAS SAYING HE WANTS TO WORK IN SALES AND KEPT ASKING ME ALL SORTS OF STUFF.
HE'S VERY ENTHUSIASTIC.
I CAN TELL.
SHE CLOSED THE WINDOW.
SHE SAW WHO USED TO BE ASSIGNED TO OUR PROJECT.
AT LEAST, I THINK...

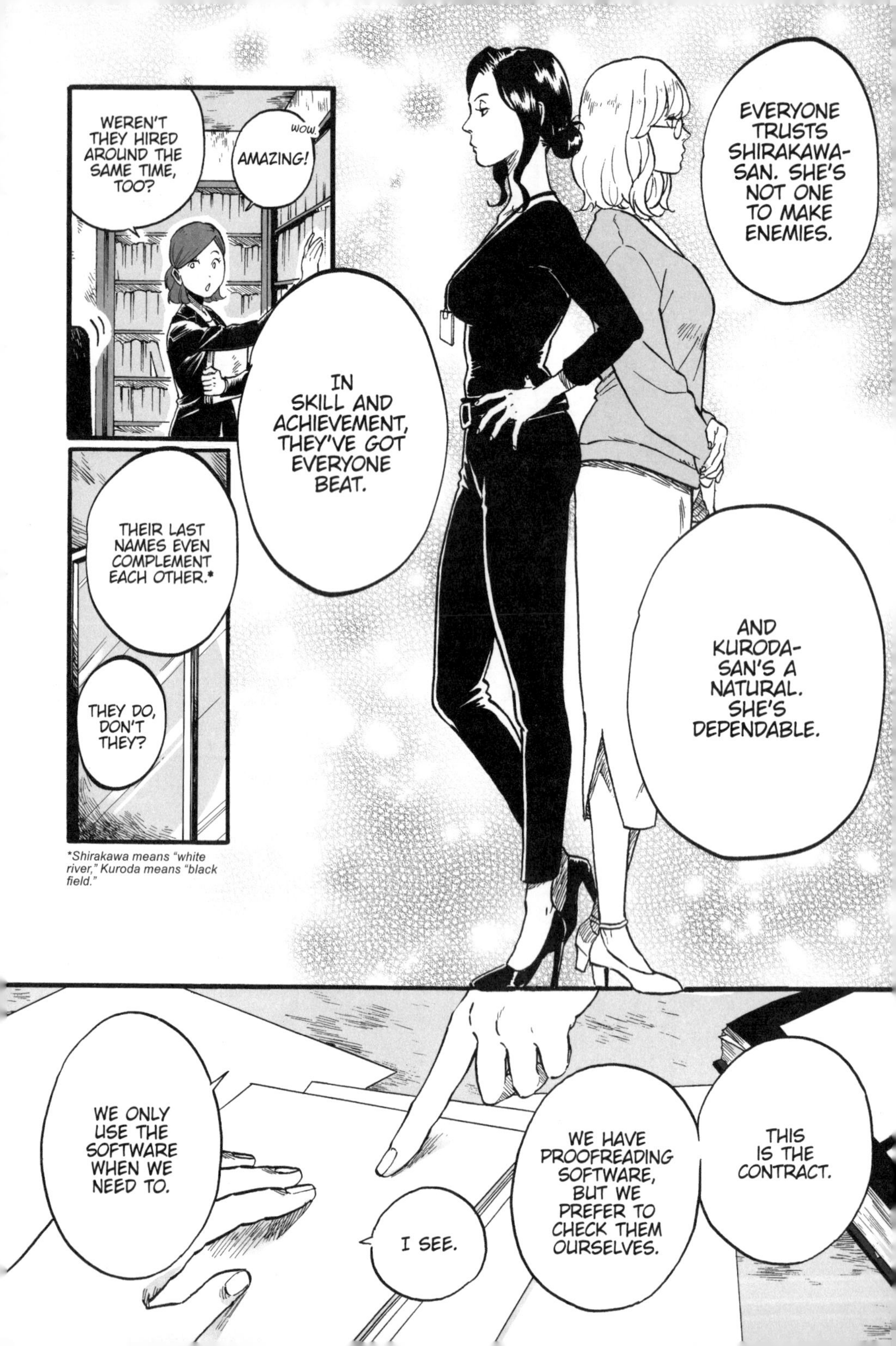
EVERYONE TRUSTS SHIRAKAWA-SAN. SHE'S NOT ONE TO MAKE ENEMIES.
AND KURODA-SAN'S A NATURAL. SHE'S DEPENDABLE.
IN SKILL AND ACHIEVEMENT, THEY'VE GOT EVERYONE BEAT.
WOW.
AMAZING!
WEREN'T THEY HIRED AROUND THE SAME TIME, TOO?
THEIR LAST NAMES EVEN COMPLEMENT EACH OTHER.*
THEY DO, DON'T THEY?
THIS IS THE CONTRACT.
WE HAVE PROOFREADING SOFTWARE, BUT WE PREFER TO CHECK THEM OURSELVES.
I SEE.
WE ONLY USE THE SOFTWARE WHEN WE NEED TO.

*Shirakawa means "white river," Kuroda means "black field."

"IT'S NOTHING TOO COMPLICATED."

"WE ALREADY HAVE A SAMPLE DONE."

"YOU CAN USE IT FOR REFERENCE."

"UH, SURE."

"I'M LOOKING FORWARD TO SEEING WHAT YOU COME UP WITH."

"SOUND DOABLE?"

"OF COURSE..."

"KURODA-SENPAI JUST TRANSFERRED HERE."

"'UNUSUAL' IS RIGHT."

"YOU'RE CUTTING HER TRAINING SHORT TO WORK ON A BIG PROJECT."

CREAK

"SHIRAKAWA-SAN WILL HELP HER."

"SHE'LL BE FINE."

"BUT SHIRAKAWA-SAN HAS HER HANDS FULL WITH THE JUNIOR STAFF."

"WELL..."

"I'M LOOKING FORWARD TO SEEING HOW THIS ALL PLAYS OUT."

TAP TAP

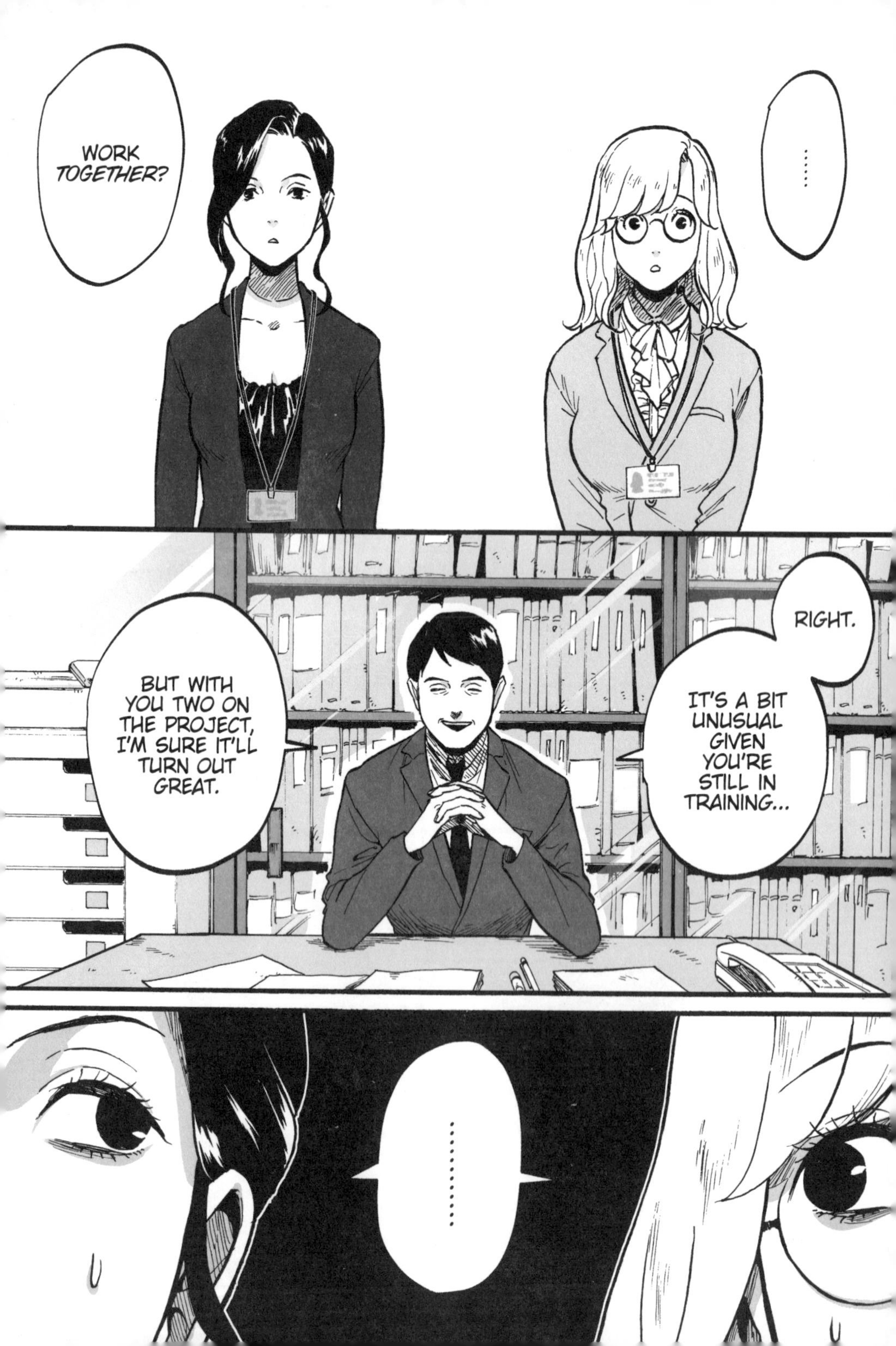
......
WORK TOGETHER?
RIGHT.
IT'S A BIT UNUSUAL GIVEN YOU'RE STILL IN TRAINING...
BUT WITH YOU TWO ON THE PROJECT, I'M SURE IT'LL TURN OUT GREAT.
......

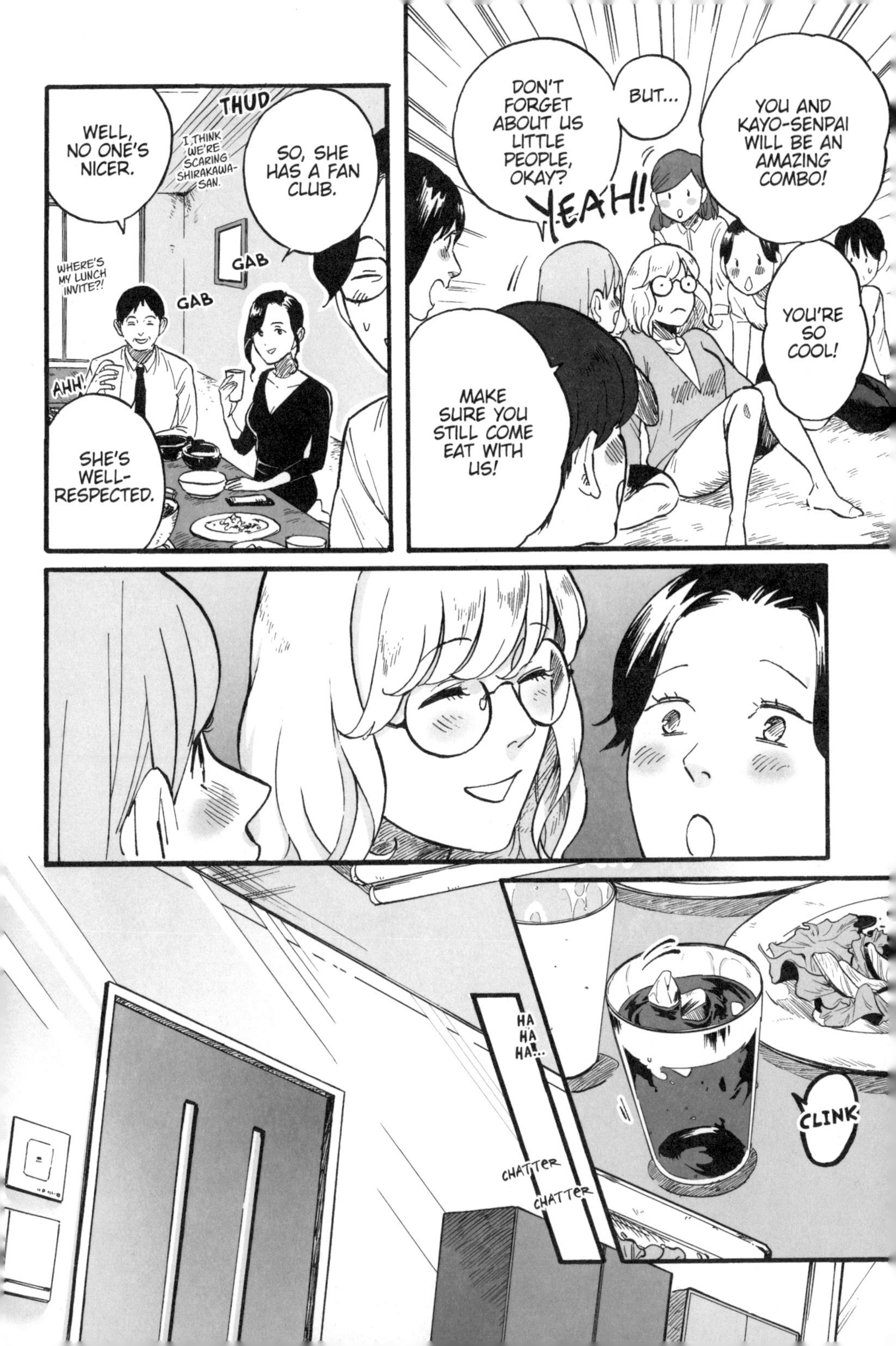
YOU AND KAYO-SENPAI WILL BE AN AMAZING COMBO!
BUT...
DON'T FORGET ABOUT US LITTLE PEOPLE, OKAY?
YEAH!
YOU'RE SO COOL!
MAKE SURE YOU STILL COME EAT WITH US!
SO, SHE HAS A FAN CLUB.
THUD
I THINK WE'RE SCARING SHIRAKAWA-SAN.
WELL, NO ONE'S NICER.
GAB
GAB
WHERE'S MY LUNCH INVITE?!
AHH!
SHE'S WELL-RESPECTED.
CLINK
HA HA HA...
CHATTER
CHATTER

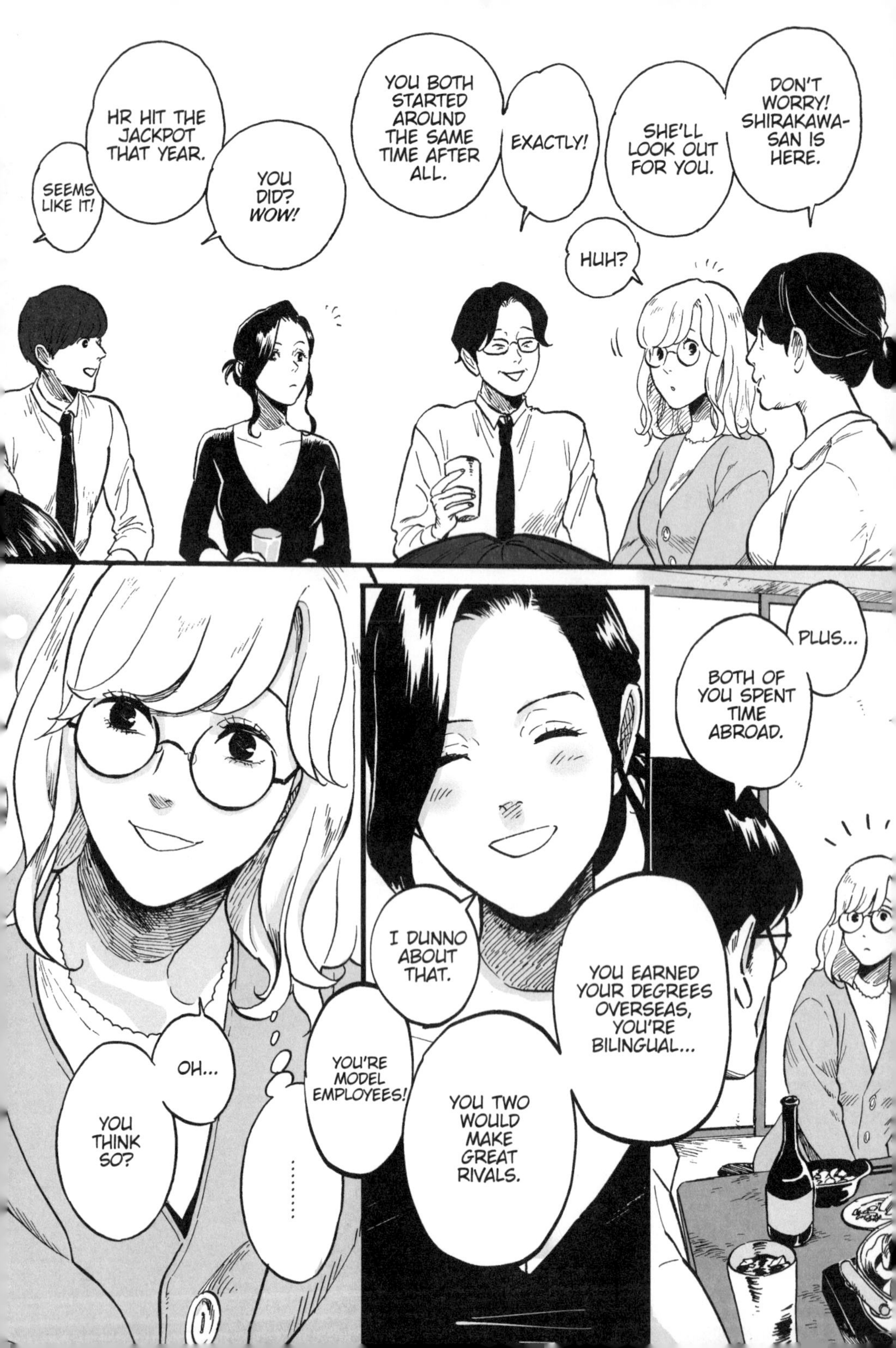
DON'T WORRY! SHIRAKAWA-SAN IS HERE.
SHE'LL LOOK OUT FOR YOU.
HUH?
EXACTLY!
YOU BOTH STARTED AROUND THE SAME TIME AFTER ALL.
YOU DID? WOW!
HR HIT THE JACKPOT THAT YEAR.
SEEMS LIKE IT!
PLUS...
BOTH OF YOU SPENT TIME ABROAD.
YOU EARNED YOUR DEGREES OVERSEAS, YOU'RE BILINGUAL...
I DUNNO ABOUT THAT.
YOU TWO WOULD MAKE GREAT RIVALS.
YOU'RE MODEL EMPLOYEES!
OH...
YOU THINK SO?
......

KURODA-SAN...
WOW!
YOU WERE A REGIONAL NUMBER ONE WITH CORPORATE SALES, RIGHT?
WEREN'T YOU INTERVIEWED FOR THE COMPANY NEWSLETTER, TOO?
I JUST GOT LUCKY.
YOU'RE TOO MODEST.
YOU'RE PRACTICALLY FAMOUS!
WE WORK IN SALES, TOO, YOU KNOW.
SURE.
BUT CORPORATE SALES IS *TOTALLY* ANOTHER BALL GAME.
DOING BUSINESS WITH FOREIGN COMPANIES...
I CAN'T PRETEND I'M NOT NERVOUS... CUSTOMS, CULTURES...
IT'S TOTALLY DIFFERENT.

WE'RE HAVING A WELCOME PARTY TONIGHT.
SMILE
IT'S AT THE BAR MENTIONED IN THE EMAIL YESTERDAY.
WILL DO!
ALL RIGHT, BACK TO WORK!
SHE'S GORGEOUS!
I KNOW!
SMILE
TANAKA-SAN, ABOUT THOSE DOCUMENTS...
HERE THEY ARE.
LET'S TOAST TO KURODA-SAN.
CHEERS!
WELCOME ABOARD!
THANKS SO MUCH.
CHEERS!
GLAD TO HAVE YOU ON THE TEAM.
CHEERS!

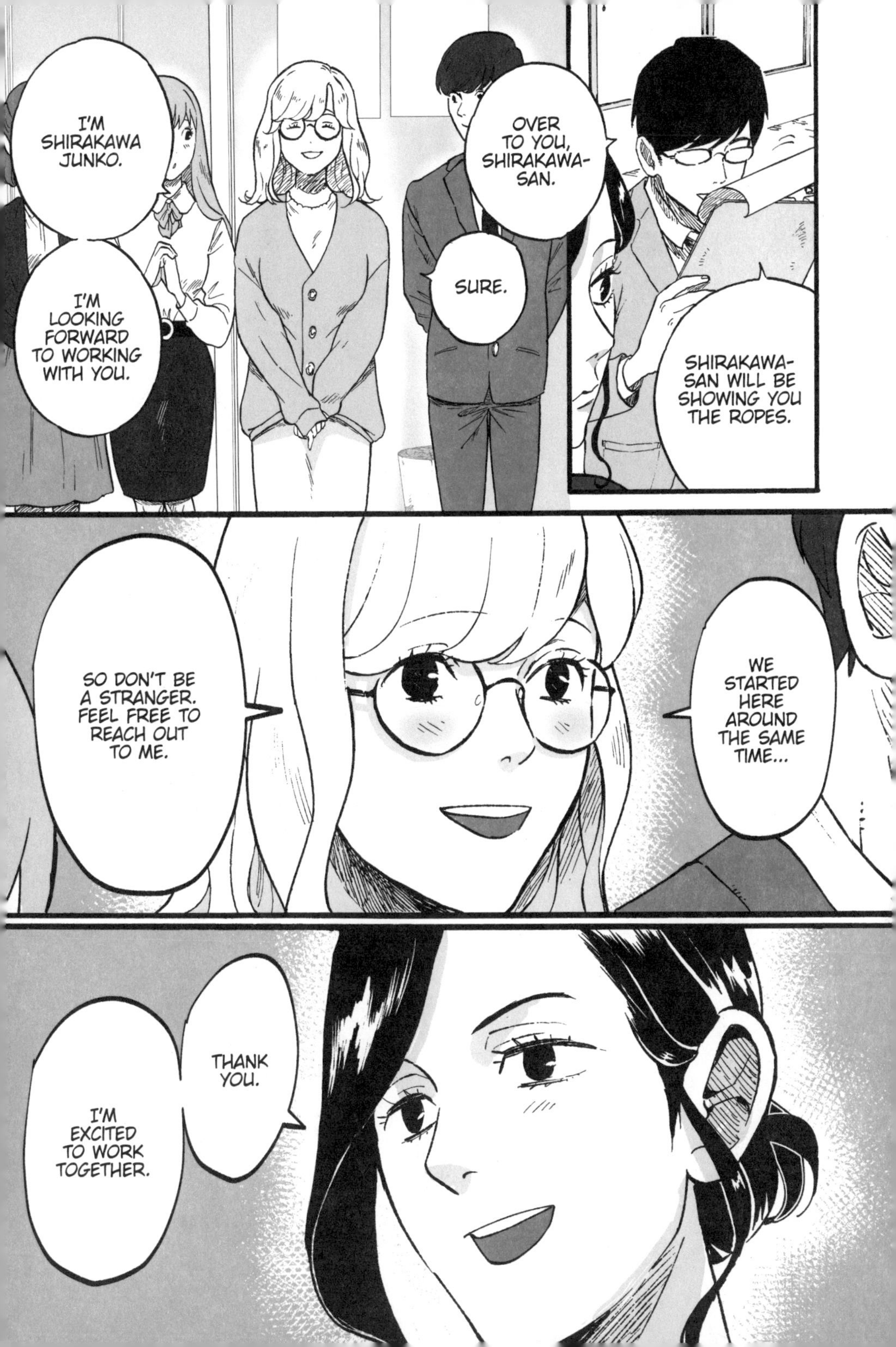
SHIRAKAWA-SAN WILL BE SHOWING YOU THE ROPES.
OVER TO YOU, SHIRAKAWA-SAN.
SURE.
I'M SHIRAKAWA JUNKO.
I'M LOOKING FORWARD TO WORKING WITH YOU.
WE STARTED HERE AROUND THE SAME TIME...
SO DON'T BE A STRANGER. FEEL FREE TO REACH OUT TO ME.
THANK YOU.
I'M EXCITED TO WORK TOGETHER.

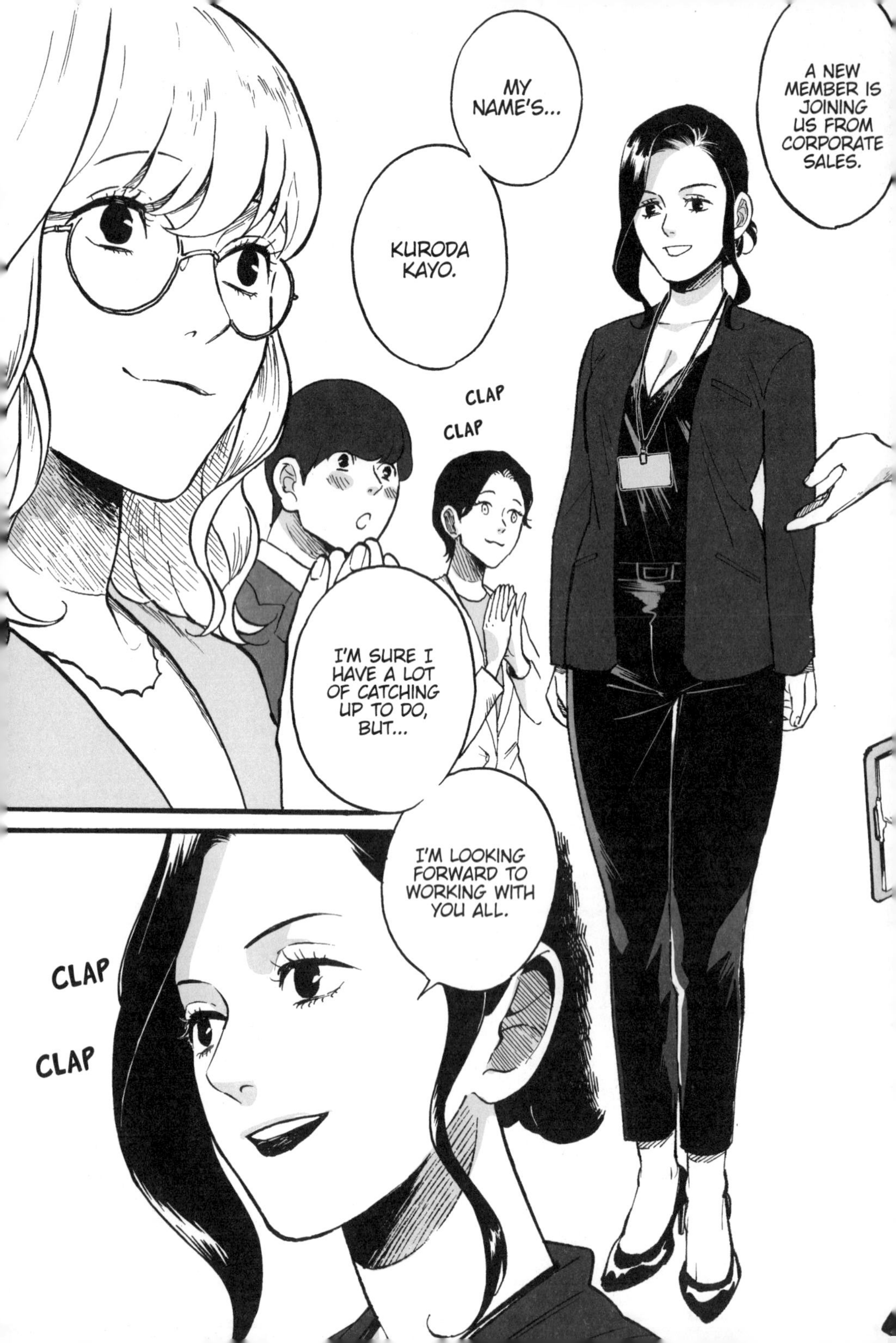
A NEW MEMBER IS JOINING US FROM CORPORATE SALES.
MY NAME'S...
KURODA KAYO.
CLAP
CLAP
I'M SURE I HAVE A LOT OF CATCHING UP TO DO, BUT...
I'M LOOKING FORWARD TO WORKING WITH YOU ALL.
CLAP
CLAP

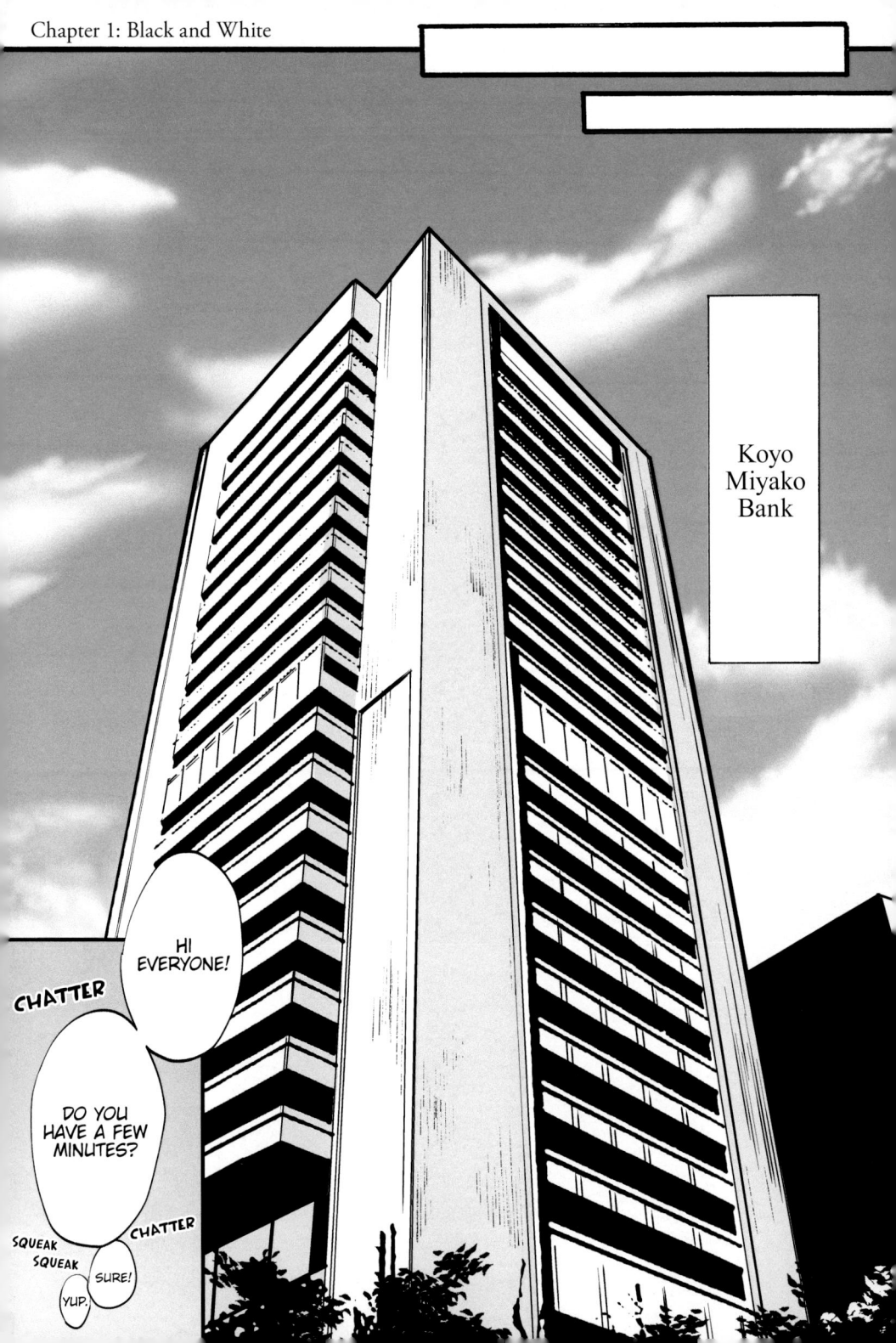

Chapter 1: Black and White

Koyo Miyako Bank

HI EVERYONE!

CHATTER

DO YOU HAVE A FEW MINUTES?

SQUEAK SQUEAK

CHATTER

SURE!

YUP.

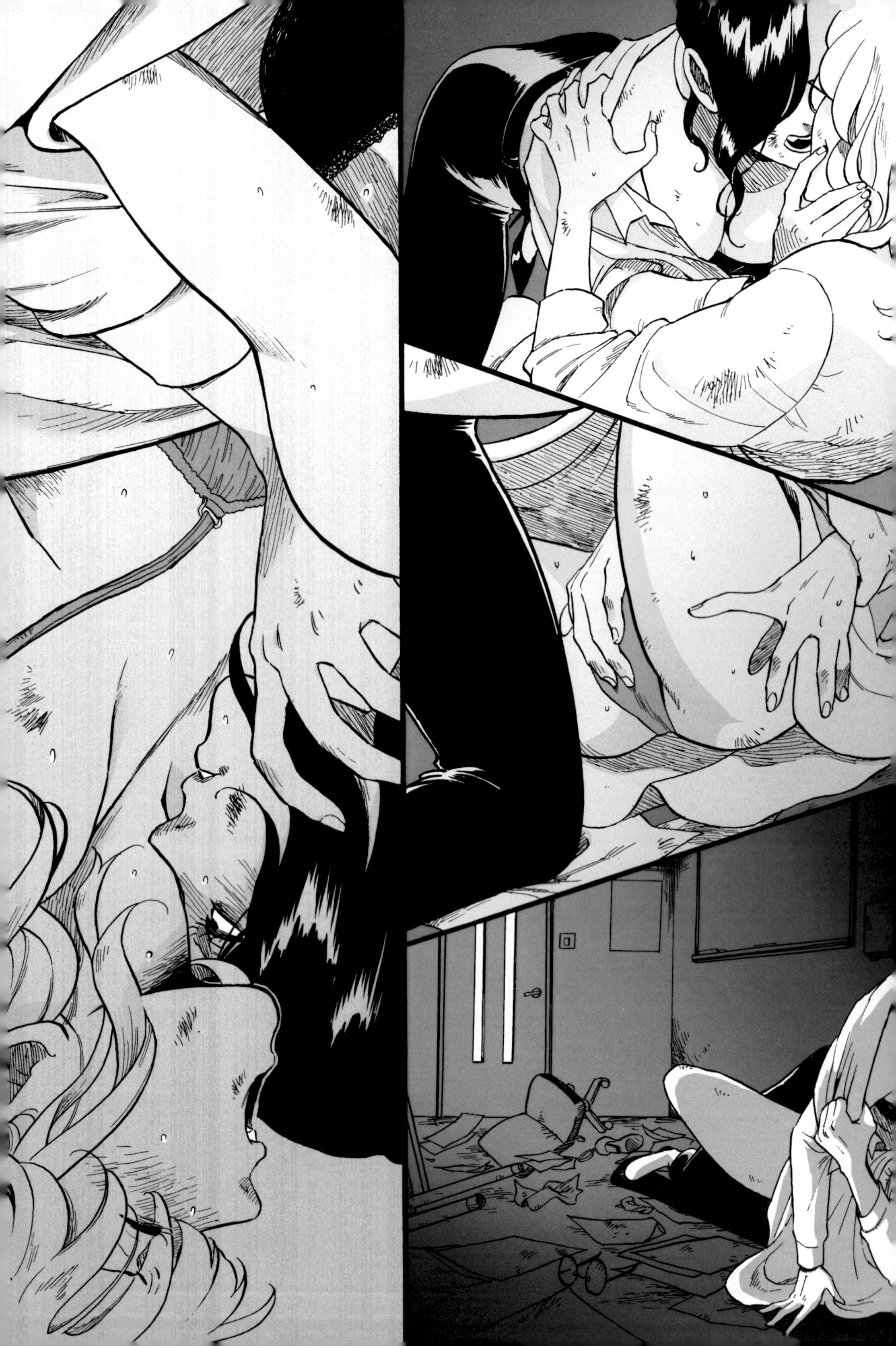

DAMN IT!
GRR!
TEAR TEAR TEAR
RIP
CRUMPLE
SLIP
THUD
WITH THE...
INNOCENT ACT!
HUFF!
ENOUGH...

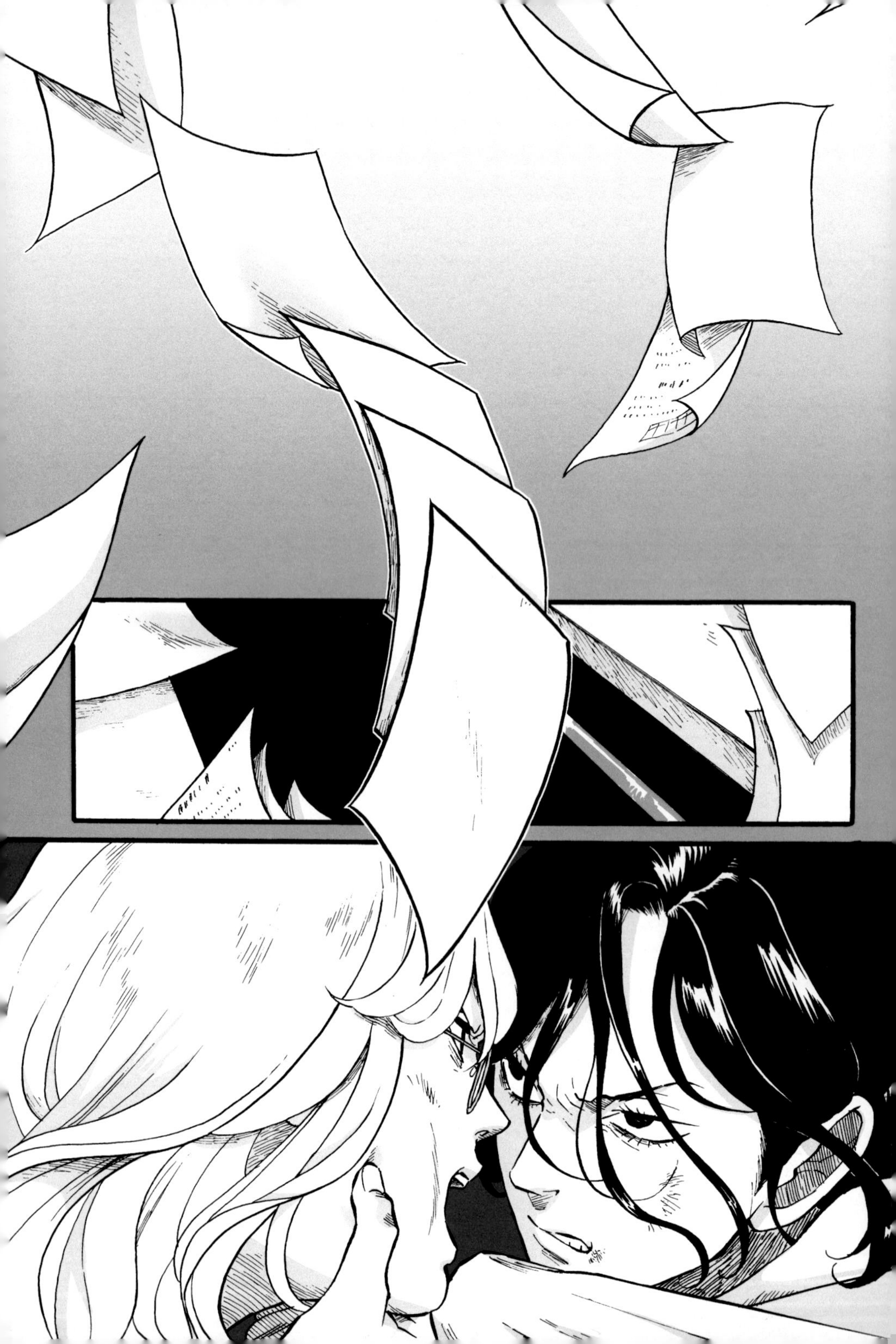

Chapter 1: Black and White —————— 5

Chapter 2: Waver —————————— 37

Chapter 3: United Front (Part 1) ——— 59

Chapter 4: United Front (Part 2) ——— 85

Chapter 5: Training ————————— 111

Chapter 6: Kouhai ————————— 135

Bonus Material ——————————— 160

Black & White
volume.one
Contents 1

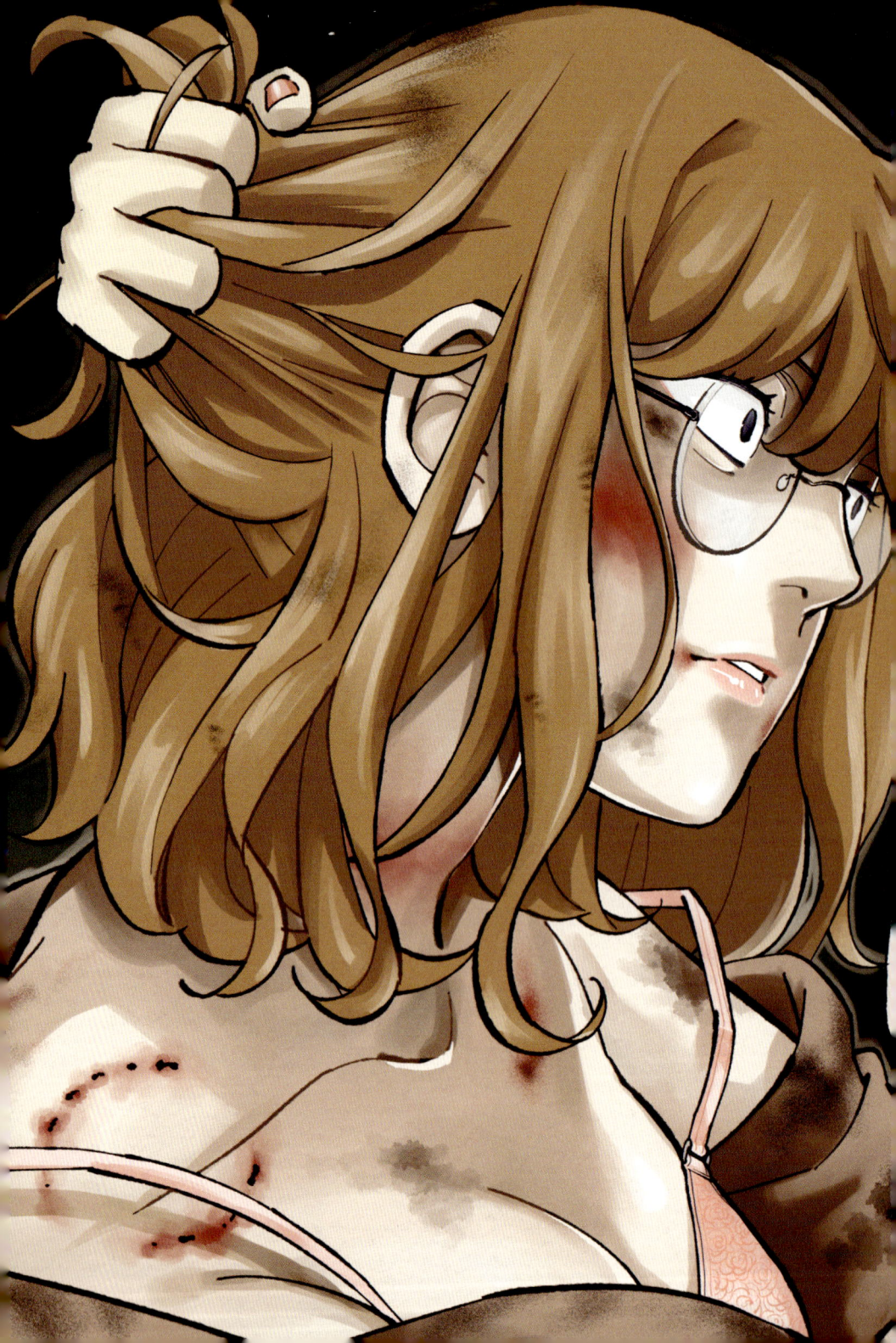

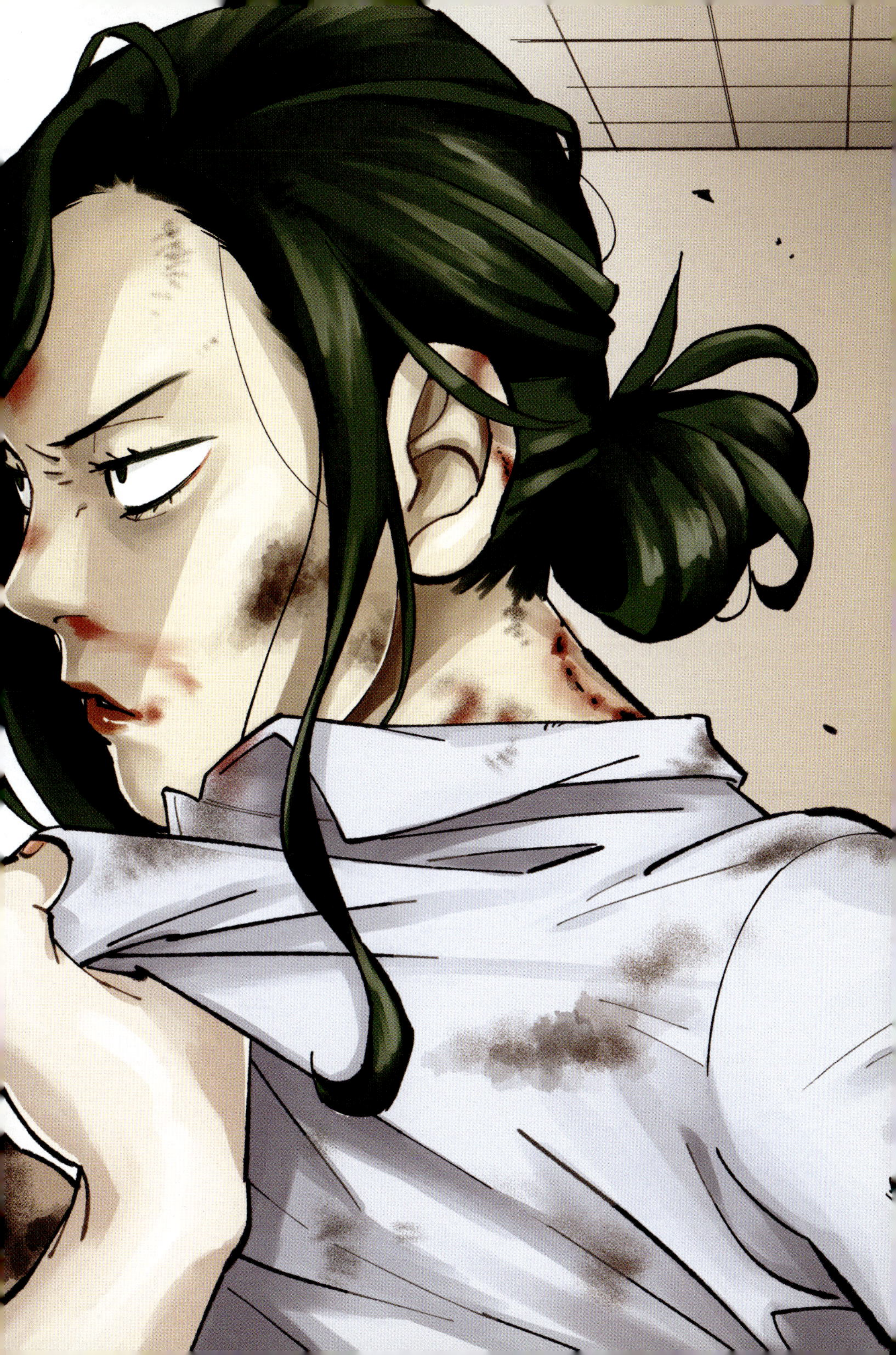

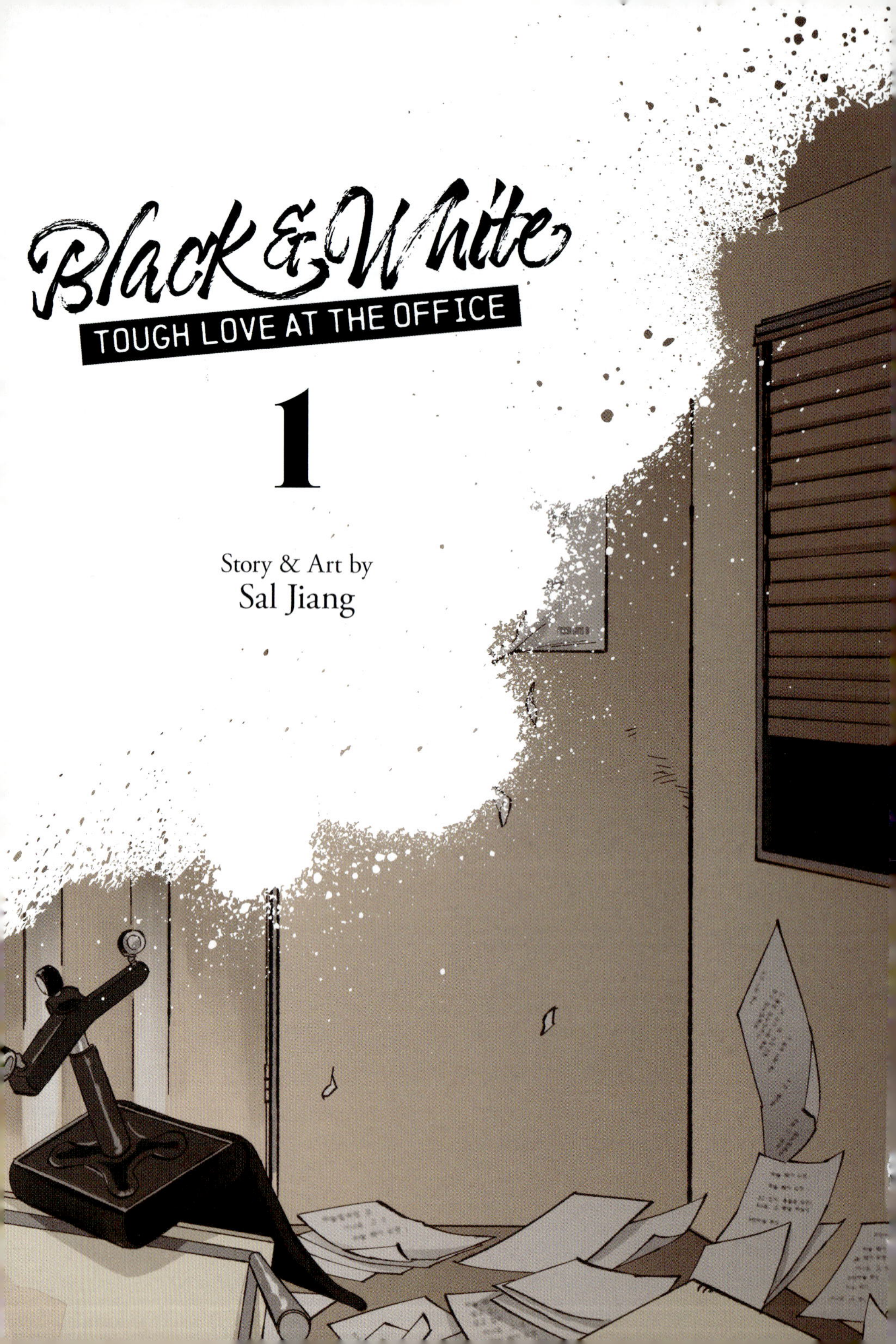

Black & White

TOUGH LOVE AT THE OFFICE

1

Story & Art by

Sal Jiang